THE FOREST WITHIN

From *A Narrative of Travels on the Amazon and Rio Negro* by Alfred Russel Wallace

THE FOREST WITHIN

The World-View of the
Tukano Amazonian Indians

GERARDO REICHEL-DOLMATOFF

"Ecoute un homme d'expérience; tu en apprendras plus dans les bois que dans les livres.
Les arbres et les pierres t'en enseigneront plus que tu n'en pourras
acquérir de la bouche d'un magister."

Bernard de Clairvaux
(1090 - 1153)

Themis Books

Published in 1996
by Themis Books, an imprint of
Green Books Ltd, Foxhole, Dartington,
Totnes, Devon, TQ9 6EB, UK,
in association with the COAMA Programme,
Colombia and The Gaia Foundation, London

Distributed in the USA & Canada
by Council Oak Books, Tulsa, Oklahoma

All photographs were taken by the author in the north-west Amazon,
Pira-paraná river region, Colombia, with the exception
of those on pages 110, 117 and 141, which were taken
by Professor Sir Ghillean Prance, Director of Kew Gardens.
They are reproduced with his kind permission.
The engravings on pages ii, 5, 6 and 9 were reproduced
by kind permission of the British Museum.

Type and make-up by Chris Fayers, Soldon, Devon
Printed by The Cromwell Press, Broughton Gifford, Wiltshire

The paper used in this book is made from wood from managed plantations,
where replanting exceeds the trees harvested. These are in
North America, coastal areas of Brazil (eucalyptus plantations,
harvested every seven years), Portugal and Spain. The paper is
acid-free and elemental chlorine-free.

A catalogue record for this book
is available from the British Library

ISBN 0 9527302 0 0

CONTENTS

Many people directly or indirectly helped and encouraged me to write and publish this book. I should like to express my gratitude to them here.

I want to thank my British friends: Malcolm Deas, the Earth Love Fund, John Elford of Green Books, Edward Goldsmith, The Goldsmith Foundation, Liz Hosken, Nic Marks, Helena Paul, Sigrid Rausing, and the staff of the Bodleian Library and Radcliffe Science Library. Without the stimulus of the Gaia Foundation this book would never have come into being.

I would also like to thank Richard E. Schultes, Johannes Wilbert, Antonio Guzmán and my daughter Helena Reichel. Finally, as always, I wish to acknowledge my gratitude for the lifelong support of my wife and colleague, Alicia Dussan de Reichel.

Gerardo Reichel-Dolmatoff
September 1993

For Edward Posey

A Taibano boy with palm (*Astrocaryum*) fibres

INTRODUCTION

This book is concerned with selected aspects of rainforest ecology, more precisely with the Amazon. But it is not another treatise of what specialists would call ecology; it is an account of how an aboriginal tribe of a remote Amazonian region copes—successfully, I anticipate—with some of the many problems of relating to their forest environment.

Our modern ecology has developed theoretical frameworks and methodological approaches in accordance with our understanding of tropical rainforest environments. This knowledge, however, is based upon recent events: the discovery of the existence of tropical rainforests and of their global importance, the first going back only a few centuries, the second of much more recent date. The Indians, however, have known the rainforest for thousands of years, and it is time we took a closer look at their experience, their *intelligence du milieu*, even if their theories and practices do not conform to our logic. But in this book I shall be concerned with another logic, which I shall try to make understandable by introducing the reader into the yet little explored field of South American ethno-ecology, defined here as the analysis of socio-ecological relationships.

The idea of writing this book arose in the course of conversations with friends in England and France, in the course of lonely readings in the Bodleian, the British Library and the Linnean Society; in the course of countless hours spent in the great and small bookshops of Oxford and Paris in the summers of 1992 and 1993. It has been my privilege and good fortune to spend most of my life in Colombia where I have been able to work as a field anthropologist among the Indians of the Northwest Amazon and of many other rainforest areas of that country, and so I can speak from the vantage point of more than half a century in a tropical land, actively engaged in research, teaching, and writing on anthropological topics. Now I feel the time has come to summarise some observation on aboriginal ecological practices.

During the nineteenth century and already before that, Colombia, the former Kingdom of New Granada, had been visited by many European travellers and naturalists whose works became required reading for anthropologists. Alexander von Humboldt had travelled widely in this country in the first years of the last century, and his biogeographical theories had been influential for many years. The Spix and Martius Expedition (1817-1820) had explored the botany and zoology of a hitherto unknown part of the Colombian Northwest Amazon, and its members had published accounts of Indian customs, languages, and artefacts, observed in their local contexts. In the middle of the last century, the British naturalists Henry Walter Bates, Richard Spruce and Alfred Russel Wallace worked in the Northwest Amazon, and opened up a vast field of research never since described as vividly, earnestly, colourfully, and humanely as by these travellers. By the end of the last century and the early years of the present one, Brazilian, French, German and Italian travellers had made their appearance. Antonio Brandão de Amorím, João Barbosa Rodrigues, Henri Coudreau, Ermanno Stradelli and others now dominate our specific area of interest, the Rio Negro and Vaupés territories. Scholars, humanists, occasional poets, occasional government agents, these authors can still be read with profit and pleasure. The last traveller in that great tradition was the German ethnographer Theodor Koch-Grünberg, who spent two years (1903-1905) in the Colombian Northwest Amazon, and who left us a wealth of ethnographic and linguistic data on the Indians of the Vaupés territory, presented in the form of an itinerary, in the colourful context of life in the forest and on the rivers. After him come years of neglect. But that is another story.

For years my wife and colleague, the anthropologist Alicia Dussán de Reichel, and I had been going over the literature on the upper Amazon. Although our interests were ethnographical and initially limited to accounts of Indian life, we soon discovered the importance of other dimensions without which our understanding of aboriginal societies lacked the vital context of environmental conditions. We had read the principal geographical works and then turned to the biologists. The Indians had taught us that a knowledge of animal behaviour was essential, and so we read about territoriality and pheromonal communication, about social insects and fishruns, anything the Indians referred to in their daily lives, or in myth and ritual. We turned to the botanists and found ourselves in good company, because they too had been learning from the Indians and had come to appreciate their knowledge of plants. And then, of course, we read up on rainforest ecology.

It was then when we began to lose contact with a reality we had come to know as ethnographers. Ecologists spoke with authority of the dynamics of biodiversity, of nutrient cycling, gap-filling and co-evolution, but they hardly ever mentioned the Indians who, as we knew only too well, were intimately concerned with the very same processes, and had thousands of years of experience to draw on. Was their knowledge of no importance to ecologists? Had the Indians perhaps mismanaged their environment? Did the ecologists not know that many rainforest Indians in Colombia (Northwest Amazon, Chocó, Catatumbo, and elsewhere) were living in that blissful state technically called 'sustained development'?

The world's great rainforests, their wildlife, their global importance and local potential, have recently become the focal point of discussions and research which have occupied the mass media as well as many highly specialised institutions in many fields of science and development. At present, in Europe and in

INTRODUCTION

North America, bibliographical sources on rainforest topics are abundant, and the interested general reader might begin with some of the many beautifully produced volumes which show the splendour of orchids and blooming trees, of evergreen foliage, cascading waters, strange animals and, occasionally, the impassive, tragic, beautiful faces of the forest people, the natives, the aborigines, or however the respective authors choose to call them. It is a sheer pleasure to leaf through the pages of these books, again and again, sometimes to admire a particular photograph for its aesthetic value, to study another for its ethnographic interest, another for its nostalgic associations.

But often enough, what these books convey to the experienced reader and beholder are images which are far removed from reality. Obviously, and necessarily, the photographs which are the book's main strength have been carefully selected by author and editor in a combined effort to attract, please, and inform a wide readership, and this selection itself has been guided in many cases by fashionable concepts of exoticism, perhaps by ecological facts and fads, vague humanitarian feelings, or simply in an attempt to illustrate the naïve adventurous exploits of a newcomer to the tropics.

Although the Amazon Basin covers almost half of the world's rainforests, sober and well-documented books of the profusely illustrated type, aimed at a wide readership, seem to be rare. This may be the reason why there still prevail the old stereotypes of an Amazonian 'Green Hell', a 'Devil's Paradise', a 'Counterfeit Paradise', a disease-ridden steaming jungle sparsely peopled by head-shrinking savages who only now are beginning to adopt civilised ways, or who are dying out. Even the educated public, not to speak of Amazon-concerned governmental circles, often show a disconcerting level of ignorance about the history, geography, and the aboriginal peoples of the Amazon Basin.

During recent years another source of information on the Amazon has come into existence: the travel reports of writers who have been there by aeroplane, cruise ship, motor launch and helicopter; who have been to Belém, Santarem, Manaus and Iquitos, the major cities along the great river; who have visited cattle ranches and gold mines, logging companies, rubber tappers' camps, and hydro-electric dams, all those places where Western technology and local enterprise combine into what is called progress. Some of these journalistic travel reports make for interesting reading but, again, they are one-sided because they rarely refer to the Indians, to their millennial experiences in adaptation, their beliefs in energy flow, their knowledge of the workings of ecosystems and ecological interdependences. It is, of course, a fact that the reporters, the analysts, would have little or no contact with Indians, who still conserve their tribal knowledge and would be willing to share it with a passing stranger. The reporters hardly ever leave the main routes of modern river transportation by motor launch and outboard motor, and do not penetrate into the hundreds and thousands of streams and creeks, much less into the interfluvial forests. In other words, they completely miss an enormous region teeming with life, the true life of the forest and the river where people still continue their traditional ways. This does not mean that these people are 'untouched by civilization'; they do have metal tools, machetes, kettles, some cloth, perhaps an old shotgun, but they have no transistor radios, no outboard motors, no electric torches, and they hardly speak any Portuguese or Spanish. Some of these Indians present conditions which are very close to those found by travellers a hundred or hundred and fifty years ago. By not mentioning these living aboriginal cultures the reporters often give the impression that the Indian tradition has ceased to exist, that the native element has become acculturated and incorporated into the national societies of the Amazonian republics. And this is exactly what many politicians would like to hear.

And then there is the growing scientific literature on the Amazon. There are hundreds of books and thousands of research articles in learned journals, dealing with climatology and limnology, soil classification, flora and fauna, agriculture and resource management and so many other fields. The scientific study of tropical rainforests is indeed a field in which the Biological and Earth Sciences have made great progress in recent decades, and the Amazon Basin has provided challenging opportunities for some of the best minds in some of the most important disciplines. These people, unlike most authors of coffee-table books, have done their field work. They have paddled their canoes and walked through the forests and swamplands with the Indians. They have lived with the natives and eaten their food and have come to admire the Indians. But they were not ethnographers. They applied their Western logic to what they saw and heard; they thought in terms of a heliocentric universe and applied the Linnean system. Many of them, especially the botanists, worked closely with the Indians and recognised their profound knowledge of the local flora, of food plants, medicinal plants, hallucinogens and toxics. However, they rarely described the use of these plants in their social and symbolic contexts, nor did the ichthyologists describe the Indians' beliefs about fishruns, or the limnologists refer to the chromatic scale of river waters, as understood by the Indians. Being specialists in the Natural Sciences they did not mention all this, because it lay outside their fields of competence or interest.

There are, then, two Amazons. One is the Amazon of modern development, of national and international enterprise, of road building and hydroelectric dams, logging, cattle ranching, rubber tapping. It is the Amazon of ruthless exploitation, of soil depletion, river pollution, the expulsion of the Indians from their homelands; the Amazon of corruption and human misery, with all the stench and violence and vulgarity which accompany progress. It also is the Amazon of national flags clattering in the wind, of army posts and bureaucracy, of international missions and national development agencies, of luxury hotels and the tourist trade. And then there is another Amazon.

From *The Hidden Peoples of the Amazon* by Stephen Hugh-Jones and
Elizabeth Carmichael

It is clear that I am speaking here of a minority, of a small number of aboriginal peoples who still retain their cultural heritage, their cosmogonic myths,
their ancestral value systems expressed in rules and rituals. But these people are
important. Not only to anthropologists but to all those who still believe in the
importance of human creativeness, no matter where; who are interested in the
varieties of adaptive strategies, of sensorial experiences, of psychological func-

From *The Naturalist on the River Amazon* by Henry Walter Bates

tions, of the imaginary, of the quest for meaning and balance. After five centuries of incomprehension, this small group of survivors, inheritors of invaluable knowledge, not only of the forest but also of man's predicament, be it alone or in society, are the owners of a wealth of accumulated wisdom we should all treasure, not as a museum relic, but as a living example, a mirror, a choice some of man's ancestors made for better or for worse. To know these people, to study them in depth and detail, is not only a contribution to anthropology, but to ecology and biology, to psychology and philosophy, to the humanities, to a better understanding of ourselves and our neighbours. Few ethnologists have made detailed studies of the ethno-ecology of Amazonian Indians, and most of them have applied Western models to Amerindian thought processes, obtaining, at best, a one-sided and distorted view, and at worst missing the fundamental issues. Honourable exceptions are Philippe Descola, Darrell Addison Posey, Elizabeth Reichel and Maria Clara van der Hammen, to mention a few; but otherwise, ethno-ecological studies largely ignore the non-economical aspects of the Indians' concept of the *oikos*.

There is, then, another Amazon. Beside the illustrated books and the journalists' reports, apart from the specialised scientific records and the mass of institutional reports by local, regional, and international corporations, there still exists an Amazon which is rarely mentioned in the literature. It is the region of rivers and creeks, of interfluvial darkness, of endless forests and scattered settlements of Indians and Mestizos who hardly ever use the word 'Amazon', but who live in a world known to them only by Indian names: *igarapé, paraná, caruru, piramirí, itapucú*. They may have heard of the great river or of the city of Manaus, but they have never been there, nor have they any wish to go there. It is the other Amazon this book is concerned with. So much of what has recently been written on the Amazon and its Indians has tended toward a mood of progressive disillusion. The present study attempts to be a step toward the rediscovery of aspects which have remained hitherto largely unexplored.

In this book I shall be concerned with *meaning*, with the ways in which the Indians interpret their lives and their environments, and how they interact and try to adapt. But meaning cannot be quantified, and so I cannot give statistics. Meaning can be found in attitudes and daily conversations, in myths and spells, in the manner in which people describe events and emotions, or in the words they use to explain rules of behaviour, the do's and don'ts of everyday existence. Nothing of this can be quantified. I shall describe what I have learned from the Indians, and I shall use their own voices, their own words in an attempt to reach a better understanding of *their* perspective of rainforest ecology.

In the anthropological literature or, in general terms, in the literature concerned with culture history, we often find references to so-called 'fertility cults'. Many of these publications speak of fertility 'goddesses', of a palaeolithic 'Venus' or a neolithic fertility ritual, and there exists an abundant iconography which illustrates these tentative reconstructions of so-called primitive religions.

Other publications speak of a kind of pan-sexualism as predominant in some ancient or present-day traditional societies. The authors of these studies tend to interpret many cultural manifestations in terms of reproductive behaviour, as if the societies under discussion were almost exclusively oriented toward hedonistic goals. And then there is the recurrent theme of matriarchy, which some authors trace from palaeolithic Europe to the myth of Amazon rainforest women.

Much of all this is a matter of definition. If we speak of reproduction, of reproductive behaviour in terms of multiplying a given substance, we can easily compare economic production, such as planting and harvesting a field, with sexual activity. If we grow wheat or rice or potatoes, if we breed cattle or sheep, if we are in the lumber business or are bee-keepers, we always depend on, and interfere with, the biological facts of procreation. Our daily food intake consists of items which were produced as part of a biological cycle of procreation: meat, milk, eggs, bread and cheese, vegetables and fruits. During breakfast or lunch we don't think in these biological terms, partly because we are much too far removed from the sources of our food items. We don't know the hen that laid the egg, nor do we know or care to know the precise origins of our bacon or roast beef, or of our orange juice or Brussels sprouts.

But there are millions and millions of people in this world who know exactly what they are eating; who know the biological processes by which their food items are produced, and who know the environmental conditions under which these processes are developing. The Tukano Indians are part of these millions. Among them, biological processes are matters of daily discussion. Copulation, menstruation, conception, pregnancy and birth are constantly being talked about, not because the Tukano practise a 'fertility cult'; not because they are oversexed and promiscuous, but because they are concerned about the continuity of life and the quality of life. They are concerned about exactly the same problems you and I are concerned about, namely: population control, soil degradation, river pollution, overhunting, overharvesting, the conservation of natural resources, together with the conservation of ethical values and personal responsibilities.

I am speaking here of a tribal society of the tropics, of a people still sometimes called 'primitives' and 'savages'; of people who, occasionally, will put on feather-crowns and sing in praise of fish or palm fruits. But I believe that the ideas the Tukano Indians have developed in the course of thousands of years of rainforest experience are of an importance that goes beyond the limits of anthropological research. We know that the Amazon rainforest is of global importance, and we cannot dismiss the Indians' experience as useless or superstitious, once we recognise that the effectiveness of their adaptation to the environment has been creditable.

In Western modes of thinking most of us are used to speaking of man and nature as if we were referring to an accepted dichotomy. It seems that the Indians do not share this view. In the first place, Tukanoan languages have no word that would be equivalent to our 'nature', our spatio-temporal world as we conceive it. The nearest expression would be *deyóri turí*, the 'visible dimension', as the Desana call it, meaning by this the perceptual universe, with the inclusion of dreams and hallucinations. But *deyóri turí* is not a term an Indian would use in conversation to describe nature in the sense of what we would call the physical environment, here meaning the forest, the river, flora, fauna, climate, the abbreviated and condensed nature of a person's existence. As the Indians see human life, man is in every respect a part of his environment, much in the same way in which thinking and feeling man is part of biological man. One might say that the Tukano feel to be part of their external environment in the same way as we inhabit our bodies. For example, if we imagine an Indian going into the forest, we should not interpret this act as that of an isolated person entering a specific part of nature; this would be as meaningless as saying that he 'enters' his skin or his digestive system.

What we call nature is conceived by them as an extension of biological man, and therefore an Indian never feels 'surrounded by nature', as we would say, when he leaves his house to go into the forest or to travel by canoe. Nor is he ever 'living in harmony with nature', much less is he a 'child of nature'. These are romantic Western notions, quite unrealistic and totally misleading when used with reference to the Indians.

We have said that the environment (call it 'nature') is an extension of man. This does not mean that the perceptual universe is conceived as a living organism. What is meant here is that man participates in the universe and in his immediate environment through the energy circuit of *bogá*, a circuit which includes all plants and animals, together with all sense data; but the universe or our earth are not thought to be alive as a system as such. What gives it life is man, by 'incorporating' what we call nature, into the human scale. The Indians have done this on many levels, on levels of awareness, of imagination, of practical use. In the first place, they have named and categorised much of their external environment. They have projected their culture upon it by saying: *'This hill is like a house'*, *'This river is like a man standing with outstretched arms'*, *'This cave is like a womb'*, *'This fish is like a woman'*. So if you see an Indian walking in the forest or paddling a canoe on a river, he is not 'in nature' but he is entirely surrounded by cultural meanings, by meanings his cultural tradition has given to his external surroundings.

This view, of course determines his ecological awareness. His protective practices and beliefs referring to what we call nature, are essentially self-protective; he knows that any damage done to nature will be damaging to his very own life, and so he attempts to conserve nature in the same way in which we take care of our own bodies, their physiological functions and their psychological stability. We all are aware of our bodies; we know something about our anatomy and physiology; as a matter of fact, we have gone to great pains in naming all the parts and functions and systems and relationships of our bodies. But, of course, there are many things we don't know about our bodies, and so we are at times concerned about certain signs and symptoms, about certain malfunctions.

Bulging-stemmed palm
(*Iriartea ventricosa*)

It has been suggested that nature is hostile, violent and unpredictable, and that the Indians try to bring order into this confusion by categorising it. This may be so in some cases and some societies, but from what we have learned from the Indians, it is man and his basic impulses: food, sex, power, security, which are chaotic and must be controlled, while nature, far from being disordered, offers many practical models for human behaviour and adaptation. Nature has its definite structures and rules, its periodicities, the Milky Way, plant growth, animal behaviour, crystals and flowers, colours and odours. The chromatic scale of the rainbow, a phosphene perceived in a drug-induced trance, a seasonal fishrun or a bird migration, a meandering river in the forest; they all are models which offer security together with a wealth of intellectual and emotional stimulation.

The Indians have stored a large amount of culturally important information in all aspects of their physical environment, as well as in their material artefacts. This storing, this coding, is multi-referential and layered; a certain aspect of nature or a certain artefact may contain simultaneously various information expressed in metaphors and metonymies. In this layering one can recognise many fields: rhetoric, narcotics, sexuality, social organisation, material culture, and others, all of which are interrelated. This interrelatedness emphasises aspects which are recurrently stated as constants. For a example, the river emphasises linearity, fluidity, segmentation, communication, complementarity, reciprocity, exogamy. These are organisational principles which express a value system and, with it, the uniqueness of Tukano culture. The forest is dark and musky. The river lies under an open sky, odourless. In water one drowns; in the forest one may be lost, entangled in a wilderness; both are liminal regions of initiation, of transformation. Myths and tales, dreams and hallucinations repeat this theme over and over.

Often enough, many of these meanings may not be too obvious, even to the Indian observer. There is a time perspective to these meanings, especially with reference to landmarks, to ancient place names, to ancient trees and boulders. Other meanings may have been forgotten altogether or may be known only to certain people. But to make a difference between nature and culture does not make any sense to a Tukano.

On the other hand, the visible, discernible structure of matter provides a set of simple models which in the minds of the Indians constitute ideal patterns of organisation. For example, the hexagonal structure of a rock crystal, together with such hexagons as can be found in a honeycomb or a tortoiseshell, is such a model. Or the segmentation of the trunk of a palm, the patterns on a snake skin. There will be models taken from astronomy, from the motions of the moon, from eclipses, or there will be the model of the central axis, the zenith. Other models are seen in the spiral: snailshells, whirlpools, dustdevils or botanical forms and embryonic shapes.

These 'natural' forms observed in the environment are being incorporated into the culture as given forms of optimal organisation. The Indians do not animate a landscape, a forest, a mountain or a river in a disorderly, incoherent way. It may seem so to us, but to the society in question there exists an underlying coherence. What we are inclined to call animism is, then, a very serious matter; it is a process of imprinting, of the naming of things which are chosen to represent cultural truths. And they are selected not in an arbitrary way. There is a consensus which has to be expressed in certain striking, memorable images. This, then, is a highly structured imagination, an imagination which is coherent, which makes sense. And that is precisely the point: the Indians have created their cosmologies, their symbolic systems, not in a casual fashion but have chosen their images in such a way as to represent sets of cultural truths, social norms, major principles of organisation.

We have spoken here about the reality of the environment in which the Indians have developed their culture. Sometimes these realities are harsh and sometimes the way in which the Indians see them and adapt to them may seem to us crude and shameless. But if we want to understand their culture we must admit that these realities are the raw material for their imagery, and that their images create ever new imaginary constructs. And these processes of the imagination are highly selective; this is not imagination run wild but imagination constructed, imagination used like a tool of precision, to achieve a certain objective. And, of course, this imagination cuts across all fields, across all these compartments into which cultures are accommodated by our theories and our models. But, speaking of realities, reality is that part of nature upon which the Indians have projected their culture.

A Note on Orthography and Abbreviations

All words in aboriginal languages are written in italics. Personal names and names of mythical or supernatural beings are also italicised.

The Tukanoan languages occasionally quoted in this book have not yet been described by specialists. There exist no definite analyses of Tukanoan languages, and the available studies made by Bible translators and others are still in a preliminary stage. Those referring to Desana, Pira-Tapuya, and Uanano, the languages I am mainly concerned with, are hardly more than brief introductions. The orthography employed in the present study is not phonemic, but attempts to transcribe words and sentences as understood by the author in the course of field research and textual analysis. The approximate English (French, German) values are:

a as in f*a*ther
e as in cl*ay* or s*e*t
ë as in qu*e* (French)
i as in t*ea*
o as in b*o*ne
h as in la*ch*en (German)
Exceptional are ö as in hören (German), and *ü* as in r*ue* (French).

A circumflex or swung dash (~) preceding a word, indicates nasalisation; occasionally it can appear on the last or penultimate syllable of a compound word, in which case it indicates nasalisation of only that part. Glottal closure is indicated by an apostrophe ('); stress-accents are used when called for and are important in tonal differences.

References to languages are abbreviated in the following manner: (T) Tukano proper, (D) Desana, (PT) Pira-Tapuya, (U) Uanano, (TT) Tatuyo, (BA) Bará, (BS) Barasana, (LG) lingua geral, the Tupi-derived Amazonian vernacular, (SP) Spanish. Other abbreviations are: lit. for literally, and cf. for compare. Since the present writer's name is frequently mentioned as a bibliographical reference, it appears in the text in abbreviated form as RD.

The more than twenty patrilineal descent groups or 'tribes' which constitute the Eastern Tukanoan linguistic family, are usually referred to in the literature as Tukano. One of these tribes, however, calls itself 'Tukano' and, therefore, as a linguistic unit, must be designated as 'Tukano proper'. In the present book I am using the terms Tukano or Tukanoans when speaking in general terms of the Indians, but shall use the term 'Tukano proper' when referring to the particular language of the Tukano tribe.

I am not a linguist but I have a working knowledge of Desana and Tukano proper, the language which is spoken by many Tukanoan Indians, irrespective of their particular language group. Whenever I quote Tukanoan words or sentences without indicating a specific language group, I am quoting in Desana, but usually all linguistic affiliations are indicated.

I should like to add a note on the problem of using certain terms for which I find no equivalent in Tukanoan languages. For example, there seem to be no abstract words for god, love, soul, nor is there a word for nature. I find it embarrassing to clutter my text with words in quotation marks, words in italics, words *sous rature*, etc. whenever I want to call attention to the fact that I use these words not in their usual sense (whatever that means), but because I can find no better translation. I shall try to be explicit. The Indians have words for ambivalence, anxiety, emptiness, energy, dimension, memory, transformation, but the meaning of these terms may vary according to context.

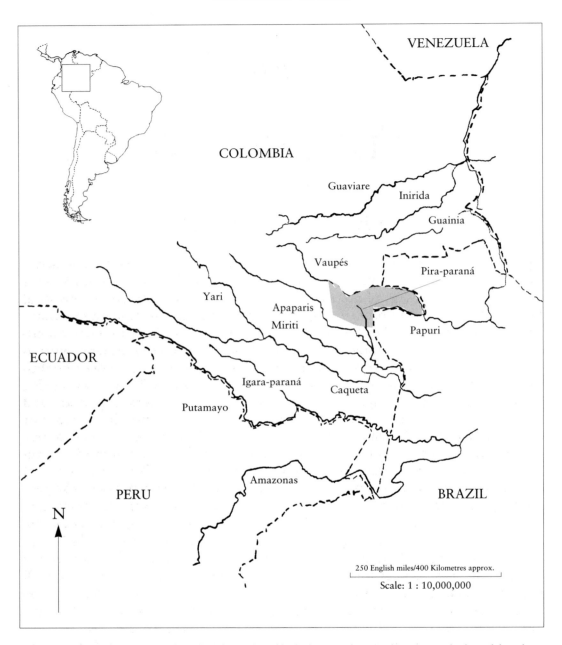

The south-east corner of Colombia; the shaded part shows the area inhabited by the
Tukanos

Chapter I

THE SETTING

An Ethnographic Sketch

The central region of the Colombian Northwest Amazon is commonly referred to as the Vaupés territory, taking its name from the Vaupés River, a major western tributary of the Rio Negro. This is a vast expanse of equatorial rainforests, level and unbroken, sloping almost imperceptibly toward the southeast and the great basin of the Amazon. The monotony of the rainforest landscape gives the initial impression that this land forms a homogeneous unit in terms of climate, soils, irrigation and biota, but this would be an oversimplification. In reality, within this apparent uniformity many different zones exist, each characterised by a significant combination of soils, rivers, vegetation and wildlife, often showing variations which form a complex mosaic of larger or smaller ecosystems. When looking out over the wide sweep of the skyline one can see, here and there, a few rocky hills, level-topped or dome-shaped, emerging over the distant horizon. Like dark towers or islands floating in a sea of green, these points are remnants of the Guiana Shield, remainders of the geological past. The forest itself is varied, ever-changing, never quite the same; there are areas of dense or more open forest, of small savannahs and *caatinga* of white sand. There are differences in species distribution. And then there are black-and-white water rivers, falls and rapids, waters cascading over boulder-strewn stretches of river, which form biological frontiers and, in themselves, are all important landmarks and ecosystems. It is clear that these many different zones have always influenced the characteristics of flora and fauna, and with it, the history and processes of human adaptive responses to the environment.

The aboriginal population of the Vaupés territory is represented mainly by members of the Eastern Tukanoan linguistic family, and are generally referred to as Tukano Indians. This linguistic family consists of more than twenty tribes or, rather, named descent groups, each one speaking its own language. Some of these tribes were known by name already in the early literature, and the British naturalists of the mid-nineteenth century collected some interesting ethnographic data. They became well known to European scholars only early this cen-

Barasana shaman with honeycomb

tury, through Theodor Koch-Grünberg's classic travel account *Zwei Jahre unter den Indianern*. At present, some of the better known groups are the Desana, Bará, Barasana, Tatuyo, Taibano, Cubeo, and the Tukano proper. The territory occupied by these and a dozen other Tukanoan tribes, can approximately be delimited thus: the Vaupés River to the North and Northeast; the Apaporis River to the West, and the equatorial line to the South.

Intensive studies of Tukanoan tribes began in the sixties, Irving Goldman's research among the Cubeo (1939-1940) being a pioneering exception. It was in the mid-sixties when the present author made an urgent appeal to the international ethnological community to study these Indians who were by then, being threatened by accelerated acculturational pressures. This initiative led to a number of detailed studies, most of them carried out by European and North American scholars.

In the following pages I shall present a brief outline of the main characteristics of Tukano society and culture. According to ethnohistorical traditions the Tukano Indians are newcomers in the Vaupés territory where they arrived sev-

Tatuyo boys with pan-pipes

eral generations ago, proceeding from the East by ascending the Rio Negro. There is no information on their original homeland, no exodus myth, no memory of the motivations for this migration. It is clear, of course, that the Vaupés territory is a refuge area which, in the past, has received wandering groups proceeding from the Amazon, the Orinoco, and Guiana.

Once such a wandering or fleeing people had penetrated above the confluence of the Rio Negro and the Vaupés, beyond the first great falls and rapids, they would have achieved a measure of security, and the interfluvial forests would have provided, then as now, a safe hinterland. But it is strange, nonetheless, that among the Tukano there should be no trace of a tribal memory recalling a time previous to their ascending the Rio Negro. In the Vaupés territory, they first established contact with local sedentary Arawakan groups from whom they acquired manioc cultivation. After some initial conjugal unions with nomadic Makú bands, the Tukano began to intermarry with the Arawakan population. After overcoming their hostility and a slow process of change from uxorilocal residence and matriliny to virilocal residence and patriliny, the Tukanoan groups assimilated and displaced most of the local Arawakans and established Tukanoan dominance in much of the Vaupés territory. During the last decades of the nineteenth century Brazilian-Italian missionary influence was strong on the upper Rio Negro, but eventually subsided. Missionary activity was renewed during the second decade of the twentieth century, when Dutch Catholic missionaries entered the Vaupés. The rubber boom had little effect upon the Vaupés Indians, but recent political upheavals in Colombia, combined with the drug traffic, the discovery of gold mines, and the activities of Protestant sects, are threatening the cultural identity and the biological survival of the Indians.

The traditional form of settlement is the *maloca* or longhouse, a self-contained unit of several nuclear families. Malocas are spaced along the rivers and creeks at distances of a day or two's journey by canoe, but occasionally are found in remote interfluvial regions. Nucleated settlements of square one-family houses are not traditional, but are imposed by missionaries, government agencies or rubber gatherers, and have led to social and economic disruption, the spread of diseases, alcoholism, and the breakdown of symbolic systems related to maloca life and ecological theories and practices.

Slash-and-burn ('swidden') agriculture is the rule, and manioc cultivation provides the staple food in the form of coarse flour and large flat cassava cakes. Women spend much of their time in the daily task of harvesting and processing the poisonous tubers. Palm fruits and wild-growing tree fruits of many different species are important food items. Game and fish are abundant and the men spend much time in the forest and on the river. The most important game animals are large rodents, monkeys, peccary, deer, tapir, as well as game birds such as guan, tinamou and toucans. Edible insects and honey are readily available. Garden crops include cooking plantains, peppers, some sugarcane, tobacco and coca, as well as cultivated fruit trees such as peach palms.

Traditionally the Tukano tribes trade with northern Arawakans, exchanging goods which, symbolically, represent women. Trade items acquired at mission stations include cloth, woven hammocks, cooking vessels, machetes, axes, fishhooks, and some minor objects such as needles and matches. Native arts and crafts include canoe-making, fish trap construction, bark-cloth preparation,

Barasana headman with a Tatuyo boy

basketry, pottery, blowgun-making, featherwork, and the manufacture of ritual adornments.

Labour division is well marked. The men make clearings in the forest and fire them, but otherwise horticulture is a female activity, while men and boys hunt and fish; both sexes are active in the gathering of forest fruits, insects, and wild honey. The daily food supply is prepared by women and girls, but only men may smoke game or fish, manufacture ritual objects, and prepare coca, tobacco, and hallucinogenic substances. Garden plots are privately owned, but hunting, fishing, and gathering territories are loosely defined as belonging to the inhabitants of nearby malocas. Tribal lands are delimited as such only in shamanic geographical terms based upon ethnohistorical tradition, but are not coherent and do not correspond to reality.

Each Tukanoan tribe constitutes a phratry which is divided into some twenty ranked and named exogamous sibs, each tracing its origin to a common mythical ancestor. Terminological uses are related to the Dravidian model. The main characteristic of Tukanoan society is language group exogamy; a person must marry a spouse speaking a different language and, therefore, belonging to a different phratry. This form of exogamy is combined with patrilineal descent and virilocal residence, real or classificatory, with cross-cousin marriage being the preferential form of union. Marriages are monogamous, but polygyny does occur. Marriage is essentially a sister exchange between men of different but preferential marriage groups. Divorce is unknown, but separation of spouses is not unusual. Until recently, the basic domestic unit was the longhouse inhabited by four to eight nuclear families which formed a tightly organised cooperative. According to Tukanoan inheritance laws, ritual objects are passed on from father to son, and constitute the most valuable property. Gardens and malocas are sometimes passed on to the youngest son. Infants and young children are raised permissively, but boys of five to six years of age are guided and controlled by their fathers. At approaching puberty boys are severely disciplined by their fathers and elders. Emphasis is placed upon exogamy, the laws of reciprocity, the conservation of natural resources, and the acquisition of traditional values. Mission-educated Indians mostly become wage labourers, boatmen or servants.

Since language groups or phratries do not occupy discrete territories in the Vaupés area, one cannot speak of 'tribes' in the accustomed sense. The principal political unit is the maloca. During the last century there still existed chieftains, but later on authority became invested mainly in shamans and elders of recognised esoteric knowledge. Some large maloca communities may still have a headman, but his authority is feeble. Women occupy a low status in society. They carry a heavy burden in food production and processing. On an idealised level, however, female-oriented imagery is strongly felt. Intermarriage with Hispanic 'colonos' and rubber gatherers is infrequent; temporary concubinage is common but is often childless owing to native contraceptives used by the women.

A Barasana shaman and his Bará sister-in-law

Recently the Colombian government has established a large *resguardo* for all Tukanoan groups of the Vaupés territory, and consequently some Indians, who have received some formal education, under the influence of Colombian national politics, have set up small groups of self-styled native leaders. [*Resguardos* are different from reservations in the US sense in that they grant legal ownership of the land to the indigenous peoples, whereas on reservations the government grants the use of the land but retains property rights.]

Early Spanish contact with Vaupés Indians goes back to the sixteenth century, but no settlements were established, and until the early years of the twentieth century political sovereignty of the area was unclear. The Indians' orientation was toward Brazil; Tukanoan chiefs were appointed by the Brazilian authorities in Manaus, and all trade or missionary activities penetrated into the Vaupés by way of the Rio Negro. Mitú, the present Colombian district capital, was founded only in 1936, when the international border was delimited. When rubber became an important item in the war effort of the forties, additional settlements were founded and some primitive roads were traced. Ever since, Mitú has been the centre of political, administrative, missionary and exploitative activities, with some health services and schooling facilities for the Indians. Since among the Tukanoan Indians, political cohesion and authority were always very weak, these recent developments have deeply affected most of the organisational structures of the aboriginal population.

Shamans continue to exercise control over many family and community affairs, and are important mediators in contacts with outsiders. The strict observance of hunting, fishing and foraging rituals, expressed in dietary and sexual taboos, constitutes a body of socio-ecological management rules which are constantly being extolled by shamans and elders. With the progressive breakdown of the maloca unit, brought about by missionary activity, these control systems are losing their strength.

Warfare, cannibalism, the forceful abduction of women and the destruction of hostile settlements, constitute frequent themes in ethno-historical tradition. The principal enemies were the Arawak of the central and southern Vaupés, and the Caribs of the western borders. Magical aggression is a serious matter and vengeance for inflicted harm may be protracted over years. Fights over women, adultery, abduction, or simple maloca gossip present everyday conflict situations. During recent years political unrest, guerrilla infiltration, the cocaine trade and the gold rush have introduced new conflicts for the solution of which the aboriginal culture lacks all mechanisms.

Turning now briefly to Tukanoan religious beliefs, we first must consider the structure of the universe. According to shamanic theories the universe consists of three superimposed layers: the celestial vault, our earth, and the netherworld. Each one can be subdivided into many smaller units. In shamanic language, the celestial vault is an immense womb, a brain, a hexagonal rock crystal, elements

A group of men: (left) Barasana headman, (right) Bará shaman

in a chain of analogues which form an all-embracing image of creation, trans-formation and growth. The sun, sometimes referred to as 'Sun Father', is the origin of all fertilising forces. The entire universe is conceived as a circuit of energy flow of limited potential. Man's task consists in maintaining this flow through balancing all ecological aspects in such a way that the interaction between mankind and the physical and social environment may not be upset. There is no sun cult, but a strong awareness of the interdependence of all living beings.

Shamans tend to specialise in ritual, dancing and singing, in reciting genealogies, in divination, healing, spells, and other fields. All exercise control over hunting, fishing, and harvesting strategies, and have a keen understanding of local ecological problems. Catholic and Protestant missionaries have had little influence upon shamanic beliefs and practices.

Belief in a supernatural Master of Animals is widespread, and fear of his retaliation constitutes an effective control to overhunting. He is often associated or confused with other forest or river spirits, some of them appearing as seducers, doppelgänger, or even as cannibalistic monsters.

The principal metaphysical experience is provided by collective ceremonies during which the men consume hallucinogenic substances under the guidance of shamans and elders. On their ecstatic flights the participants return to the cosmic/maternal womb where they visit different dimensions in which they become witnesses to cosmogonic episodes. Male initiation rituals introduce the novices into the lore referring to historical origins, and the importance of exogamy and male dominance. Periodic exchange rituals are celebrated between complementary exogamous units, reaffirming lineage origins and alliances. In all these ceremonies hallucinogenic substances play a prominent role.

Dancing and singing are important art forms. Many objects, both of ritual or of everyday use, are decorated with design motifs perceived during hallucinatory trance states. Since many of these motifs are culturally coded with reference to marriage rules and fertility concepts, this applied art constitutes a body of visual reminders of important cultural truths. The shamanic orchestration of the multiple sensorial experiences during collective ceremonies, when hallucinogenic substances are consumed, are important artistic acts.

Herbal lore is highly developed and the Indians' knowledge of botany (pharmacology, toxicology, narcotics, etc.) forms one of the most interesting aspects of Tukanoan culture. Shamanic diagnostic practices include the interpretation of hallucinations, dreams, and crystal gazing. Curing practices combine medicinal plants, dietary restrictions, chants, the blowing of smoke, asperging with water and the sucking out of supposedly pathogenic substances.

Death originated in mythical times from incest and adultery. Canoe burial or pit burials are the rule, sometimes inside the maloca. The soul-stuff wanders over a perilous trail to a land of blissful annihilation or, in the case of a person having led a sinful life, he or she is transformed into animals and thus enters into the abodes of the Master of Animals, where he replenishes his charges. Funeral ceremonies are of little importance and consist mainly of shamanic spells and chants. Old people are sometimes abandoned on an uninhabited river island, or in a lonely spot in the deep forest.

In the preceding pages I have presented a bare outline of Tukanoan ethnography. It is a telegraphic summary, something for a handbook, written in a leaden, abbreviated style. But this book is not meant to be a monograph, and this section cannot offer more than a generalised overview, to provide the reader with a few points of reference. To speak, however, of a generalised Tukanoan culture in the Vaupés territory is in itself an oversimplification. In the first place, an often repeated mistake is the belief that the Cubeo Indians, known through Goldman's monograph, are representative of Tukanoan society and culture. They are an Arawakan tribe, linguistically Tukanoised in recent times, but culturally different from the Tukanoans in many ways. A similar situation prevails among the Tariana, another Arawakan group largely assimilated by neighbouring Tukanoans, but still conserving many traits of their Arawak tradition. The Makuna of the lower Pira-paraná are another example of cultural divergence; although they speak a language of the Eastern Tukanoan family, they have ceased to practice the strict rules of exogamy, and other aspects of their culture are strongly influenced by non-Tukanoan Indian groups living to the south of Makuna territory. Another common mistake is to believe that the Colombian Tukanoan Indians are as acculturated as the Desana, Uanano, Tuyuka, Tukano proper, and others of the Brazilian Rio Negro. The Indians of the axis Yavareté-Saõ Gabriel have been exposed to strong economic, religious and political influences for more than two centuries. Moreover, on the lower Rio Negro these Indians occupy part of the Amazonian floodplains (*varzea*), while the Colombian Tukanoans are mainly concentrated on *terra firma* which is not seasonally flooded. Recent ethnological studies carried out along the Brazilian Rio Negro obviously describe cultural and ecological conditions which differ from those prevailing in the Colombian Vaupés. Contact areas or routes, such as the Rio Negro to the East, the Isana River to the North, the Caquetá and Mirití-paraná Rivers to the South, are major factors in cultural diversification in the Vaupés core area of Tukanoan tribes, and should always be taken into account.[1]

The Creation of Geography and the Ecology of Creation

To introduce the reader to the Tukano and their land, I shall begin by presenting a condensed version of the Desana origin myth, as it was told in my presence on several occasions by shamans and knowledgeable elders. The creation, the advent of mankind, and the beginnings of social life develop, according to the Indians, in a well-known geographical dimension.

It is said that in the beginning of time the Sun Father sent his representative called *Pamurí mahsë* ('progenitor') to descend to earth in order to establish mankind on it. The Progenitor carried a staff called *yeégë*[2] and he was searching for the precise spot where he would create man. While travelling on all the rivers of what today is called the Vaupés territory, in the Colombian Northwest Amazon, the Progenitor stopped here and there, standing in the prow of his canoe, and would thrust his staff into the riverbank as if to probe the ground, as if to test the fertility of the forest soil. He was searching for the spot where his staff would stand upright without casting a shadow. The Progenitor went on and on, but every time he thrust the staff into the ground, it stood askew and cast a shadow. At long last the Progenitor arrived at a place where the staff stood straight and cast no visible shadow. Now drops of sperm fell from the staff into a deep pool in the river, and from it the first Desana was born.

So far, this is a very simple tale and one might want to go on with it and learn more about that first human being. But this would lead us astray and we must proceed gradually. To begin with, the reader can imagine that even as artless a story as this can be expanded and embellished in many ways. There may be colourful descriptions of the way-stations the Progenitor visited before finally locating the 'exact' spot; there may be accounts of the obstacles he had to overcome, the hardships he had to endure. There also may be descriptions of his powerful staff, of his canoe, of the qualities of the soils he found on the riverbanks. All this would depend upon the speaker, his eloquence, his memory. However, the bare facts of the tale were few: a fertilising solar principle, an earthbound agent and his tool, and a certain spot where the task had to be accomplished.

To understand this constellation of givens, we must provide the reader with a broader scene, the one the native listener has in mind when he hears the first sentences describing the Progenitor's voyage on the rivers of the Northwest Amazon. Let us stop, then, here and discuss some of the details this story implies.

The territory of the Colombian Tukano tribes is approximately limited by several rivers. To the north and northeast we have the Vaupés River which, after first running in a west-to-east direction, turns sharply toward the southeast until it joins the Rio Negro. Following this river we come to the Tiquié, an affluent that runs from west to east, almost exactly along the equatorial line. From there, the upper Pira-paraná is pointed out as a northwestern limit, while the Ti, a small affluent of the middle course of the Vaupés, runs from southwest to northeast and thus closes the territorial outline.

This, of course, is but a figure drawn with a stick in the sand, by people who cannot read a printed map but who, nevertheless, have an approximate idea of a wider geographical unit. Some of the Indians I talked to, over the years, would correct or expand this delineation, but most of them would agree that Tukanoan territory was, in all essence, of hexagonal shape, an idea which corresponds in many ways to geographical reality.

There is, however, an abstract concept involved. The model of this shape is the rock crystal, the principal power tool of Tukanoan shamans who see in its recurrent hexagonal structure an element of order and continuity which express a primordial energy. This energy manifests itself in the rainbow pattern of the colour spectrum one can observe in the depth of a crystal when handled under varying light conditions. I shall return to this aspect later on; at this point it should be added that the concept of hexagonal space is ever-present in Tukanoan imagery.[3] The entire tribal territory is imagined as being subdivided into innumerable invisible hexagons, some larger and some smaller, ever changing in size, depending upon the specific context in which the hexagonal image is being used. For example, all headwaters are thought to be enclosed in hexagons, and so are

Rock formations near the Vaupés River, at Urania near Mitú

all confluences and rivermouths. A hill, a lake, rapids, indeed any landmark is thought to lie within a hexagonal space, and the same is believed to be true in the case of a maloca, a cultivated field, a port, or a burial ground. Even people, notably shamans, are at times believed to stand within a hexagonal space. The human heart is hexagonal, the womb, the brain. The hexagon's power is the power of the rock crystal which contains the colour energies, the all-important concept of Tukanoan shamanism and cosmogonical theory which teaches that these crystals contain solar energy, the energy of the Sun Father.

After this long digression we must return to the Creation Myth. It was said that when the Sun Father's staff stood upright, drops of semen flowed from it into a pool, a whirlpool. This act marks the creation of man; not of mankind, because the latter term would include woman. It was man who was created there and then. Woman was not created; woman always existed, she existed already when man was not yet born. Because woman is the land, she is identified with the earth and the Indians of the Vaupés have no creation story for the earth; it always existed.

A creation story of the Barasana Indians of the Pira-paraná, one of the major rivers of the Vaupés territory, parallels the theme of pre-existing womanhood. It is a long and complex story but it can be condensed into one single scene of high drama. The story tells that Whippoorwill fluttered down into primeval darkness and silence. Whippoorwill was afraid and called out: '*Who am I?*' Out of the darkness a voice said: '*You are man!*' Whippoorwill cried out: '*Who are you?*' and the voice replied: '*I am woman.*'

There exist many different versions of narratives describing where exactly the first human beings or tribal ancestors emerged or were created. Some say that it was at the Rock of *Nyi*, a large boulder with a petroglyph, standing on the eastern bank of the Pira-paraná, almost at the spot where it crosses the equatorial line. Others will mention some rapids in the territory of the speaker. Most myths, however, will agree that it was at *Ipanoré*, a place located on the lower Vaupés River, just north of its confluence with the Tiquié. *Ipanoré* is famous for its dangerous rapids; on many boulders over which the waters cascade one can see deeply engraved petroglyphs and natural pot-holes, and many origin myths point to this spot as points of emergence and dispersal. It is told that it was at *Ipanoré* where the Tukanoans first established contact with the Arawakan Tapir People.

Some of the pot-holes are shaped like shallow cups of about 30 cms. diameter, and here again Tukano imagination perceives a series of female associations. In some origin myths these shallow depressions are said to represent basketry trays in which the local women offered food to the Tukanoan invaders; in other tales, they are said to be the impressions of women's buttocks when the Tukano took possession of these lands and peoples. In still other contexts the pot-holes are said to represent the cooking vessels in which those women prepared man-

Dense forest near the Pira-Paraná river

ioc gruel for the strange hungry men. Some whitish veins of crystalline intrusions in the dark rock surface are pointed out as the overflow of the boiling gruel, but others are inclined to see in these streaks the traces of sperm. In any case, it was at *Ipanoré* where bands of Tukanoan invaders, hunters and foragers who travelled in canoes made of large pieces of tree bark, and who were short of marriageable women, first made contact with sedentary agriculturalists, manioc-growers who lived in large longhouses and whose women were not averse to give the newcomers a friendly reception.

At *Ipanoré* we learn for the first time of tribal subdivisions and distinct language groups. The central theme of many myths and tales is the progress of a group of men travelling in a canoe shaped like an anaconda, or inside an anaconda swimming in the depths of the riverbed. The men are variously described as being the ancestors of phratries, the founders of ranked sibs, the representatives of different ethnic groups: Tukanoans, Makú, Whites. The key motifs are migration, colonisation, and the slow development of marriage patterns, from violent abduction of women to formalised exogamy.

The men's search for marriage partners is a dominant theme. From dozens of texts recorded in the field, it appears that from the very beginning in mythical times women are associated with manioc planting and processing, while the Tukanoan male is described as a hunter, sometimes as a fisherman, and only marginally as a horticulturalist. In many narratives it is said that Tapir Women introduced horticulture among the Tukanoans who, during the early stages of their contact with the Arawakans, were condemned to servitude in the manioc fields of their fathers-in-law. It took generations before virilocal residence and patrilinear descent rules became established, accompanied by highly formalised forms of exogamy.

The idea that horticulture and its produce are associated with the women of 'other people', that a man 'marries into horticulture', is expressed in many metaphors. It is part of the female image, and the development of strict exogamous relationships between nominal hunters and nominal horticulturalists forms the background to ecological principles of the first order, not merely in economic terms or a simplistic carbohydrate/protein link, but in the sense of psychological compatibilities and energetic combinations as formulated by Tukanoan shamans. The division into hunters and horticulturalists does not correspond to reality, but neither does the Tukanoan division into people of inherent odour categories, technological preferences, or ritual participation. However, all these and many other concepts express the predominating need for reciprocity, not only in a social context, but also between human beings and nature. This idea is deeply rooted in the Tukanoan world-view, and we cannot but call this an ecological theory.

In Tukanoan understanding, the organising principle of the universe is the life-force called *bogá* which produces semen/pollen, leading to insemination, growth, and maturity, followed by death and the regeneration of semen/pollen. This mechanistic evolution is not purposive, but neither is it permanent. It must be regulated and controlled by man, because otherwise people are likely to interfere with these cycles. The Indians are aware that this evolution is an ongoing process, that soils become degraded and must be allowed to fallow; that seeds can evolve or degenerate, that overhunting can decimate or even exterminate a given species. They know that they must be managers; not mere stewards of a given state of things, but active administrators of resources and controllers of people's needs.

The Indians do not believe that the universe of their environment is in any way a self-regulating, self-maintaining system. Their strong belief in the land as a legacy of the ancestors who continue to be a 'living presence', calls for obedience to a multitude of responsibilities and restrictions which must govern man's interaction with nature, always taking into account the limits of nature's resources and the pressures exercised by increasing demands. The biosphere is not a living organism. It is like a maloca; a maloca has no life of itself, but it harbours life, the life of its inhabitants, and the maloca's usability will last only as long as its occupants keep it in good shape.

This sounds coarse and conceptually crude. But the Indians will explain: to live (*mari ohokaríri në*) is to interact by following harsh rules. 'Our contemplation' (*mari pepíri ne*) will lead to abstract thought (~gunyári) and hence to 'our existence' (*mári ~ariri ne*) which demands from us 'to think and tread firmly' (*keranyeári*): marry the right woman, eat the right food, and obtain both in the right manner!

Chapter II

THE COSMOS

Cosmic Energies

According to the Indians, the principal energy in the cosmos is generated by the sun and is called *bogá*, a fundamental life force of an essentially spermatic character.[1] There are two suns: one, called *abé pagë*/Sun Father, which is the true source of all cosmic energy and which is invisible to human eyes, while the other is our visible sun, called *ëmë abé*/Day sun, which radiates heat (*ahsirí*) and light (*gohserí*). The invisible Sun Father is hardly ever mentioned in cosmogonic myths or shamanic discourse; he is not conceptualised as an anthropomorphic being but as a male principle vaguely associated with an immense translucent rock crystal.

The visible sun is the Sun Father's representative and pervades the entire universe with an immediate spermatic life-force. This sun regulates the seasons and, through them, controls all animal and plant-life. One might say that our sun controls what we call 'nature', but does so in a somewhat inconstant way, because a prolonged dry season or heavy rains will be harmful.[2]

The invisible sun is always beneficial. It emits *bogá* (pl. *bogarí*) and this concentrated energy is composed of many distinct parts. In the first place, *bogá* combines male and female principles in which the concept of 'force' (*turári*) is clearly distinguished from that of 'energy' (*bogá*), the former providing motion and intensity to the latter.[3] Many *bogá* energies are set in motion by *turári* forces. As one shaman put it: '... *turári pushes and bogá is being pushed; the latter is the true energy.' Bogá* is understood by the Indians as a compound of sensorial experiences conceptualised in abstract arrangements. A colour, an odour, a sound perceived in any dimension of consciousness is given an abstract meaning, and the totality of meanings provides a knowledge of rules men must follow in their daily interaction with the environment.[4] There is no homeostasis, no escape from personal responsibility; people must act in accordance with the facts of *bogá*.

A significant category of *bogárí* energies is perceived during narcotic trance states, but can also be observed during fleeting states of dissociation, day-dreaming, hypnagogic states, isolation, sensorial deprivation, or other situations of stress. The invisible sun is said to emit a spectrum of chromatic energies called *dári*, meaning 'rays' or 'threads' (*abé dári*/sun threads). This is a plural form and the singular is *da*, a word that can be applied to a string, a thread, or a vine. The so-called *dári* threads are said to flow in space in a straight line or in a broken line, and appear in a multitude of yellow, orange, and red hues which represent an energy range from male insemination to female fecundity[5]. *Dári* threads contain energies not only in a biological sense, but also transmit cultural norms referring to the traditional knowledge of environmental adaptation. Shamans explain that, at first, people might be unaware of receiving *dári* rays, but that eventually they will come to 'understand' them, and then begin to incorporate them as guiding principles in their behavioural patterns. Shamans say that one can see this process of energy transmission, for example, by watching the sun's rays falling into the dark, smoke-filled interior of a maloca, or through the dense forest canopy. Dust specks are compared to seminal matter, such as tiny tobacco seeds, pollen, or fish spawn. Or one can observe a rainbow or drops of water, one can watch the night sky and see a shooting star with a luminous *dári* effect. The *dári* phenomenon, the Indians say, can also be observed in lightning, or in sparks flying from a fire in the dark. *Dári* threads or dots do not move very rapidly, it is said. While *dári* threads are brilliant or of yellowish hues, being related to male reproductiveness, a group of wavy threads called *daríri* has a colour range from green and blue to violet. It transmits energies to women, mainly with reference to their menstrual cycle, and also to plants in which it determines their growth cycles. A third group of threads is called *~náriri*; in trying to explain this sensation, shamans mention phenomena such as heat waves, a slight tremor of the hands, or a scintillating, glimmering sensation on water or wet leaves. These are closely serrated lines which appear in all colours of the spectrum. These three energies: *dári*, *daríri* and *~náriri* form part of *bogá*, but, as we shall see further on, play an important role in the energy output of the visible sun.

Another group of *bogá* energies is related to intra-uterine developments and consists of dot-shaped elements called *~marári*, *noméri*, and *dobéri*. We must turn, then, to some shamanic theories of conception and foetal development. The choice of the two colours—yellow and red—is based upon the belief that the human embryo is a product of male sperm ('yellow') becoming mixed with female blood ('red') proceeding from the woman's liver. The entire concept of colour energies can be said to revolve around this fundamental idea which, in turn, is based upon the certainty that female blood must be an essential component of a new life, because menstruation stops as soon as conception takes place; the blood does not 'putrefy', as the Indians say, and is not expelled, but is retained.

Petroglyph on the Rock of Nyi

A woman's womb is said to be like a gourd vessel, like a cooking pot, a filter, and in many shamanic images is compared to a hexagonal rock crystal. The uterus is called ~*maró*; at conception, the woman's blood and the man's sperm form a substance which is called ~*marári*, a term designating a kind of powder, a very finely structured element which is retained in the uterine sieve. ~*Marári* is the plural of ~*mará* and refers to tiny luminous spots or particles people are said to perceive during drug-induced hallucinations, in hypnagogic states, or in a variety of states of high emotional involvement. The appearance of ~*marári*

Tatuyo with ritual stick-rattle

spots in hallucinations or similar states is technically known as phosphenes.[6] In the literature they are described as very small, many-coloured glowing points, dancing and moving, which the Indians compare with pollen, sand, smoke, sperm, very small seeds, the Milky Way, fish spawn in a river. All these and similar phenomena in nature or in imagination are said to have a seminal character and, according to the Indians, to perceive ~*marári* dots is to become aware of a seminal element, of insemination, of potential biogenesis.

The ensuing process is believed to be as follows: during the first month of pregnancy the ~*marári* element becomes more and more solid; the tiny individual particles grow, and soon a yellow and red component become distinguishable. After the first month these particles grow rapidly and, as shamans say, 'become heated'. During this stage the yellow component predominates and the biological process is visualised as a bright yellow background upon which a number of moving, luminous yellow and red dots are projected. This image is designated as *noméri*, literally, 'to paint with small dots'. These *noméri* dots are said to contain female energy and to manifest themselves in fleeting sensations perceived by people during states of stress, for example in fear, rage, or during the sex act. They are somewhat larger than ~*marári* dots, but fewer in number, and appear in well-defined colours, and move and mingle before the viewer's eyes, representing (yellow) male fertility and (red) female fecundity. The word *noméri* is related to *noméo*/woman (pl. *nomé*) and describes the act of painting small red dots with which women adorn their faces in preparation for social/ritual activities, thus indicating their fecundity potential.

It is said that during sexual intercourse women see dancing *noméri* dots before their eyes. The idea is that *noméri* represent a developmental stage of ~*marári*, a stage at which male and female energies are clearly differentiated and ready to fuse into one single element. The Indians will see *noméri* dots in many aspects of nature, in flowers, pelt marks, feathers, seeds, stars.

At the approach of the third month of pregnancy, the red element increases in quantity and temperature, and now begins to 'cook', in shamanic terminology. The respective imagery is described as a swirling multitude of large luminous red dots which now dominate over the yellow element. This image is called *dobéri*, literally, 'to paint with large dots', a phenomenon associated with male energies. The *dobéri* state continues throughout the entire period of foetal development. These dots move slowly, forming groups in which one colour begins to dominate—yellow or red. The appearance of these dots signifies that fertilisation has been achieved. At the end of this period a change occurs; when the time of birth approaches, the dots begin to reshape. The dots begin to turn into threads, they turn into *dári* threads. And so, when the infant is born, it has become the carrier of the solar energy.

These elements, then, are all-important factors in the generation and continuity of life. The entire sequence of images represents a belief system which is not limited to human physiology alone; on the contrary, it constitutes a fundamental theory which underlies practically all aspects of Tukanoan culture and of the shamanistic worldview. The Indians see in these sequential phenomena the image of procreative energies which have their formal and functional analogues in nature: sperm, pollen, spawn, seeds, comparable to smoke, sand, sediments, the Milky Way. These concepts, then, find their expression in the visual code of what we would call 'decorative art', painted on house fronts, on bark cloth aprons, used in body paint, painted on ritual objects and many other artefacts.

The idea that cosmic energies, however defined, find their visual expression in phosphenes, that is, in a neurophysiological phenomenon, is of special relevance. In some images, the Indians compare the celestial vault with a human brain, the two hemispheres being separated by the Milky Way; in other images, the cosmos is compared to a womb, '... *a dimension where there is everything, where there is gestation, a potential*', it was said. We shall find this uterine concept again, when we speak of other dimensions of awareness.

Bogá contains another pair of energies which serve quite specific ends. They are called *savéri-da* and *yëbëri-da*, and relate to different stages of plant growth.[7] The term *savéri* refers to incipient growth, to dormant and axillary buds, while *yëbëri* indicates ripeness. These two categories of 'threads' (*dári*) energise all plant-life, from the smallest herbs to the tall canopy trees of the dense rainforest. In shamanic practice, a small scandent plant (*Sabicea amazonensis*) provides the standard model, and is called upon in spells and songs whenever plant anatomy and growth stages are mentioned as metaphors of human developmental stages.[8]

All these energies emanating from the invisible sun—the seminal threads, embryogenic dots, and budding sprouts—are associated with a complete colour spectrum, a range of odours, flavours, sounds, shapes, textures, temperatures, and other properties which, in turn, are subdivided into categories indicating hues and intensities. A shaman's power (*turári*) consists in his ability to arrange and harmonise this multitude of energies, to interpret them, and balance them in case he should become aware of any disequilibrium.

I have said that the invisible sun's energies are always beneficial. The same is not true of the energies emanating from the visible sun and, occasionally, from the moon. In the first place, our sun's light (*gohsíri*) and consequently its colours, are not the same as those of the invisible sun's which is called *boyóri*, a kind of dawn-like reflection, quite different from the harsh primary colours full sunshine reveals to us. In the second place, our sun produces heat (*ahsíri*) which can be harmful to all life forms, while the invisible sun produces *kunyu poréri*, a kind of heat that hatches, the 'heat' of the womb, of an anthill, or of the decaying litter on the forest floor from which spring seedlings, mushrooms, and all medicinal plants. Our sun can produce severe headaches (*dihpúru niári*), especially in women.

The moon contains energies of which 'blackness' (*nyiró*) and 'coldness' (*gëhsari*) are associated with negative, life-destroying forces which originate in a colour range defined as 'pale green' (*yahsé gohseró*), 'pale yellow' (*bo're gohseró*), and 'red mixed with dark blue' (*diabiri nyirí*). The greenish aspect of the moon is associated with the initial, unripe stage of plant growth, called *saveri*; the yellowish aspect is associated with ripeness, here called *bogé*, and the purple (i.e. reddish-black) aspect, with putrefaction (*boáro*). Venus transmits a colour spectrum similar to that of the visible sun, but the most prominent hues are pale yellow and orange, that is, colours symbolising fertility. The stars and the Milky Way also emit energies, but to a minor degree. Some solar energies are concentrated in the rainbow which is said to 'look downward', meaning that its arc opens toward the earth. Since solar energies penetrate vertically, the rainbow's energies are thought to be a 'rebound' (*dea deáro*) which produces a rain-shower. Shamans elaborate on this saying that the term *dea deáro* should be replaced by *ka doáro*, an abstract concept which refers to a cove, an inlet (*kaë*) where 'river energies' accumulate. In this image the rainbow is a repository of colour energies which can be called upon in curing spells. Lightning contains *bogá* because it is a heavenly ejaculation manifested in tiny quartz splinters said to be found at the spot where the discharge struck the ground.

All men and women receive at birth an equal amount of *bogá* colour energies transmitted to them by the sperm of their fathers and the 'blood' of their mothers. At death, these energies return to the original source. *Bogá* is also contained in game animals, in fish, and in plants; in all food resources the environment offers to man and beast. In the case of human consumption, the highest food energy is associated with the state of *bogë*, described as a condition of ripeness which, in turn, is associated with an orange-brown colour, an appetising odour, and a specific flavour. The term *bogë* can be applied to cultivated or wild-growing fruits, to tubers, seeds, nuts, berries, insects, but also to rodents and other mammals, and to a wide range of other potential foods which show this state of 'ripeness'.

In sum, the sun, moon, stars, Milky Way, thunder and lightning, winds and floods, all act upon what we call 'nature'. This impact, often enough, is perceived as an interference leading to dysfunctions. It is at this point where shamans feel called upon to intervene by using *bogá* emanating from the invisible sun. They will invoke in their spells all the life-giving forces upon which plant and animal life is based, to strengthen with them the processes developing under our sun.[9] These concepts are not only formalised in ritual, but tend to orient any social interaction in which shamans and elders might be involved in everyday life. The rules and norms these people establish are of ecological importance; they are norms of survival. Shamans are not concerned with teleological questions about cosmic energies and prior causes, but with the hard facts of environmental limitations to food resources, of illness, and of human lawlessness. Their task is to foresee ecological calamities and to control maladaptive behaviour.[10]

The above is, necessarily, a highly abbreviated scheme, but at this stage of inquiry we are only beginning to explore Tukanoan energy concepts. I should add here that words like 'energy', 'life force' or 'emanation' are inadequate translations of Tukanoan terms. I am fully aware of this dilemma and must warn the reader that, whenever I use these English words I do so for lack of better terms. In the pages that follow I shall use the word energy in the sense of *bogá* and its components, and not in the sense of modern physics.

Dimensions and Circuits

The Desana divide the universe into two fundamental components. One is *deyóri turí*, the visible or transparent world which comprises what we would call 'nature', and everything we can perceive in it with our senses as a material dimension of colours, shapes, smells, movements, sounds, tastes and textures. The other is *deyóbiri turí*, the invisible world. It contains a different set of phenomena, not hidden but different in their relevance to mankind. It contains Sun, Moon, and the Milky Way which, although visible to the eye, pertain to *gahí turí*, another world. The meaning of the word *turí* depends upon the context in which it is used; it can mean 'world', as in the present case, but it also can mean 'dimension' in the sense of an intellectual field, an imaginary or hallucinatory sphere, or a spiritual experience. A cerebral hemisphere is called *turí*, alluding to its functions, but *turí* can also refer to a distinct unit in a sequence of abstract but interrelated concepts.

To be visible is *deyóri*, and *kuiru deyóri* is the capacity of the human eye to perceive form, movement, and colour, but it also means to be able to recognise the unseen qualities of things in the visible world; it conceptualises and interprets. The verb *boyóri* means 'to shed light upon something', and the word for dawn—*boyóro*—is derived from it. It can be employed in the physical sense of 'lighting up', of 'seeing clearly', or in the sense of the English expression 'it dawned upon me'. Shamans say that in order to live well in the visible world, one must look at it through insights gained in the invisible world. Not all people are able to do this, and only 'knowledgeable people' (*mahsá deyoke iia*) can recognise, translate, and transform the meanings of *deyóbero*, the invisible, and can thus spiritually nourish themselves.

The universe is called *ëmësée*, a concept of space imagined as a hexagon, after the model of a transparent rock crystal. This term is difficult to translate; *ëmë* is 'man' and *ë'mëtári* is 'to precede', 'to be a precursor', while *sée* is related to the verb *~seeri*/to contain, in the sense of 'to enclose' (a germ in gestation). For example, a pregnant woman would be referred to as *~seego*. It is in this sense that the hexagonal universe is referred to as *~see ~piru*, lit. 'gestating anaconda', an image of uterine incubation in which the anaconda is only one in a large number of analogues. In sum, the universe is a womb which, being continuously fertilised by cosmic *bogá*, brings forth animate life in many different forms.

Within the hexagon are located several other dimensions. The most important one is *emekóri mahsá turí*, lit. 'man-period people dimension', a term derived from *eme*/man, *ko*, a particle referring to a time period or an orientation, with the underlying idea of 'fundamental tradition'. *Mahsá* means 'people' and refers here to timeless and nameless ancestors who established the tradi-

Tatuyo man with harpy down feather-crown

A mat made of two *Mauritia flexuosa* leaves

tional ways and institutions of the Tukanoan peoples.[11] Knowledge of these traditions is the realm of the *kumú*, the priestly sages of the Tukanoans.

Next comes *vaí mahsë turí*, lit. 'animal-person dimension'. The abstract
realm of the Master of Animals.[12] This Master is associated with the fertility of
game. For this very reason his celestial trajectory is the Milky Way, called the
Trail of the Master of Animals, because the succession of stars and constellations
on the horizon marks the season and, with them, the abundance or scarcity of
game, the onset of rutting and nesting seasons, fishruns, the nuptial flights of
edible ants, and all kinds of other events of a cyclic nature. The Milky Way is a
calendar for most human activities throughout the year, and in its image as the
Master of Animals' Way, it is a blueprint for the hunter and forager, and much
less so for the horticulturalist. In some mythical contexts the Milky Way is the
Sun Father's stream of semen fertilising an Amazonian Danae. On this earth, it
is the rainbow that represents the Master of Animals' ejaculation. In his
humanoid form he is imagined as a red dwarf, a phallic being, in charge of the
propagation of the animal world. He is first and foremost a gamekeeper who
protects his wards, and who constantly has to admonish the hunters and fishermen not to exceed themselves in their pursuit of the prey. *Vaí mahsë* will appear
to people in many disguises and, as he is said to be a very strict administrator of
all game resources, his appearance in time of scarcity is feared because to the
hunter it might be an indictment of having exceeded himself. But in times of
abundance his fleeting appearance is taken to be a propitious omen.

To the Master of Animals, the entire earth is an enormous horizontal spider-
web, hexagonal in shape, the cartwheel structure of which symbolises the network of prescribed pathways on which men and beasts must move without
straying off them. The Indians say that, just as a man might crush such an orb
web he encounters on his forest trail, so *Vaí mahsë* dominates the animal world.
It is said to be a fragile world, easily upset and disturbed, and this is why the
Master exercises so unremitting a control over it. He himself might appear to the
hunter in spider form (*bëhpë*), and the spider is sometimes identified with thunder *(buhpú)*. *Vaí mahsë* often wanders over the Milky Way and from this vantage point he watches the doings of men and animals. He then descends to the
'white cloud level', below which lie the dark rain clouds and hence, in the form
of lightning, he will project himself to the ground.[13] He is imagined then as hurl-
ing thunderbolts of white quartz splinters or, rather, of turning himself into a
bolt that strikes a hill, a tree, or even a maloca. When this happens, people say:
'*vaí mahsë mohó yuriaya*' (*vaí mahsë* weapon let fall) or they might say: '*yee
mohó yuriáya*', the word *yee* standing for either jaguar or shaman.[14] In fact, the
Master of Animals is both; in jaguar form he dominates all other animals, and
among his creatures he is the shaman, the protector, the mediator between the
hunter and his prey. He also might manifest himself in a storm, or as a cock-of-
the-rock (Rupicola) displaying his bright orange-yellow plumage, or as a lizard,

a fish, or a cacique bird. Sometimes, again, he might manifest himself in the strong smell of lichens and mosses after a rain shower, which grow on the forest floor in some parts of the forest, in the odour of youthfulness, *mamári*, as the Indians call it, alluding to its erotic connotations and its similarity to the scent of small bundles of fresh aromatic herbs young men wear tucked under their belts at dances. In sum, *Vaí mahsë* is conceived as an immediate force of nature.

Another abstract dimension is *yuhkë mahsá turí*, lit. 'tree-people-dimension', which includes all plant-life, with special reference to fruit-bearing trees of the forest. This is an extremely important dimension, because plant-life is said to depend directly from the *bogá* energy of the invisible sun. There exists no Master of Plants, no intermediary like *Vaí mahsë*, but only a direct dependence on cosmic energy. On this abstract level, the 'Tree People' are not imagined as anthropomorphised, but as a category of animate beings, containing a variety of 'heat energies' which are essential to human life on earth. On the concrete level of everyday experience, they are incorporated into the kinship system, as we shall see further on.

The next dimensions refer to the concrete level of common sensorial experience in the 'visible world'. The dimension of *vai ~mëra turí* comprises the wildlife of the forest, especially all game animals. In this category, the expression *vai ~mëra* is a key concept. The word *vai* (D T PT U) is commonly used in the sense of 'fish', but it is also applied to all game animals of the forest, as in *Vaí mahsë*, the Master of Animals. The term *vai* may have its origin in *bari*/to eat and may simply refer to a concept of 'food', but this is unproven. If nasalised and pronounced *~vai* (D), this word is a kinship term and refers to father's brother. This difference in pronunciation and in meaning lends itself to intentional wordplay or to unintentional misinterpretations of myths or spells. The Desana say that, in general terms, all animals of the forest are related to a person's patriline, while all fish are linked to one's matriline, being associated with the Pira-Tapuya, Uanano and Tukano proper. In that case, the root element *va*, or *vai*, can be traced to *vameó* (T), *~vamé* (PT), *~vamá* (U), the kinship term for mother's sister.

As to the term *~mëra*, the meaning covers the following range: ancient ones, ancestors, ancestral sages; *mahsá ~mëra*, lit. 'people-ancient', is an expression used to refer to the ritual flutes which are being played during male initiation, each flute being associated with a certain ancestral voice. Combining *~mëra* with the nasalised form of *vai*/fish, i.e., *vai ~mëra*, the expression means 'old fish', referring to matrilinear and patrilinear descent. This may sound contradictory, but is explained through the consensus that *vai* means, first of all, food, be it in the sense of nourishment, or be it that of prey in the widest sense, including the women of 'other people'.

The domain of *Vaí mahsë*, understood here as the physical environment inhabited by animals, is thought to contain in all its manifestations, the same

interrelated set of energies (*bogári*). First, all animals, both as taxonomic categories and as individual specimens, are said to contain the same series of chromatic energies which are derived from the visible sun and other sources, respectively. The exact proportional distribution is of importance and, in the case of
game and fish, is described thus: a large component of 'blackness', occupying
about half of the colour scale, is accompanied by a lesser amount of 'redness'
(i.e. female growth potential), and a still lesser amount of pale, weak 'yellow-
ness' (male generative potential). Second, all animals contain their inherent
qualities of odour, with a range of musky, oestrous, and floral; of temperatures,
such as 'warm' and 'cold'; and of flavours, such as 'sweet' and 'bitter'.

Whereas, in this system of thought, men and women participate in the original solar energy (*bogá*), with which they share in an equal amount of colour
energies, animal-life is said to be entirely dependent upon mankind. This idea is
expressed in several ways. In the first place, the Master of Animals is imagined
as a hunter walking over the Milky Way, from east to west, as if returning from
a chase. On his back he carries his prey, a game animal symbolised by a certain
constellation or a star that has just risen over the horizon. Throughout the year,
vaí mahsë will thus be carrying game over his celestial trail, for all to see. As
soon as a certain animal species becomes aware that its constellation or star is
rising, it knows that its breeding season is near, and that its specific food such as
fruits, berries, leaves or roots, will soon be available. Since the Master of
Animals is a mediator between the hunter and his prey, a relationship of dependence is being established. Human energy is transmitted through the circuit and,
at the death of a person, returns to its cosmic source. But animals do not participate in this human circuit; theirs is the circuit in which man, by consuming
animals, transmits their energy and transforms it into their life-force which is
restricted to this world. Animal energy does not return to the cosmos. Game animals will weep at the death of a person, because then a potential carrier, a link
in their energy circuit, has disappeared. These ideas are of considerable ecological importance, because in this view, animal procreative energies are described
as feeble and are made to depend to a large degree upon the spells, incantations
and restrictions shamans pronounce, in order to protect wildlife. Animals are
thought to depend on shamanic fertility rituals, and on the distribution of game
resources by the Master of Animals who, in their midst, is a representative of the
hunter.

The other division is 'fish-dimension' (*vaí turí*), also called 'water-dimension'
(*dehkó turí*). It includes all rivers, streams, creeks, lakes and swamps, together
with all species of fish and other aquatic creatures. This dimension is imagined
as divided into three superimposed layers according to their relative depth; the
deepest layer is said to be inhabited mainly by 'black' and 'cold' fish, middle
layer by 'red' and 'cold' fish, while the upper layer is inhabited by 'brown' and
'warm' fish.

Chapter III

DAILY LIFE

The Maloca

The natural environment in which the Indians live is structured on a horizontal scale, but is always understood as having a time dimension. In this manner, any environment is part of *deyóri turí*, the visible dimension, as well as of *deyóbiri turí*, the invisible one. The environment forms a tapestry of meanings which make it a blueprint for behaviour, an inexhaustible source of intellectual information and aesthetic pleasure, a guide into the known and the unknown. It is a home in which all occupants share, but which has no owner, because it serves all, as long as all associates participate in its maintenance. This feeling of a home is based upon a precise knowledge of all the components of the environment, of the ways how they interact, and of the manner how this interaction can be furthered and preserved. Much of this knowledge is not scientific in our sense but, having been acquired over thousands of years of close observation, it contains a wealth of sound facts on wildlife and biological rhythms, on meteorology and soil properties, on human adaptability and human frailties and failures.

We must distinguish here between the way in which the Indians see their natural environment, and how it is in objective reality. The Indians' view is closely related to their overall belief system and, therefore, contains attitudes and practices we consider irrational. This impression, however, may be partially wrong, because irrational beliefs occasionally may be adaptive devices which, in the guise of magic can be much more effective than if looked at from a practical, rationalistic point of view. On the other hand, as the Indians do not share our concept of nature, they divide their natural environment not only into what we would call ecosystems, but also segregate certain parts of the environment for their specific atmosphere. Now this is not quite the right word and I must try to explain this concept. There exist spots or spaces such as a beach, a watershed, or a tree, where people are said to be subject to unusual sensations, although

Overleaf: A Taibano longhouse (*maloca*) in the interfluvial forest

45

there seems to be no obvious reason for it as far as the environment is concerned. But there is something in the environment that triggers off these reactions. These places or spaces do not constitute ecosystems, but the Indians mention them in any enumeration of ecological subdivisions as essential parts of the environment. They are liminal spots where transformations are likely to occur, places where all values are abolished and replaced by others, places that lie outside of time. It is obvious that we are entering here a dimension of the imaginary, but as these places do exist in reality as landscape features, and are singled out by the Indians as components of *their* concept of nature, I shall include them in the discussion which follows.

The Tukanoan Indians recognise at least 20 named subdivisions or areas of their environment. I am not referring to the Vaupés region as a territorial unit, but to the environment as perceived by the individual, by the contact a person has with an area with a diameter that would take three days to cross on foot. These environmental subdivisions are the following:

1   the maloca (*vií*) and its immediate surroundings or patio (*vií keráro*).
2   productive garden (*poé*)
3   recuperating garden (*poé seári*)
4   old abandoned garden and house sites (*viadó*)
5   dense forest (*nëngë*)
6   open forest (*nëngë varo*)
7   caatinga forest (*tara boa*)
8   riverine forest (*dia vehká*) (not flooded)
9   swamp forest (*dia vehkópe*) (occasionally flooded)
10   hills (*ëhtëngë*)
11   hillocks (*búru*)
12   river (*dia*)
13   rapids (*ëhtámu*)
14   pools (*dihtáru*)
15   streams, creeks (*~maë*)
16   headwaters (*dihpári*)
17   confluence (*piró*)
18   island (*~nëngëro*)
19   beach (*imipa ~nëngëro*)
20   salt-lick (*~nerédu*)
21   sites (*sorogóro*)

All these subdivisions of the environment are believed to be charged with energies which continuously emit messages to which humans react in different ways. Many of these environments are resource areas of food or of raw materials of daily consumption, and in this manner the individual is in permanent contact with several subdivisions, and in occasional contact with most, if not all, others.

In the following pages I shall discuss these contacts and relationships, in order to show how strongly the individual is linked to his physical environment, and how predominant are non-material aspects in these linkages and interactions.

The first environmental subdivision is the house, the maloca (*vii*). Malocas are multi-family longhouses which do not form nucleated settlements but are spaced along the rivers and streams, at distances from one to several days travel on foot or by canoe. They usually occupy higher ground and are located a few hundred metres away from the river, to be protected against flooding at the height of the rainy season. Malocas are artefacts, and very elaborate ones, and this book is not concerned with material culture as such, but only in so far as it articulates man with his environment in a significant way. I shall therefore omit descriptive details of maloca construction, and limit my observations to more abstract points.[1] The choice of raw materials, such as house posts, beams, rafters and struts, together with a roof thatch and vines for fastening the parts together, follow traditional rules which are controlled by shamans and elders during the process of construction. The thatch has to be renewed approximately every six years, but the wooden structure will last for many more years. The individual parts are associated with cosmological models, astronomical phenomena, anatomical and physiological functions, kinship notions, ritual dimensions, and landscape features, in short, with all spheres and scenarios of human experience. The maloca is a cosmic model, it is a forest, an assembly of kin and allies, a womb, a grave, a tortoise, a microcosm in which every part is named and every relationship between parts is seen as a link in a coherent whole. It is the most complex of Tukanoan artefacts, and as an abstract model it can be found in the sky, in nature, or in the depth of a lake.

The immediate surroundings of a maloca, the ring of level ground we might designate as a 'patio', is called *vií ~kerára*, lit., 'house-weeding'; from *~kerári*/to weed, to clear the ground. The limited variety of plant specimens the occupants of a maloca cultivate nearby, represents an interesting selection. There will be a few peach palms, some small trees bearing seasonal sweet fruits and, perhaps, a few aroids. Obviously, these are not food resources for daily use, but emergency foods or mere snacks. What is needed at hand, daily or frequently, are plants used for seasoning, dyes and pigments, some fish poisons and a few narcotics. The near absence of medicinal herbs is due to the Indians' belief that these must be left to grow in their natural environment, if they are to conserve their healing power; people know where they are to be found when needed.[2] In the course of analysing these words, mention was made quite unexpectedly of the fact that a maloca stood, metaphorically, upon a large horizontal grate made of strong poles in parallel open order. The Indians construct these grates or grids (*keyá*, pl. *keyári*) in the forest, over colonies of edible ants, at about 40 cms. above the ground, to protect themselves when gathering ants during their nuptial flights.

Coca plants

A cucurbit

A climbing palm (*Desmoncus horridus*)

Basket with seeds of *Monopteryx angustifolia*

Manioc procesing with sieve on tripod

Processing grated manioc roots

Cassava bread

Pulverising toasted coca leaves

Medicinal plants: *Clidemia sp.* (left); *Tococa sp.* (right)

A Tatuyo man burning *Cecropia* leaves, for coca processing

Fruits of yërë

Manioc roots soaking in a creek

Preparing *Cecropia* leaves for burning, as part of coca processing

Grates of all sizes are essential pieces of furniture in the forest, in the mountains, indeed anywhere among Indians or rural Creoles. Three or four stout rods are stuck in the ground; at any convenient level above the floor, three or four horizontal bars are tied to the upper ends of the rods, and the bars are covered with parallel sticks or canes to form a table-top. Such a grate can be used to smoke or dry game or fish, to make a seed bed, or simply to protect all kinds of perishable things from humidity, loss, damage by children, dogs or insects. Inside a dwelling, a small shelf-like grate may be suspended in the kitchen area where it will serve to keep condiments, or near the walls of the living area. The rudimentary nature of this piece of furniture should not keep us from recognising its symbolic associations. The grate, as seen by the Indians, is a divider, a protector; it isolates from damaging external influences, it screens and safeguards. All these concepts appear in shamanic texts, principally in purification and curing spells. In view of this grate symbolism, it is not surprising that, in one image, the maloca is imagined as standing upon a grate similar to the one people build to catch edible ants.

A spot of importance is the place at a neighbouring creek where women and children gather to wash, soak and peel tubers or palm fruits. Such a spot is called *game ~neréri goró*, lit., 'together-gather-place'. These three words have alternate meanings which point to the more covert aspects of these spots. The term *game* is related to *gaméri*/to love, to desire. The verb *~neréri*/to gather (people, animals), if stressed on the last syllable, means 'to lick' and is associated with the image of tapirs wallowing at a saltlick, or licking each other. Mutual licking and grooming, as observed among animals, has strong erotic connotations among the Indians and the image of tapir gathering at a saltlick is related to male sexual fantasies in which prey animals and women are equivalent. It should be added here that there are specific spots called *doári goró*, lit., 'to sit-place', with the implied meaning of 'resting place', a place to find privacy for sex. These spots are usually located near the trails that lead from the maloca to the fields, in the underbrush surrounding the fields or between the tableroots of a large tree. One consideration is privacy but another, not less important one, is comfort. In a rainforest environment where it may rain for weeks on end, climatic conditions can form a serious impediment to normal sexual activities which, as a rule, are not allowed inside communal dwellings. These spots, then, have a very special purpose. In myths, tales and everyday banter they may be referred to as 'dancing places' or 'places of transformation', or other liminal concepts.

From a maloca radiate a number of well delineated trails which lead in all directions: to different resource areas, to the port, or to neighbouring malocas, and now another image arises, that of a spider and its web. Although a grate usually has a square shape, its basic structure of two intertwining elements can easily be compared with the circular structure of a spider-web. If we add to this the approximately wheel-shaped plan of the maloca environment, with its

A Barasana Indian toasting coca leaves

Palm grubs before toasting

A Barasana woman with toasted ants

Taibano man with honeycomb

numerous trails radiating from a centre, the comparison becomes more accept-able. The imagery, as explained by the Indians, is as follows: the maloca is seen as being placed on a horizontal spider-web (*bëhpë keya*/spider-grate) covering a hole in which hides a spider, a black hairy species which is common in manioc gardens and is greatly feared for its poison. The spider is called *bëhpë* (D T PT U). Underneath it, that is, right below the centre of the maloca, is located a large log-drum (*toá toré*, lit. 'to sting-cavity'). The hole in which the spider is hiding is connected with the hollow interior of the drum. In this context, the spider rep-resents a vagina, the drum is a womb, and the drumsticks are phallic elements. The sound of the drum (if it were a real drum) could be heard over great dis-tances, and the drum-beat is coded in the form of rallying calls, invitations to allies. While the sound of the drum is compared to thunder (*buhpú*, cf. *bëhpë*), the spider's sting is compared in its suddenness to lightning. The entire image of maloca-spider-web-spider-drum was said to be one representation of *ëmëkó mahsë ~simpóra*, lit.'ancestral-people-soul', the term 'soul' being an unsatisfactory translation of a word the meaning of which is unclear but the literal translation of which is 'that little flame'.

This is not the place to go into the complexities of this image; further discussion of it would make us digress too far from the central theme of man-nature relationships. A few general observations must suffice to outline the main trend of thought, as far as I was able to understand it. Spider is often associated with scorpion, generally as complementary sexual symbols, but occasionally the spider will play a somewhat ambivalent role; it can appear as a hunter and his prey, but also as an initiatory female, or as representing the female character of the maloca.

Maloca analogies do not stop here. In former times, the Desana used circular dance shields called *vabéro*, made of closely woven wickerwork, of a diameter of about 60 cms. In a further image, the maloca is seen as standing upon one of these shields, the inside of which is turned upward so that the cone-shaped protuberance (*kuu sáro*) of the shield's centre, forms a funnel, a recipient, a hole. In this position, the shield is meant to protect the maloca by providing a solid base which, at the same time, is a receptive space. With this shield image and its vocabulary is associated an informal institution called *vaberí mahsá*.

Mahsá means 'people' and these people, maybe three or four couples of neighbours, will go to a maloca several days in advance, to help the hosts in preparing a major gathering. The women will prepare a weak beverage, all the while gathering the ingredients for food and drink during the coming days, and there will be a lot of joking, laughing and singing in preparation of the event, but there will be very little or no drinking. Everything the women prepare has to be tasted and approved by the men, and the quality of beverages and dishes will be heatedly discussed by all. The word *vaberí*, with the stress on the last syllable, as in *vaberí mahsá*, refers to this preparatory activity. Moreover, the verb *vabéri*, with the stress on the second syllable has several interrelated meanings: 1) to assemble, construct (i.e. an ant-collecting grate); 2) to stir a beverage or a culinary preparation and season it well; 3) to prepare all the culinary aspects of a ritual gathering during which food items will be exchanged and fermented beverages will be consumed by a large group of people. The ideas underlying this vocabulary are concerned with the supposedly aphrodisiac effects of smoked ants, the well-balanced food, in terms of ritual purity and compatibility, and the corresponding social combination of kin and affines. The expression *vaberí mahsá*, which is applied to the group in charge of preparing these culinary/sexual/exogamous mixtures, i.e. of assembling the components and ingredients for a successful gathering, means just that: 'the assemblers'. They are imagined as sitting upon the upturned shield, contributing through their well organised activities to the stability of the social unit.

One last observation: I mentioned that the cone-shaped protuberance in the centre of the shield was called *kuu sáro*; *kuu* (PT U) is the land tortoise (*Geochelone carbonaria*), and *~saaró* (D P PT) means 'place where something is to be deposited', a common allusion to the female genitals and to impregnation. Tortoise often appears in myths and spells, ribald tales and everyday metaphoric language, appearing as a womb symbol, a female trickster, with devouring connotations. Some of these attributes are related to the unusual behavioural patterns of this species: they can often been seen feeding on carrion, they cry out during coition, and they are known to have an iron grip should they bite someone's finger (or testicles, as is told in many narratives). In some shamanic images, tortoise is identified with a maloca, located in the centre of the shield, this time with the outside turned upwards. The total environment of a maloca, including its port, gardens, and forests is referred to as *maríya nihkú*/our land, and is said to be the legacy or, rather, the property, of *vaí mëra*, lit. 'beings-ancient', also referred to as *mahsá mëra*/people-ancient, the ancestors.

With this last image we leave the maloca and its immediate surroundings, and take the trail that leads to the port. There are other images of the maloca and its setting, but the few examples I have given here have shown how intimately the longhouse is related to the all-important spheres of procreation, kinship bonds, animal and plant life and, above all, to the entire structure of the cosmos.

The Port

The main link between the maloca and the outside world is the port or landing place on the river. There may be a cove, an inlet—in any case there will be a stretch of sandy beach during the dry season when the water level is low. The occupants of a large maloca may have a number of canoes which are moored there. The front of the maloca, with its main door in the centre, is oriented toward the port and although the river and the port may not be visible from the dwelling, the inhabitants would always, even in the darkest night, know the exact direction and distance between the maloca and the landing place. Apart from canoes, some of them pulled up on dry land, others tied to poles stuck in the sand, there will be some other signs of human activities; sticks and fishing rods, an old basket, a rotten palm-leaf mat will be lying there, and there might be a broken gourd vessel or a bundle of firewood someone brought from some spot on the riverbank. There may be a *miriti* palm or two, an *umarí* tree, but hardly any other fruit tree. At a port, the fresh air coming from the river will mingle with the peculiar odour of rotting wood, of plant remains half submerged in water, of excrement and decay. In the dry season, or whenever the beach emerges, there will be footprints in the sand, and the eye of the hunter is always interested in tracks and marks left not only by animals but also by

Tatuyos at the port

humans. The marks left on the sands of a maloca port can tell a great deal about the doings of its inhabitants; the port is the bathing place for both sexes, and it is the destined spot for sexual activities, real or fantasied.

Already before dawn, some of the young men will go down to the port to bathe, while others will arrive there by canoe, after a night of fishing. At the port people feel *kunyu ~poréro*/warmth-dehiscence, a sexually arousing atmosphere. The air will be cool, but the temperature of the water is warm and the young people will splash about and beat the surface of the water producing a hollow sound: *to to to*. This is called *pihtu guári*; from *pihtúri*/to sound, and *guári*/ to bathe. This drumming is an invitation to the girls and young women of the maloca to come down and join the youths; it is still dark when they hurry down to meet their lovers and then return to prepare the first meal of the day.

The young men will stay at the port and there will be a good amount of horseplay and laughing. At the same time they will drink large quantities of river water, and absorb liquid peppers through their nostrils with the help of small funnels made from green leaves. After much sneezing and vomiting they will feel purified and, eventually, will be ready to go hunting that day. The basis of this belief is the observation that peppers act as powerful deodorants by neutralising body odours; the game animals of the forest won't perceive the scent of approaching humans. Just before sunrise the youths will return to the maloca while playing on their pan-pipes little tunes with coded erotic messages to the young women who hear them coming. The verb for 'to bathe', in four Tukanoan languages, is as follows: *ku'asé* (T), *kusáye* (PT), *kusáa* (U), *guári* (D). The verbs based on the root *ku*, *kus*, convey the sense of 'to become hardened', a term referring to physical fitness and, in a covert way, to sexual prowess. The Desana verb for bathing is *guári* and has the same meaning of 'hardening', but in addition it means 'to become enraged', 'to become fierce'. From this, and many other verbal statements, it becomes clear that, in Tukano thought, bathing is connected with male-dominant behaviour.

The erotic atmosphere of the early morning bath of the young men is paralleled by the activities of girls and women who go to the port any time during the day. The port is a meeting place for women of all ages who go there for their intimate toilette, for gossip, for talking about men and sex and lovers and of running away. This sort of atmosphere leads to stock situations and stereotypes. For example: it is part of a woman's daily task to go to the river to fetch water. A girl will get a pitcher or a gourd vessel, and will say: '*I am going to fetch water*', and then will run down the trail and out of sight. Among some people of the maloca this might cause some sneering remark about the girl's true intentions, but even if nothing is said, everybody knows the double sense of 'to go to fetch water'. Now when dipping the pitcher or gourd into the river, there will be a gargling sound the Indians imitate with the words: *kuru kuru kuru*. This daily occurrence is a reminder of women's wiles and tricks, because the sound is interpreted as a

Taibano hunter, carrying aromatic herbs in his belt, goes to embark in his canoe

mating call, ~koré being the vagina and goró being the 'place of origin', which simply is but another way of saying it. Sounds carry far over the water, and the woman 'making *kuru kuru kuru*' is a recurrent stereotype in tales in which a faithless wife calls her lover from a neighbouring maloca.[3] Another stereotypical phrase from the oral literature, is: '*The girls went down to the port to sit and eat ants*'. This sentence makes sense only if one knows that there are no ants at the port, and that edible ants are thought to be a sexual stimulant.

The port, then, is an institutionalised space for sexual activity, conventional, illicit, ritualised. It is of importance in male initiation rituals and is often mentioned in mythological contexts when institutional origins are being discussed. A recurrent theme in these myths is the scene in which the father admonishes his pubescent son to rise early and find at the port the 'thing' the father has hidden for him and the boy must possess to become a man. A mid-Victorian view of

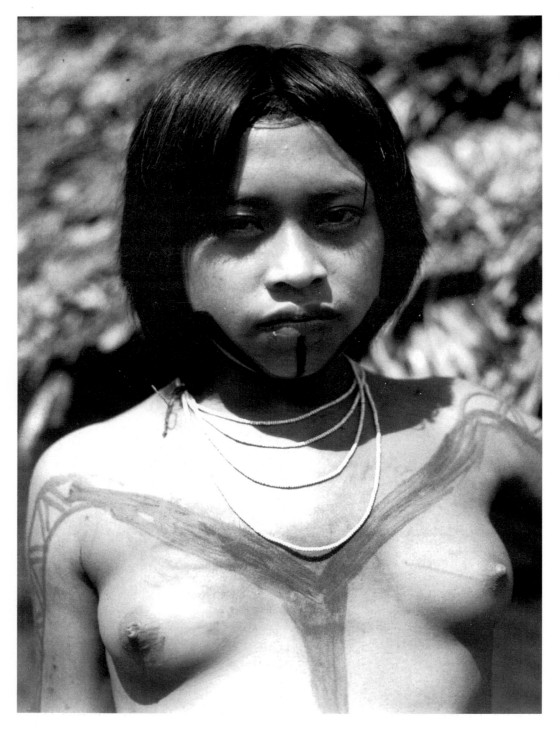

Barasana girl

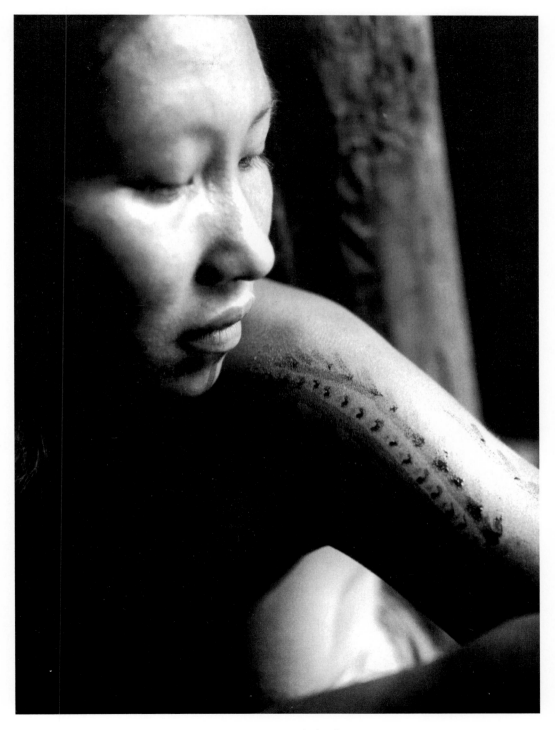

Barasana woman with body paint

Bará woman

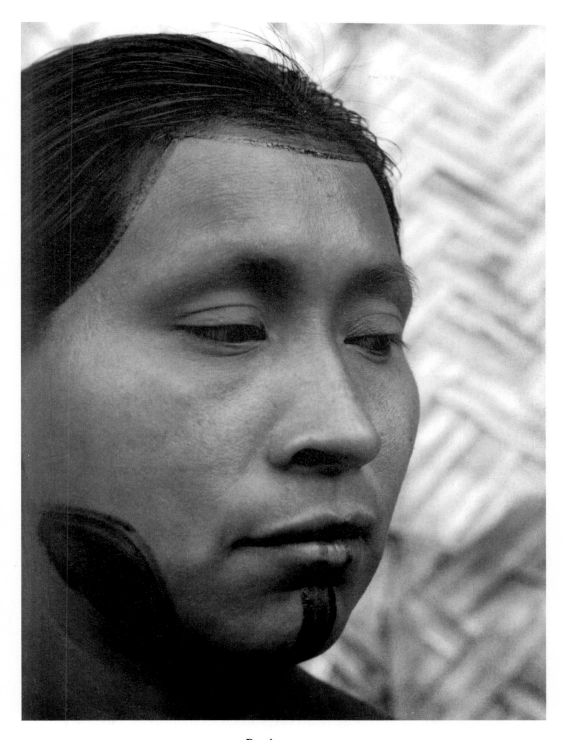

Bará woman

what was going on at a Tukano port is expressed by Alfred Russel Wallace who wrote 'in very dreary blank verse', and 'in a state of excited indignation against civilised life', the following lines:

'The young girls carry water on their heads
In well-formed pitchers, just like Cambrian maids;
And all each morn and eve wash in the stream,
And sport like mermaids in the sparkling wave.'[4]

By now we are beginning to see the port with different eyes; we recognise its liminal nature, its power of transformation. At the port, at spots where there are excreta in the sand, swarms of yellow butterflies will gather and during the dry season one can see hundreds of them flying upriver, forming long undulating chains. Their presence at the port, near human tracks in the sand, their fertility-associated colour, and their meandering flight toward the headwaters form an emotion-charged scene which appears regularly in mythological and other narrative contexts. Butterflies at the port are a pleasant thought in Tukano imagery.

At this point we must take a look at some linguistic aspects of the port image. The word for port is *pehtá*, in all four Tukanoan languages we are concerned with. This is related to the verb *pehtasé* (T) which has several interrelated meanings. The most common meaning of *pehtasé* is 'to lie down, to copulate'. In the context of some tales, *pehtasé* is used as a noun and refers to the act of a jaguar lying at rest in a tree fork. This behaviour one can occasionally observe, but to the Indians it means more than a simple trait of feline resting postures. It belongs to the conceptual domain of bifurcation in nature, in plant and animal life, with emphasis on the human body. In many contexts, jaguars symbolise male sexuality in its aggressive forms, while bifurcations represent the female body. In a ritual context, the verb *pehtasé* describes the act of putting on a feather head-dress, an image which is associated with the idea of 'covering the head' by introducing a male element (the head) into an open circle (the feather-crown, a vagina).

Apart from its overtly sexual association, the port has its darker side on which its liminal nature introduces the visitor into otherworldly dimensions. When standing on the edge of the water and looking down upon one's mirror image, one notices that one is linked, articulated to it, by the soles of one's feet. The same is true when one looks at one's own shadow, or other people's shadows. Then there is a time at dusk when people don't cast a shadow at all, and that means that they may not be people but spirit-beings. Dusk at the port or twilight in the forest contain moments of danger. What is feared is the appearance of the *vearí mahsá*, phantasmal beings in human shape, male or female, who appear impersonating close kin, perhaps a brother, a cousin or an uncle, and talk his prospective victim into following him into the oncoming darkness. These beings will imitate people in all their personal details, even in their peculiar body odour, and will make them accompany them, only to 'lead them astray'. The victim will return to the maloca after days, sometimes after weeks, haggard and incoherent, telling of starvation, mistreatment and rape, and of having been forcefully kept in a thorny thicket deep in the forest. We have some indications as to the nature of these fantasies. For example, it is said that the best defence against them is to chew peppers in these situations. This is a standard procedure of purification, in the sense of neutralising the dangers of illicit sex; the *vearí mahsá* are seen as sexually impure or forbidden. Furthermore, linguistic evidence points in the same direction; the term is derived from *vearí*/to abduct (D); the expression *inya veári* is used to describe the act or ability to 'look and seize', in the sense of 'looking through' a person and so finding out his or her most intimate thoughts and desires. The underlying problem seems to be incestuous fantasies which are then acted out in an imagined 'thicket'.[5]

The Garden

Radiating out from the maloca, a number of trails lead to the gardens. These lie in the surrounding forest, at varying distances, usually near a creek or stream. Gardens are private property and belong to the families that live in the same maloca, each family owning four or five gardens, at different stages of production. The clearing of a new garden is a task accomplished by communal labour.

A Tukanoan garden is not an artificial environment; it is a natural environment which hardly alters the ecosystem of the forest and which has only slightly been modified to harbour and nurture outsiders in the form of plant species which are no more than guests. In a wider sense, this articulation is brought about by female labour. The men fell the trees, are active in the burning of the clearing, and supervise the first planting, but practically all subsequent gardening tasks are taken care of by women; gardens have a female, reproductive character and, in many ways, are feminine as if they were female bodies.

When a new clearing has been made and when, after firing it, the soil is ready to be planted, the shaman will say some fertility spells over it and will spit here and there on the ground, in a symbolic act of insemination.[6] A garden may measure one hundred metres in diameter or more, and is planned according to principles which, at first view, are difficult to discern. In any case, the place certainly does not look like a garden; it rather looks like a tree-fall, caused by windthrow, a large gap in the forest cover, a mass of fallen trunks and branches, and only when approaching more closely can one recognise the food plants which grow between this confusion of branches and shrubs.

But there is order in this green tangle. Most of the area is occupied by manioc which is the principal root crop, and of which several varieties of the same species are planted, but next to it there will be a number of other food plants.

On the slope toward the creek will be some cooking plantains, followed higher up by tubers such as Dioscoreas and Aroids, and perhaps some groundnuts. Peppers are planted here and there, and some leafy greens to be added to soups. Sugarcane is planted in a patch toward one edge of the garden, and maize is equally segregated in another section, because it has an altogether different vegetative cycle. Pineapple is planted on the slope; two or three rows of coca shrubs occupy a small patch, and there will also be some ichthyotoxic plants for occasional fishing. There won't be any fruit trees; the productive life of a garden is too short (two or three years) for their full development, and so there will be only one or two Inga trees, a few Pourouma shrubs, and some shrubs of Solanum, the fruits of which can be made into a refreshing drink. A small cashew tree may also be present.[7] The Tukanoans always practice selective weeding and should the women find a tree seedling growing through the litter, they will carefully preserve it.

Although most of the area is occupied by manioc, the emphasis is upon diversity. Tukanoan cultivated lands are not fields in our sense, but are mixed gardens with a variety of cultigens. According to the Indians, plants grow better as parts of a diversified plot than in monoculture. People are equally opposed to the idea of domestication; in their view, fruit trees, medicinal plants, toxic or narcotic plants develop best if left in their original environment where they can grow in permanent interaction with the local climate, soil, flora and fauna. A fruit tree, they point out, has its pollinators which, in turn, interact in their own way and have their own cycles. A tree may have its insect pests or vertebrate predators, but it also has its defenders; it has its vines and creepers and epiphytes, but they all have a function to fulfil in the tree's life, and if this interaction is disturbed, the tree won't thrive.

Part of the diversity one finds in a Tukanoan garden plot consists in the tangle of metre-high charred stumps, fallen trunks, upturned roots, lopped-off branches, vines and underbrush. The Indians run like squirrels over the skeletons of fallen trees, but a city dweller will have difficulties in balancing along the slippery or rotting trunks, and in passing from one to another. To call this a garden and to claim that this could be a model for sustained development seems ludicrous, but we soon shall learn otherwise.

What may look to us like a primitive clearing in the rainforest, in reality is an intentional combination of many components. In the first place, the litter of rotting wood, leafy shrubs, and carbonised branches is, in the Indians' view, an important part of the process of cultivation; it contains nutrients ('energies') not present in the soil, but which come 'from above', and which provide the cultivated species with an articulation with the forest environment, an interaction the Indians believe to be essential. This is not a 'clearing' in the forest or a 'cultivated' spot in a hostile environment, but a safe-hold, a second home where things may be grown thanks to the forest. In the second place, the felled litter

Above: A manioc garden   Below: Cucurbits (*Koa*)

attracts several important species of prey animals: paca, agouti, cavi, deer and armadillo. In this manner, a cultivated plot is an excellent place for what has been called garden-hunting. As the Indians see it, it is a bait, a trap set right in the forest. Next to attracting game, this environment attracts many insects, butterflies and beetles, and these in turn attract birds and lizards. In this variety of life-forms the Indians see a condensation of energies, of pollinators and activators of the cycles of insemination, growth and decay.

A new clearing in unmodified rainforest should always be made by taking into account the particular quality of the trees which have to be felled. The place is carefully selected because, as the Indians say, a garden is a spot where seeds are going to be selected.[8]

In the first place, the plot to be cleared should contain a number of tall mature trees, fruit-bearing or otherwise useful.[9] These trees contain a large amount of *bogá* and related energies. In the course of its long life, a tree 'takes care' of its immediate surroundings by transmitting to them a steady flow of additional energies; leaves, flowers, seeds, branches and twigs, bits of bark, insects and bird droppings will fall down upon the ground, and this litter will have specific characteristics in terms of colours, odours, textures, temperatures; and then there will be mushrooms, mosses and the entire understorey flora and fauna which come to form a very specific environment. In other words, a given tree species and its micro-environment the Indians designate as 'hatch-insemination', admittedly an inadequate translation of words referring to fermentation, gestation, and insemination.[10] The Indians say that a garden is planted 'with the energy of dead people', of 'Tree People' (*yuhkë mahsá*), and suggest that trees are immortal because 'they spring up in gardens'. The ashes of trees are ancestral energies.

After having felled such a tree and its neighbours during the dry season, and after the garden plot has been burned, the first breeze that enters the clearing is referred to as Smoke People, a personification of a seminal concept in which smoke, ashes, pollen and other seminal analogues are combined into an energetic principle which is now being set in action.[11] At that time of the year the air is saturated with pollen and with the scent of the great trees; in fact, 'smoke is like pollen', say the Indians, and it now begins to inseminate the soil. The scent of tree saps and resins attracts the most colourful and largest beetles, such as Buprestis and Longimanus, together with a host of smaller ones. This change of air, of sunlight, of odours and of a fresh breeze entering the gap in the forest is often mentioned in conversation as an emotion-charged time of the year; the humming of insects, the sudden crack of a seed pod scattering its contents over leaves and branches, all this is said to have a peculiar effect upon the Indians who see in this new atmosphere an increased energy flow which can be sensorially perceived in many ways.

This brings us to an important aspect of rainforest horticulture. According to the Indians, each tree species, notably those mentioned above, produces a particular kind of ashes which contain energies propitious to the growth of certain food plants. Some ashes will be of an orange or yellowish colour, while others will be grey or white, and the Indians will distinguish a range of shades.[12] During the first few days after firing the garden, these ashes will be clearly visible and now it is their quality and distribution which determines the pattern of planting.

Accompanied by the women, the men will see the burnt plot as if it were a multi-coloured mosaic, a checkered patchwork of energy-charged 'fields', and will examine the ashes and point out the best spots or section where specific food plants should be cultivated. With the first rains these ashes now begin to mix and blend; they add the fallen trees' energies to the energies of the trees' microenvironments and it is now this combination which constitutes the true fertility potential of a garden. What is of importance are the colour associations of the ashes, the degree of heat developed by the burning of different woods, and the ways in which this is believed to combine with the energies the live tree used to contain. In correlating ash distribution with planting, the Indians claim to be following a natural model instead of creating a cultivated field.

Planting is done with great care, in order to maintain the right combination of energies. For example, manioc, yams, aroids, plantains, sugarcane and pineapple should always be planted in the ashes of the tall forest trees, or near the foot of still standing carbonised tree trunks, because these plants 'need charcoal', as the Indians say, and this need is expressed in the particular odours which now establish a bond between these plants. Odour peculiarities determine a plant's relationship with insects. For example, the *Inga* tree 'needs no charcoal' because it has its own peculiar smell, and with it attracts insects. Plants of fish poison also attract many insects and need neither charcoal, ashes or shadow, but the shadow of fast-growing manioc is essential for peppers. A variety of *Inga*[13] will attract many insect larvae which otherwise would attack the manioc. These interactions are well known among women who will calculate in detail where to locate insect-attracting plants, so that they will protect the staple food and other cultigens. It is very likely that these ashes-charcoal-odour interactions are playing a major role in controlling bacterial, fungal, and viral plant pathogens, as well as plant nematodes. A minor function of the tree trunks lying dispersed all over the garden, consists in their providing a grid of references to the location of plants or soil characteristics.

In the course of a manioc garden's productive life there are no distinct planting or harvesting seasons; women plant as they harvest, slowly advancing across the garden, replanting selected seedlings in the loose soil from which they have just extracted the tubers for daily consumption. The harvesting life of the garden is about two to three years, after which begins a period of fallow that may last from eight to ten years. A nuclear family may work two productive gardens simultaneously, one in advanced stage of production, after more than one year,

Barasana girl burying *Micrandra spruceana* seeds in *Heliconia* leaves

A Taibano with manioc sticks for planting

while the other is still in an initial stage, having been cleared and planted only four or five months ago. During the second year the ashes are diluted; women now scrape together the earth to make small mounds for planting manioc and other cultigens that have superficial roots. However, the quality of the tubers soon declines.

A major point of interest which must be kept in mind is that of women's general attitude toward horticulture in the Northwest Amazon. The idea that women have a close emotional relationship with the land they cultivate is, I fear, a Western stereotype, not applicable at all to the Vaupés. In the first place, in a society based upon virilocal exogamy, women do not work the traditional lands of their own people, but those of their authochtonous husbands. In the second place, a Tukano woman's work in the manioc gardens is very hard and tiresome, especially for younger women who have small children to look after. The rains will last up to nine months a year, and during much of this time the women will be drenched and mud-splattered, following the same routine of planting and harvesting, processing and replanting, week after week. They hardly ever complain, but neither do they show any sign of emotional attachment to their gardens.

Manioc gardens, however, play a considerable role in women's gossip patterns. While processing manioc or whenever they meet in the gardens, women will talk about different food plants, about the many different kinds of manioc they cultivate, and will praise their respective qualities. This is a matter of personal prestige and each woman will refer with pride to *her* garden which provides food for her family. This means that the talk is of *poé*, which is the word for garden. But from there, by a turn of phrase and apparently in a quite casual way but in reality following a patterned conversation, they will talk of the *ucuquí* fruit, called *poé*, not as a fruit but as a bait, as a female element which one exogamous unit offers the other, in exchange. Speaking of 'other people's' marriageable women, it will be said, for example: '*She is like ucuquí; she has a pleasant colour; she has a pleasant taste*', thus identifying the fruit with the women. *Ucuquí*, as we will remember from the creation myth, symbolises Fish Woman, the mythological First Woman, who was courted, seduced and finally conquered by the First Man. This talk goes on and imperceptibly changes to *poé*, the word for husband's sister. This word play: *poé/poé/~poé*, refers back and forth, from garden to fruit to alliance and, in this manner, assigns to the manioc garden a specific function in the representation of social organisation; it is the husband's land which articulates the ideal woman with the social woman. It is a talk of everyday matters—the garden, fruits, other women—but it is a patterned discourse of mnemonic and moralising significance.

Gardens should not be places for sexual intercourse, although often enough women will take advantage of their solitary environment for adulterous escapades. Childbirth, on the other hand, always should take place in the garden, so that the newborn child can partake in the condensed energy of the plants. And there are other reasons for childbirth to take place in the garden. One is privacy; another is the ready availability of large Cecropia leaves (*boré-pu*) for cleaning and swaddling the child, and of a vine (*tegá-da*), the coarse sprout of which is used to cut the umbilical cord. Menstruating women should avoid gardens, because their state of non-fertility would harm the plants. The female nature of gardens is furthermore seen in the 'female' character of its habitual fauna. A garden attracts above all armadillos and a variety of rodents, many of them large and of excellent meat, and all of them metaphorically associated with women, because of their odours, pelt marks[14] or other traits. A cultivated plot, then, is a good spot for 'garden-hunting'.[15] Peccary do not invade the garden because the poisonous variety of manioc would kill them.

Apart from the shaman's chanting and spitting, Tukanoan horticulture is devoid of ritualisation. Or so it seems. The men live in a world of hunting, fishing and foraging, which is highly ritualised and socialised, but a woman's world is closed; not secret but closed upon itself, upon the yearly round of planting and harvesting which keeps them occupied from dawn to dusk in an unvarying cycle. In a man's daily activities there is much of the unforeseeable, of the incidental, the dangerous. The forest and the river are not open storehouses, but will yield their fruits only under conditions which may be very demanding. The abundance of ritual prescriptions and prohibitions, together with the ever-present pressures of reciprocity behaviour, make the hunter's life a tense and even anxious one. A woman's life is endless drudgery, but the garden offers few real dangers, and good harvests are foreseeable. There is no such thing as crop failure; there will always be manioc and, should the worst come to the worst, some fruits, some tubers, something to fill empty stomachs will always be available. A garden provides security; a woman always knows where to find food; a hunter does not. And, quite apart from this, among women there is no great concern about ritual purity or about the endless balancing of relationships with one's allies. In many ways, the hunter and the gardener live in different worlds.

To put the Tukano garden into its conceptual context, I shall refer to some myths in which mention is made of the origin of horticulture. One mythical personage who frequently appears in these narratives is *Boo-bari mahsë*, Starch-eater Person. One myth (in highly abbreviated form) reads as follows: '*Starch-eater taught First Woman to plant manioc in the centre of the garden, so there would be yellow, red, and brown tubers, but he strictly forbade her to do two things while planting: to touch her vagina, and to look toward the edge of the garden where all the weeds and garbage had been thrown. But the woman did not obey; she masturbated and urinated, and when she looked up, all seedlings were burned, and the garden was invaded by weeds.*' The lesson of this, and similar stories, is said to be that the onerous tasks of planting and weeding constitute a punishment for women's lack of control of their sexuality.[16]

A Taibano in his garden

A manioc garden with dense forest in the background

Another myth explains the origin of the garden fauna. An abbreviated version reads: '*After having copulated with the women for the first time in the garden, the men changed into bluebirds and flew up into a high tree. One of them threw down some seed pods; the dry seeds made a sound:* ke ke ke[17], *and from them sprang agouti. Another threw down a kind of* purí[18] *and it turned into paca. He threw down* Inga: *and it turned into monkey. Then he threw down* umarí *fruits, and now macaw and green parrots arrived to feed on them. He threw down more* umarí, *to create peccary. He threw down* uacú *seeds, but there were too few and they fell at the edge of the garden, and peccary came to feed on them. He threw down flowers of Pokeweed[19], and deer came to eat the leaves. Finally he threw down a manioc squeezer, so that little* cavi[20] *could hide in it. By that time the* uacú *tree had grown and now the old grandmother of the women turned into a sloth and climbed up into the tree.*'

It will have become clear by now that a manioc garden is far more than a random clearing in the rainforest where a band of primitive people try to wring a precarious living from a hostile environment. These are stereotypes which have done harm to the Indians' achievement. Nothing could be more misleading than the expression 'slash-and-burn' agriculture, an expression that makes one think of people carelessly hacking away at the forest, and then setting fire to the destruction they have brought about. The truth is that selective clearing of the forest, selective weeding, crop diversity and awareness of soil-plant-animal interaction, constitute a complex procedure based upon thousands of years of experience and continued experimenting. The result is the manioc garden as a model of sustained development.

To sum up, let me briefly return to the *poé/poé/~poé* thought sequence. The sequence: garden-*ucuquí* bait-potential spouse, is mentioned in shamanistic spells; in other words, it is a clearly institutionalised formula. In discussing this patterned conversation of women, the talk turned to the abstract value of the land, and peoples' opinion can be summarised as follows. The value of gardens resides in what the women learned in their families of origin, and in the manner in which they subsequently apply this knowledge in working their husband's land—knowledge being here the rules of reciprocity behaviour. In this manner, it was said, gardens condition social interaction. The energy of the forest is converted into food energy, and the consumer must eventually return this energy by letting the soil recuperate, but it is not the caloric food the soil provides which gives it its value; it is its role of being an articulation between family members, between exogamous units and, last but not least, between the forest and the people. This was the Indians' consensus.

After approximately two years a garden will be left to lie fallow so it can recuperate. The name for such an abandoned garden is *via'do*, lit. 'that which has been given back', almost in the sense of a reserve. The word is derived from *viarí*/to return, to give back, and this verb is related to *piarí*/to let something ferment, and to its nasalised form ~*piarí*, meaning 'to unbury something', in the sense of 'recuperating from the earth'. From this is derived the expression *piárisamo*, referring to a woman of childbearing age but who is childless, the image of a latent potential of future fertility, as is the case with a fallow garden.[21] In fact, a recuperating garden is never entirely abandoned, but is occasionally visited by its owners to dig up some manioc or collect firewood and is even used for certain special purposes. For example, sweet-potato (*Ipomoea batata*) is not planted in producing gardens, but in *via'dó* because, according to the Indians, it can spread out there over the ground without interfering with other food plants. As the Indians practice selective weeding and allow fruit trees to grow wherever they might spring up, the further one moves back in time, the more fruit trees one is likely to find in gardens that lie fallow. Now the quick-growing pioneer vegetation, usually *Cecropia*, begins to close in. At this stage the garden is compared to a basketry tray, and the circle of *Cecropia* trees is said to 'shape the garden' (*viadó tiarí*), as if the basket-maker were putting in a hoop or two to strengthen the periphery of the basket. The common *Cecropia sclerophylla* in particular is ant-infested. The ants are attracted by the nectar of *Cecropia* which is said to contain a substance called *piarí*, comparable to a raising agent, a ferment. For example, a married woman who is childless although still being of childbearing age, is called *nomé piarí*; or the fermented residue from three-day-old *chicha* beer used to start a fresh beverage is called *peyáru piarí*; the term *piarí*, in both cases expressing a fertility potential. These ants, which are endemic of gardens but not of the forest, are very small and are called ~*moá* ~*mera*, lit. 'salt-old beasts, or ~*moa* ~*koará*, 'salt-carriers' (from ~*koarí*/to carry). The term ~*moa* refers to salt or salt-like substances, with the underlying meaning of 'bait' and a group of concepts related to condiments, stimulants, and incentives. The idea is that ~*moa* is a generative, seminal energy, and that ants, being pollinators, are the carriers of these energies. Next to *Cecropia* we find among the pioneer vegetation the *oyodigë* tree, the name of which translates as 'bat-blood-tree'. Bats (*oyó*) are attracted by its fruits, while *di* (blood) refers to the blood-red sap of this tree. Apart from being pollinators, bats are very active in seed dispersal, and spots covered with bat dung can be recognised by the multitude of seedlings and saplings. Bat-blood trees make good firewood, and are mentioned in shamanic curing spells. Another pioneer is the *meré* tree (*Inga sp.*), one of the most common cultivated fruit trees. It is clear from the above that the Indians see in the invading vegetation of fast-growing plants rich in pollen and visited by many animals active in seed dispersal (toucans, bats, sloths, squirrels, etc.), an important mechanism of energy transmission.

While discussing this process of gap regeneration and fallows an interesting parallel was mentioned. A gap in the forest, it was said, was similar to an open wound (*kamí*) in a human body, wounds being imagined as a crack through which a vital flame was escaping. To cure a wound is *kamí yaurí*/wound-to extinguish, just as if one were to extinguish a fire (*peáme yaurí*). Shamanic curing spells said over a wound are similar to those pronounced occasionally over a recuperating garden, in trying to 'close the gap'. A survey of a large body of these spells suggest that, whenever a 'wound' is mentioned, a river crab is associated with it, its name being *gamí*. Metaphorically, these crabs represent a vagina. This category of curing spells is not to be taken literally, in the sense of trying to cure a case of medical pathology, but metaphorically refer to social ills, in this case to conflicts caused by illicit sex. The suggested homologous chain of: forest gap-open wound-vagina-illicit sex-intergroup conflict-disease aetiology may sound farfetched but deserves further study.

Ancient garden or house sites, the precise ownership of which is not within the memory of present generations, form a very special category of ecosystems. As they are usually located outside the range of daily activities, somewhere in the forest, they are called *nëngë via'dó*/forest-reserves. Some of these sites are located on oxbow lakes or channels of old meander belts, far from the present meander belt. These spots of secondary vegetation are called *rastrojos* (shrubbery), in the Spanish vernacular, and are referred to as *terra preta* (black soil) in Brasil, alluding to the patches of humus produced in ancient times by human activity. The modern Tukanoans are well aware that these sites were once inhabited by 'other people', supposedly by the Arawakan Tapir People and, as we shall see further on, they approach these sites with respectful awe.

Ancient garden and habitation sites can be recognised by the presence of certain cultivated trees and other plants. In the Vaupés territory we can observe the following: peach palm, umarí, Inga, calabash tree and papaya; other plants are Aroids, tobacco, achiote, genipa, *Banisteriopsis* and *Virola*. The entire aggregate is known as *ohtéri ~mëra*, lit. 'seeds-ancients'. None of the food plants should be eaten; their consumption would cause serious dysentery, but all seeds can be used. As a matter of fact, these places are considered to be valuable storehouses where present generations can find a supply of seeds of the best quality. Ancient gardens, however, are approached with ambivalent feelings, because the ancestral Tapir is also the ancestral enemy. Consequently, precautions have to be taken when visiting an ancient site, spells have to be said, dietary restrictions have to be followed before advantage can be taken of the legacy of the ancients.

To go to an ancient garden site to collect seeds for planting, is called *ohtéri ~aíri*/seeds-to take, but a more precise expression is *ohtéri sa'tári ~aíri*, lit. 'seeds-isolated-to take'. The noun *sa'táro* refers to something (plant or human) which has no present relationship to any other of its kind, which is quite isolated. The term can be applied to plants or to women; to call a woman *mëë sa'táro*/you-isolated one, is an insult, because it means: you do not function as a member of society, although you are potentially fertile. In the case of plants, what is referred to is that the seeds one can collect now, are not contaminated (cross-fertilised) from the outside. Tukanoans are always greatly worried about the polluting qualities of women, and as these garden sites (and any food prod-ucts) are thought to have been planted and tended by 'other women', the seeds, i.e. their fertility potential, is handled with great care. The seeds selected from an ancient garden are said to be highly productive, because they developed in a ritually pure environment. To use ancient garden sites, some of them going back for centuries, as genetic reservoirs of wild varieties, points to a degree of aware-ness of plant evolution which certainly deserves further study.

Chapter IV

THE HILLS AND THE RIVER

The Master of Animals

Over the vast flatness of the rainforests of the Vaupés territory rise, here and there, isolated hills, small rocky formations with steep walls that emerge over the canopy of trees like dark islands. Many of these are the remnants of the ancient Guiana Shield which, billions of years ago, covered the land. Because of their different geological structure, geographical isolation, and somewhat higher elevation, these hills are biological islands where flora and fauna vary from that of the surrounding forests. The hills, with their cliffs and crevasses, surrounded by dense undergrowth and ancient trees, are the home of a varied and teeming wildlife. And there are good reasons for this; the dark hills of the Vaupés are the abodes of *Vaí mahsë*, the Master of Animals.[1]

No other landmarks in the Colombian Northwest Amazon are as important to the Indians as these abrupt, towering elevations frequently topped by a small flat plateau. These 'hill houses', as shamans call them, have a womb-like character. They are places where the game animals are said to multiply and whence they emerge to roam in the forest. They are spirit-malocas, imagined as hexagonal enclosures in which a process of gestation is developing.

These 'hill houses' have their counterparts in the 'water houses'. The deep and dark pools which form at the foot of the large rapids or waterfalls figure prominently in mythology and shamanic geography. They are dwelling places of fish, of anacondas, of all aquatic creatures. At the bottom of these pools large malocas are said to exist where all these creatures live, just as people would live on land. They live there under the care and protection of the Master of Fish, one of the manifestations of the Master of Animals. Here, too, a continuous process of gestation is taking place. A hill is called *~ëhtëngë*, a word related to *ëhtagél* stone; if referring to a particular hill inhabited by *Vaí mahsë*, the term *~ëhtapel* rock, would be used, with the implied meaning of a luminous spot. A 'house of the waters', that is, a rapids, waterfall or deep pool, is called *ëhtámu*. The root *ëht (a)* is found in many words which express the idea of 'excretion', in terms of

Detail of painted Taibano longhouse; the figure represents the Master of Animals

a seminal substance and a principle of transformation associated with it.[2]

In every ecosystem, as defined by the Indians, there exists a 'house', a maloca (*vií*) where a Master of Animals dwells. The house may be a rocky hill, a lake, a pool in the river, a large boulder; in any case it will be a permanent feature of the landscape; it won't be an ancient tree or an old maloca, though it could be an old house site. Such a place is called *vaí mahsë vií* and is believed to be inhabited by animals and plants invisible to ordinary human beings, but clearly visible to shamans. Above all, among the plants there are palm trees and the Tabebuia, and the Indians will point out that the two represent female and male principles.

These 'houses of *Vaí mahsë*' are referred to as *goró* (pl. *goróri*), the approximate translation being 'place', 'site', 'spot', with the implied meaning of 'isolated spot', 'scented place', 'place of origin'. The imagery refers to genital, uterine concepts. The odoriferous aspect includes both sexes, and in this context mention is made of aromatic plants which are said to grow in profusion at these spots. Each of these places is in sight of another, so that the entire landscape is imagined as being covered by a network of scented landmarks, rocks and rapids, hills and caves, lakes and saltlicks. This is expressed in the words: *inyá me peóro*/sight-as far-reaches, meaning that each spot or 'house' can be seen from another spot. People who go to visit another maloca for a ritual should always bathe, paint and adorn themselves at the 'house' closest to the festive gathering. They are places where great vital energies are supposed to be accumulated in the form of colours, odours, sounds and flavours, and in the tangible form of wildlife. People tend to avoid these spots, fearing an encounter with *Vaí mahsë* in his role as protector; and for this very same reason these places are small reserves, not only of animals but also of seeds and forest fruits. These spots are interrelated in a complex way. I have said at the outset that cosmic *bogá* is energy reflected by the visible sun upon our earth. This concept of 'reflection' is furthermore applied to the entire surface of the land, the major centres of energy reflecting their fertilising power upon minor centres. *Vaí mahsë*'s houses are arranged in a power hierarchy, the rocky hills containing a maximum of energy, followed in importance by deep pools in the river and then, in a descending scale, by hillocks, lakes, and so forth. The energising *bogá* reflections are paralleled by reverberating sounds. People are aware that the reflection of sound-waves can produce an echo, and know that this phenomenon can best be observed in the vicinity of hills with steep walls of naked rock. This observation has led to the belief that there exists an acoustic relationship between *Vaí mahsë*'s many abodes, 'the voices of the ancestors', as the Indians would say. The different representations of *Vaí mahsë* can thus communicate, and shamans can take part in this system. Most people cannot perceive these 'echos' (*keorí*), but some do, particularly when in a state of acute awareness brought about by dietary restrictions, social isolation during hunting or fishing, or under the influence of a narcotic drug.

The Tukanoan concept of the Master of Animals and his abodes has important ecological implications. The belief that the Master might make his appearance at any time at hundreds of landmarks attributes to these spots a certain atmosphere of danger. The Master will not appear to a group of people, but rather to one or two lonely hunters or fishermen: persons who, in any event, are apprehensive and predisposed to sudden encounters with animals or unusual situations. A solitary hunter will have undergone an irksome ritual purification

Tatuyo with blowgun and poisoned darts lying on a bench

before going into the forest, and once there, he will be in a state of tense receptiveness, trying to interpret the multiple sensorial impacts he is exposed to. Under these circumstances, the sudden association between, for example, an odour, and the whole range of iconic and echoic memories, may lead to hallucinatory flashes in which the person believes they see otherworldly beings. The Master, it is said, is likely to appear as a stern gamekeeper trying to protect his wards from overhunting and any other form of depletion, such as bird-nesting, honey-seeking, ant-gathering, fishing with poison, or overharvesting fruit trees. An encounter with the Master of Animals is therefore a warning, which often enough is followed by punishment in the form of illness. The Master will manifest himself mainly to people who themselves are acutely aware of ecological problems, people who are actively involved in environmental disturbances, who have consciously or unknowingly violated the norms. He will appear to them in the forest or the garden, in dreams, nightmares or hallucinations, and since these apparitions are emotionally troubling, they are likely to be communicated to a shaman who then will warn the dreamer.

The 'acute awareness' I mentioned above will be recognised by shamans and is called *maría ~aríri*/our being, our way of being, and consists of two qualities: *mahsá pepíri*, lit. 'people-feel', and *~simpóra pepíri*, lit. 'soul-stuff-feel'. The verb *pepíri*/to feel, contains the root *perí*/to hear, referring to the 'inner ear', the capacity of the person to 'hear' the multiple messages of his physical environment. These two qualities constitute *mári deyóri*/our presence, an expression derived from *deyoári*/to appear, to make itself (oneself) visible, meaning that the person must be perfectly 'open' to the Master's sudden apparition. This mechanism is consequential in aboriginal ecological thought. The figure of the Master of Animals is a projection of a man's conscience; if he sees him, or feels his presence in any way, he knows he has violated some fundamental norm. In this manner, a shaman's way of interpreting apparitions, dreams, premonitions, or any sign of the Master's presence, are of ecological significance. The Master of Animals is not a mere gamekeeper but an ever-watchful guardian of man's actions impinging upon the environment.

In view of these threats, which are frequently being emphasised by shamans and elders, people tend to avoid *Vaí mahsë*'s houses or, at least, when passing nearby, do so quietly and without causing any disturbance. The result is that these spots, especially the islet hills, have become natural sanctuaries, natural game reserves. Many animal and plant species will thrive there undisturbed, and since the animals are not being persecuted, species such as deer, rodents, monkeys or game-birds are observable, and sometimes may be quite tame when approached by an occasional intruder. These aspects—unusual species density and the unafraid behaviour of the animals—have led to many local beliefs. In the first place, any spot in the forest or on the river where occasionally or frequently an unusual abundance of animals can be observed, is thought to be the dwelling-place of a *Vaí mahsë* and, as such, is taken to be a reserve, a breeding-ground people should not interfere with. Correspondingly, a spot where there is a noticeable absence of animals, or a sudden decrease of the fauna, i.e. of fish in a deep pool in the river, or of monkeys in a certain section of the forest where formerly used to be many, is believed to have been abandoned by its Master in retaliation for game depletion. On the Papurí River I was told of a hunter who was sitting on his stand, at a saltlick, drowsily watching the arrival of more and more tapirs. He had already killed two of them and now was looking forward to killing another. When the tapirs came, a voice could be heard in the forest: *'Two are missing!'* It was *Vaí-mahsë*. The hunter fled and from then on refrained from killing more game than was strictly needed for his family.

The behaviour of the game animals which occupy *Vaí mahsë*'s hill houses or other abodes, is often compared with that of human society. They are thought to have their social organisation and hierarchies, their gatherings and dances, their fertility rites and ceremonial exchanges. This belief is reaffirmed by observations the Indians have made in the course of time. Shamans who have visited

Taibano hunter with ritual facial paint, blowgun in left hand, quiver in his right

Vaí mahsë's houses, especially those located in the rocky formations of the Guiana Shield, or hunters who have gone astray and have found refuge in a cave or rockshelter, have come upon deposits of faunal remains, probably the vestiges of ancient or fairly recent hunting peoples who, more or less temporarily, occupied these spots. These finds, occasionally associated with artefacts such as necklace beads, stone axes, bone tools or pots, are interpreted by shamans and other people as proof for the existence of *Vaí mahsë*'s ghostly company. It is also a fact that on overhanging rock surfaces one occasionally finds pictographs in ochre or in black, representing animals and geometrical design motifs. Pecked or incised petroglyphs can be observed on many large boulders or slabs lying near rapids and pools, spots which are almost always connected with mythical events and the presence of guardian spirits.

From the foregoing it is obvious that the breakdown of the native belief system, brought about by missionaries, Bible translators, government agents, irresponsible tourists, uncontrolled colonisation and development, leads to severe ecological damage. Ignorance, bigotry, and ruthless government planning destroy this ancient belief system designed to preserve natural resources. By killing off the fauna and by torching these carefully protected reserves, untold damage is being done, not only to the physical environment, but also to an intellectual heritage. We may call the Master of Animals a creature of imagination, a focus of primitive superstitions held by savage jungle dwellers. This is true in a sense, but on a deeper level, what we call superstition is based upon sound observation, on hard biological facts. There can be no doubt that many Indian thinkers know quite well that magical threats, in the sphere of hunting and gathering, are more effective than biological reasoning. In a very important sense, *Vaí mahsë* is the representative, the tool of the shaman; he is the extension of the shaman's intellect and experience as an ecologist and administrator of resources.

What I have said so far is hardly more than a bare outline of the Tukanoan concept of the Master of Animals, and of its extraordinary importance to ecology. In the following I shall go into a more detailed account of these beliefs, to make the reader aware of the elaborate mental processes which underly and accompany the construction of this hunter's universe.

Shamans claim that they visit the Master's abodes, and penetrate into their interior during their narcotic trances. This they have to do in order to talk to the Master of Game, and convince him to release some of his charges for the hunters and fishermen, so people may eat. Let us see first of all how these abodes are structured. When saying that these places are wombs and places of gestation, the meaning is that they are places of transformation. As a matter of fact, they are the most important spots in all nature, where transformations take place. A hill house can be recognised as such because above it one can sometimes observe a spiral-shaped cloud formation, or a large funnel-shaped dust-devil. This funnel or spiral is said to be a vagina, it is the entrance to the womb which is the mal-

Fish trap from the Vaupés River near Mandí

oca inside the hill. The cosmic fertilising communication which enters vertically into the house, consists of *dári* energies in different colours. In the opposite direction, rising from the house to the surface, run, what shamans call, 'wind-threads' (*miru dári*) which transmit smells, animal odours. Hunters, when they approach such a hill, say they perceive the penetrating scent of aromatic herbs, together with the musky smell of rutting game animals such as deer, peccary or monkeys.[3] They know then that there will be a good hunting season. It is important to keep in mind that the hill house is imagined as having a hexagonal ground plan topped by a conical structure, that is, the funnel-shaped dust-devil or spiral-shaped cloud.

A house of the waters is imagined like this: the spot will be marked by whirlpools or eddies, large or small. These funnel-shaped formations, too, are interpreted as female organs which communicate with the 'House of Fish' at the bottom of the pool. The cosmic energies, once more, consist of coloured *dári* thread which penetrate vertically with the sun's rays as they fall into the water. In the opposite direction rise chains of bubbles, called 'foam-threads' (*súmu dári*) in the shamanic idiom, and which are a standard symbol for male, seminal energy. Again, the House of the Waters is imagined to be of hexagonal shape, combined with the spiral of the whirlpool.

A Barasana Indian told me quite casually of a recent walk in the forest, when he happened to pass near a hill. '*My elder brother and I*', he said, '*heard the Fish People playing their pan-pipes... it was a pleasant sound: the long flutes, the deerbone flute, the short flute. We heard all that; we also heard the laughter of the women. 'That must be a big maloca', we said. Paying close attention, we noticed the smell of the aromatic herbs the men and women of the Fish People use.'*

As happens so often, odours trigger fantasies, and this is a field shamans try to control and manipulate. Now it is a fact that *Vai mahsë*'s houses, being distinct micro-environments, have their specific odours. For example, the humid air near rapids, the spray and the mossy boulders have a peculiar smell, and so have rock formations in the forest where abundant aromatic herbs are present. When, after a long walk in the forest, one suddenly emerges upon a sun-drenched clearing, the olfactory sensations are striking and are likely to bring to mind associations, memories or—perhaps—lurking dangers.

The Barasana Indian and his brother had heard Fish People feasting inside a hill, but we have said that *Vai mahsë*'s houses sheltered animals. We must clarify this point in detail. In the first place, we have to realise that the interior of the rocky hills is 'known' to us only through shamans' accounts of what they have 'seen' there in a narcotic trance. The entire imagery has, therefore, a hallucinatory quality of changing perspectives and metamorphosing actors. It is said, for example, that in the dark interior of these ghostly malocas exist the gigantic prototypes of each species, manifestations of drug-induced macropsia. In another image, hundreds of game animals are seen gathered there, but in a somnolent state, lying on the ground or hanging from beams and rafters, as if unconscious, curled up foetus-like. *Vai mahsë* is not only their guardian but, in some ways, their procreator. He is a phallic being, a male principle in nature, constantly inseminating.

It is the shaman's task to visit periodically *Vai mahsë*'s abodes in order to negotiate with him a new supply of game for the hunters. When approaching the hill, its guardian, the cock-of-the-rock (*Rupicola sp.*) will screech loudly in warning; the spiny-tailed lizard (*Plica plica*)[4] will receive him open-eyed, in sign of recognition, and so the shaman will enter through one of the crevices and penetrate into *Vai mahsë*'s abode. The shaman does not ask for individual animals, but for a herd of peccary, a band of monkeys, a flock of game birds or, in general, for a good hunting or fishing season. These negotiation will take some time. *Vai mahsë* will consider the shaman's wishes and will choose the animals, 'wake them up' and release them in pairs into the forest.

We must stop here and try to see through this uncanny scene, and recognise behind it a clearly structured process. We are in the presence of a most important ecological brokerage. An Amazonian Indian mind is about to establish the rules by which wildlife can be exploited for human consumption, but at the same time will be protected. The shaman is the broker; he demands game animals, fish, forest resources. What can he offer in exchange?

The shaman pays with human souls. He must pledge himself to kill a number of people - of his or of a neighbouring group - whose soul-stuff must then

Fish trap on the Vaupés River at low water level

enter the Master's realm.[5] The victims are those who disobeyed the norms, who depleted local resources, killed too many game animals, cut down trees, poisoned whole creeks to catch a few fish. These people destroyed the environment and now must pay the price. All this sounds dramatic and is clearly meant to impress the hearer when shamans speak summarily about these matters. But if analysed in detail, the underlying ideas fit into the wider picture, and are far less violent than shamans make them appear.

Two energy circuits are involved here: one is the cosmic circuit of cosmic *bogá*, in which all living beings participate, and the other is the local circuit which links the hunter to his prey, the fisherman to his catch. *Vaí mahsë*'s houses, be they hills, pools or whatever, are imagined as repositories of energies represented by game, fish, and fruits, womb-like storehouses and breeding-grounds from which the surrounding environment has to be constantly replenished. In order to achieve this, new energies have to enter *Vaí mahsë*'s domains, and these consist of human life forces. When animals die a natural death, their energy returns to the cosmic *bogá*, but if they become the prey of humans, their energy enters the local circuit of hunters and their game. What is needed are mechanisms of control which will keep people from depleting wildlife, and these mechanisms are instituted and formulated in shamanic threats of becoming transformed into a vulnerable and 'energetically' limited game animal, in punishment for ecological misconduct.

The assumption that the shaman will have to kill people in order to use their soul-stuff or 'energy' for ecological ends, must be taken metaphorically. He may cast evil spells, throw magical pathogenic substances in someone's direction, or he may sing and threaten invisible enemies in a narcotic trance, but all this aggressiveness is acted out in an imaginary sphere. Time is always on the shaman's side; eventually, people will learn that someone who lived far away has died; that someone has had an accident, fell ill, disappeared in the forest or on the river. These things do happen. And then the shaman will let it be known that it was *he* who cast the spell and who had the evildoer punished.

Vaí mahsë's animals participate in an energy circuit of birth, copulation, and death, paralleled by man's, by that of plant-life, of seasonal periodicities and biological cycles visible everywhere. Animals may behave like humans, smell like humans, cry like humans, but they are not people. They are *like* people and this likeness has its reasons. I have mentioned in another place that hunting can be compared to courtship behaviour, and that the hunter, purified and scented, tries to 'make the game animals fall in love with him'. This equation between hunting and courtship corresponds to an equation between hunting as an economic-ecological activity, and exogamy as a sexual-social institution. This situation can be illustrated thus: For most Tukanoan groups, tapir, i.e. the Arawakan autochthone, continues to be an ancestral figure. Tapir is referred to as *vëhkë* (D)/father-in-law, and as such is conceptualised as the owner of women and, eventually, the wife-giver. The hunter who enters the forest crosses a threshold and finds himself in another dimension (*gahí turí*) where he has to confront tapir by understanding that the prey he is looking for will be one of tapir's people, i.e. a sister or a daughter, appearing in the shape of a 'female' animal, perhaps a deer. Among the animals coterminous with tapir in the dense forest will be collared peccary; this prey is called *yehsé*, and *yehsé porá* (collared peccary-sons) is the name of a Desana sib. Desana girls, at their puberty ritual, are referred to as *yehseru*, lit. peccary-thing, and eventually marry river-oriented men, such as Pira-tapuya or Uanano. This model of hunting (and fishing) and exogamy is largely non-factual, but details of it linger on in hunting lore and, above all, in restrictive behaviour. Pregnant women must not eat animals of the dense forest, such as tapir, deer, peccary, woolly monkey, trumpeter bird, curassow, and tortoise, because they should avoid the spermatic energy of the forest dwellers; instead they should eat garden-associated animals such as paca, agouti, cavi, armadillo, guan, tinamou, and toucan.

The relationship between the hunter and his prey is expressed in a fundamental concept to which, for lack of a better term, I shall refer to as 'abstinence' (*beréri*). This verb has two meanings: the usual, literal one being 'to fast', in the sense of food restriction, of abstaining from any excess in hunting, fishing or harvesting. The other meaning is more complex. A hunting dog is trained to point at game by raising one foot, an action designated as *bererí*. The same stance is adopted by dancers, and is referred to with the same term. The meaning of this position is that the hunter is alerted by a scent; he is approaching his prey in a state of expectancy. He has 'fasted', saving his energies for his impending courtship. A concept closely related to *bererí*/to fast, is *mererí*, lit. 'to appraise', and is used to describe the regulating and controlling of the following situations: marriage rules, hunting and fishing, food preparation and consumption, exchange rituals, music and dance. These form a homologous chain, and each individual link must be well regulated, well orchestrated, the watchword being *mereké*/combine well! It is noteworthy that by nasalising this verb and pronouncing it ~*mererí*, it comes to mean 'to become intoxicated', i.e. to pass from the measured to the unmeasured, the unrestrained.

The hunter/prey relationship is but one aspect of a much wider concept expressed in the words *gamé bohsarí*/mutually to consent, used in the sense of 'to establish an alliance'. This expression is used in the following contexts: women (*nomé gamí bohsarí*), game and fish (*vaí mëra gamé bohsarí*), forest (*nëngë gamé bohsarí*), river (*dia gamé bohsarí*), plants (*yuhkë gamé bohsarí*). The concept of alliance, then, is not limited to social organisation; it extends to all of nature. Man is allied with nature, and this fact implies the observance of rules of measure.

Vaí mahsë exercises his control according to certain categories of game. The animals he is in charge of are referred to as ~*ehkará* (D), a term which can be

Barasana shaman with *taríra* (LG) fish

A Barasana making a quiver for poisoned blowgun darts

translated as 'his breed'.[6] *Vaí mahsë* is said to be a 'breeder' in the sense of having a sexual relationship with game animals, not in fact, but in the sense of his representing a spermatic force in nature. The release of mammals such as tapir, deer, peccary and monkeys is severely restrained, as is that of curassow and Furnaridae; among fishes, certain catfish (*Pseudoplatystoma sp.*) and the *aracú* (LG) (*Leporinus copelandi*). On the other hand, paca, agouti, armadillo, and most small fish are not in need of special protection.

Game animals are said to vary in their specific 'energy' content, depending upon their local environment. For example, mammals, fish, insects, and forest fruits from the Papurí River or the Pira-paraná drainage are 'energetically' quite different. The Indians will say: '*They seem to be the same, but they are another thing*' (*yuhúro deyoárima obo gahiropa arima*). Even the animals' behavioural patterns won't be the same. The differences will then find their expression in the physical constitution and personal traits of the local inhabitants who consume these resources: '*Different people different forces-energy*' (*gahí mahsá turári bogá*). The differences in animal 'energies' depend to a large degree upon differences in the availability and abundance of their respective vegetable foods. These considerations provide the basis for food restrictions and for certain culinary preparations. The entire food chain—real or imaginary—passing through *Vaí mahsë*'s 'houses' and thereby regulating people's behaviour, has to be seen as an organised plan of ecological norms in which birth control and the preservation of natural resources are the principal values.

We are approaching here a conceptual field of great ecological interest. In the dense forest exist about a dozen trees, the fruits or seeds of which are consumed by game animals as well as by humans. Most of the seeds contain oils (*ëye këri*) lit. 'oil-to have', and this oil (*ëye*) is thought to be a very critical substance. It is recognised as having a high nutritious value but, at the same time, is believed to be too sexually arousing, leading from laxity to promiscuity; any discussion of *ëye* is likely to take an emotional turn with slightly ambivalent overtones. To consume the meat of game animals that feed on oily seed—tapir, peccary, deer, monkey—is thought to greatly increase illicit sex. The quality of *ëye* differs according to its plant source and local environment, and can vary from a saliva-like texture and transparency to yellowish viscosity. The *ëye* element is also present in game birds such as curassow and large oven-birds, but not in guan or tinamou. Large catfish contain *ëye*, but most smaller fish are harmless.[7] To this are added other factors; two animal species of the dense forest have a strong musky smell referred to as *oma sëríri*, lit. 'carry-odour', associated with sexual activity. They are collared peccary, which 'carry' the stench of the whitish fluid of their scent glands, and monkeys, which have a pungent odour. Tapir and deer are not mentioned in this context as having a strong odour, but tapir is said to symbolise a mythical progenitor's virility, while deer is said to have the attractions of female sex. The expression *óma sëríri* (from *omári*/to 'carry' a scent) is

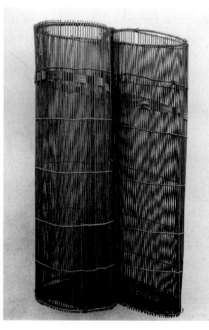

Above: A Tatuyo boy tying kapok to a blowgun dart

Left: Tukanoan fish trap from the Vaupés River

said to be the manifestation of procreative energies and of female fecundity which, if not restricted to reciprocal marriage arrangements, would lead to socially disruptive behaviour. The aim is not verbalised as population control, but as the control of extramarital sex. The underlying key concept is *ëye*, a word whose root points to a complex of meanings related to seminal substances, to human sperm and its metaphors.

As a rule, the meat of game animals of the forest has to be smoked in order to eliminate its musky or pungent odour and, what is most important, to keep it ready for an exchange ritual with one's allies. The process of smoking the meat (*siyurí*) is, in itself, an important symbolic transformation by which an implicit critical sexual potency is neutralised and cured in a manner which makes it an appropriate exchange item. The rodents—paca, agouti, cavy—form a game category apart. Although they too consume oily seeds, their meat is bland and healthy and, what is most important, rodents have a 'pleasant' smell (*sëríri*) and do not possess the strong odour (*oma sëríri*) collared peccary share with monkeys. This distinguishes the rodents from other game, even if they are forest dwellers and 'oil eaters'. Rodents are said to be friendly animals which participate in people's food by feeding on manioc peel, bananas, and kitchen refuse. They are referred to as *vií tero mahára*, lit. 'maloca-nearby-belonging' or *poé tero mahára*, 'garden-about-belonging'.

Vaí mahsë is not alone in his role as Master of Game. In the depths of the interfluvial forests dwells another ghostly being, the *Boráro*[8]. In the Amazonian vernacular this forest demon is known under the name of *Curupíra*, and has been mentioned by travellers, missionaries, anthropologists and folklorists. In the Vaupés area, the Indians describe the *Boráro* as a tall naked man, with a huge penis. Some people say that his eyes are red and glowing; others mention his large ears and his curved fangs, similar to those of a jaguar. An evil stench surrounds him and attracts many large blue butterflies (*Morpho*) and other insects. All people agree that his feet are twisted, the toes pointing backward and the heels forward. His knees have no joints, and should he fall he has difficulties in getting up again.

The *Boráro* has his maloca in the dense forest, but often visits *Vaí mahsë*. Most of the time he spends wandering in the forest, sometimes accompanied by his wife, described as a horrible hag with only one breast. They will roam on the headwaters catching crabs, which are his favourite food. He often visits large stands of palm trees, especially those of *mirití* (*Mauritia flexuosa*), *caraná* (*Mauritiella cataractarum*), and *piassaba* (*Leopoldina piassaba*). *Caraná* palms grow on riverbanks, in swampy terrain (*muhí boa*) or caatinga, and their broad leaves, dry or still green, offer him shelter at the foot of the tree. The fruits of *caraná* are inedible but many forest animals feed on them, and the same is true of *piassaba* palms. The third palm, *mirití* bears abundant edible fruits, and the *Boraró* is often seen in dense stands of this palms of the swampy (*tara boa*) sections of the forest. Occasionally a hunter will come upon a disturbance in the closed-canopy forest, a gap not created by man. These spots are called *mirúnye poé*, the wind's gardens; people avoid them because these places are visited by the *Boráro*.

In many aspects, the *Boráro* is a gamekeeper and protector of palms and other fruit-bearing trees, but he differs from *Vaí mahsë* in that the former appears in many guises as a rather benevolent force, warning and advising people, while the *Boráro* appears as a cannibalistic monster feared by all. It is possible that the two represent one and the same concept, that of a personification of a phallic-ambivalent fertility concept. In any case, the *Boráro* exercises an effective control over hunters and foragers who venture deep into the forest. Many Indians I have met assured me of having seen or, at least, heard the *Boráro* while hunting,[9] and of having abandoned their pursuit, at least on these occasions.

The Measure of the River

The rivers of the Amazon basin represent braided stream regimes forming innumerable meanders of loop-like bends. Due to lateral shifting of the river course, meander loops are cut off, turn into lakes and eventually into swamps, and in this manner an ever-changing pattern of channel sequences and relict channels cover the land.

The relationship of rivers and streams to the adjacent forests must be looked at from the Indians' perspective if we want to grasp the theory of Tukanoan ethno-ecology. In a simple hydrographic image, a river is seen as lying between the headwaters and its mouth, its course being divided into straight stretches where you can see ahead, followed by bends or loops; a bend and two stretches—one before the turn and one after—form a unit. Rapids and falls are major divisions, and near them are deep pools. During the dry seasons there will be many sandy beaches, and then there are backwaters, lagoons, and inlets. There will be promontories and islands, innumerable confluences with smaller streams and creeks, until finally the rivermouth is reached.[10]

I shall try to enlarge this bare outline with the ideas and images the Indians have developed with reference to the river. Let us first see how the river obtains its energies. Although rivers receive some cosmic *bogá* their principal energy proceeds from the adjacent forest. The riverbanks are mostly covered with open forest and some caatinga which might become flooded during the height of the rainy season. This riverine vegetation is very important in native ecology, because most fish are said to depend on it,[11] and the tendency of 'civilised' people to cut down the vegetation of the riverbanks is rightly condemned by the Indians. The forest begins only at some distance inland. However, at some spots the forest will advance to the water's edge. Forming a more or less narrow corridor, the forest will come in direct contact with the river and these spots are of significance to the Indians. It is where tapir, deer, peccary, and monkeys have their trails leading to the watering places, and where they go at certain hours, *'just like people'*, to drink water. In the Indians' understanding this is an exchange of energies in which the river receives a potent charge of life-forces which benefit fish, turtles, and all other aquatic creatures. To maintain this link between forest and river is an ecological law to the Indians, and nothing could be worse than the destruction of the riverine forests, or the depletion of game animals at their watering places.

Along the river there will be some topographical features which shamans point out as important spots. These features are protruding rocks, sandbanks, and small peninsulas. Together with the forest corridors coming down to the water's edge, these spots are mentioned in myths, spells, and songs, and shamans will explain that they are energy-laden places where a 'male' element (forest, rocks, specific trees) contact and 'penetrate' a 'female' element (river, ponds and pools, fish, turtles).

Recurrent features of the braided river systems are, of course, the individual meanders. It is obvious that the overland distance between two bends will be shorter than the waterway and, in view of this, on long and tiresome canoe travels a few passengers might want to go ashore and walk straight across the forest, and then wait for the canoe to catch up with them. People might do this for a number of reasons: to do some hunting, to gather fruits, or simply to stretch their legs. The crossing of such a loop may be a matter of a few hours but, occasionally, it could take a day or two. To take this kind of shortcut (*vahti*) through the forest is said to be dangerous and people, especially the older generation, strongly advise against it saying that one might get lost, be bitten by a snake or hurt by a falling tree and—what is emphasised—this lonely walk might provide an occasion for forbidden sex. And then, of course, one might come across *Vaí mahsë* or one of his avatars.

In reality, people crossing a loop are likely to encounter oxbow lakes and relict channels situated on older meander belts. Apart from being good hunting and fishing grounds, there are likely to be old clearings, ancient habitation sites recognisable by clumps of peach palm or other trees believed to have been planted by the ancient inhabitants. The prohibitory injunctions for crossing these meander loops may not be very severe, but they are sufficiently strong to keep people from depleting the local flora and fauna whenever they travel by canoe. In this manner, meander loops have become biological reserves of a sort, which are not negligible. Next to the natural resources available in a forested meander loop, shamans mention ancient ports as being most significant power spots where ancestors and 'other people' have accumulated energies which are still active and continue to nourish the environment. Occasionally these long-forgotten 'ports' or 'houses' are remembered as named landmarks of shamanic

The confluence of the Papurí and Vaupés rivers. In the distant right is Yavareté in Brazil

geography.

Rapids and falls are significant because they form distinct micro-environments and divide a river into sections. I have mentioned already the pools where *Vaí mahsë* has his abodes as Master of Fish; the boulders, the ancient petroglyphs[12], the patches of white foam floating on eddies. Confluences are said to be crucial points of energy convergence and exchange, and so are bifurcations and islands. Finally, we have the headwaters, another distinct region believed to be charged with forest energies.

Limnologists (e.g. Sioli, 1975) classify Amazonian rivers into white water, black water, and clear water categories, a range mainly based on ecological conditions prevailing in the headwater regions. White-water rivers are said to originate from erosion in the Andes; black-water rivers come from sandy, caatinga-like open forests; and clear-water rivers originate in the brownish clays of deep forests. There are many other factors involved, but these do not concern us here. According to this basic classification, the Vaupés and Apaporis Rivers are white water, the Papurí and Pira-paraná are black water, and clear water would be the many small streams and creeks. The Indians, however, recognise many more categories, apart from 'white water' (*dehkó boréri*), 'black water' (*dehkó nyíri*), and 'transparent water' (*dehkó siriría*); for example, there is 'greenish water' (*dehkó yasári*) in many small creeks, 'red water' (*dehkó diári*) in some larger streams, and a whole range of more or less transparent waters. Since colours are associated with energies, shamans will distinguish many shades, and will combine them with aspects of odour, flavour, and temperature, all of which are said to influence aquatic life forms, and, through them the health and wellbeing of people.

The Indians say that fish are like women. This association is referred to in many contexts, but its emphasis may depend upon the phratry of the speaker. Pira-Tapuya, Uanano, or Bará women are quite definitely 'fish women', while Desana women belong to the forest. But these are Tukanoan stereotypes; the overall consensus is that fish are a female element. Some people will say that First Woman was a Fish Woman, a forest dweller caught with hook and line; others will make comparisons with women when speaking of fishruns and spawning behaviour, patterns of swimming, odours, textures, flavours. 'To go fishing' is a common metaphor for going in pursuit of amorous adventures, and most anything connected with a man's fishing gear, rods, types of fish traps, fishing strategies, and so on, is metaphorically related with the world of women. There are a few exceptions. The *unyú* fish originated from a penis, when a betrayed husband emasculated his wife's lover, and forced her to eat it, whereupon she vomited it into the river. There are a few other, 'male' fish, but otherwise all are female and some, e.g. the *piranha*, are voracious and cannibalistic.

Seen from a wider perspective, fish are 'just like people'. They live in their 'houses', they follow strict visiting patterns and celebrate their exchange rituals;

their spawning behaviour is ritualised and they have their shamans and lead dancers. Their relationships with humans are similar to those of game animals. Fish communicate with people through their behaviour, the ease or difficulty with which they let themselves be caught; or they communicate through certain signs (we would call them apotropaic eye-spots) which carry messages from *Vaí-mahsë*.

The major falls and rapids of a river form physical obstacles for some species, a fact which, together with changing limnological and ecological conditions determines the distribution of species among a river and its affluents. The Indians are greatly concerned about the feeding habits and strategies of fish, and distinguish between carnivorous, omnivorous and other species, applying criteria of 'impurity' or 'purity' on a detailed scale of edibility. In a certain river (a stretch of the Pira-paraná) fish that live in the depths are said to be 'black and cold', those near the surface are 'hot and brown', while those of the middle stratum are 'red and cold'. In a curing spell to alleviate postpartum pains, the shaman will invoke a specific range of black-water nuances. This division into various ranges of depth is emphasised in the case of deep pools that lie at the foot of many rapids, and at the bottom of which *Vai-mahsë*, in his manifestation as Master of Fish, has his abodes. Some fish, notably those of the lower parts of a river, are said to contain *ëye*, and can be eaten only by adults who know specific spells; small species inhabiting creeks and headwater regions are said to be harmless.

For the consumer, much depends on the correct combination of fish species, culinary preparation, and age-group of the eater. Cooking, broiling and smoking are only basic procedures, the true test being the 'mixture', the addition of vegetables, seasonings and strong condiments like peppers.

Fishing, like hunting and unlike gardening, is strongly ritualised. Dietary and sexual restrictions are the rule before going on a fishing excursion, and under certain circumstances a man is not permitted to go fishing for a number of days. Should a woman touch his fishing gear it would become polluted and days might pass before is can be purified. Shamans and elders will spend hours singing to fish, often with quite overtly erotic allusions to the fish/women analogy. When, during the dry season, groups of people go to fish with fish poison, shamans or elders will control the quantity and toxicity of the preparation, so it won't affect too many fish in a given pool or stretch of the river.

Fish is one of the most important protein sources in the Vaupés region, and is almost a daily food item. There is no scarcity of fish in regions where civilisation has not yet introduced commercial fishing and fishing with dynamite, and where traditional ecological controls are still in force.

All along a river are visible landmarks, called *vií goróri*, lit. 'house-sites', many of them related to mythological or historical episodes, others being features of the natural environment, but all of them believed to be charged with varying

The Meyú Falls, Pira-paraná river in Barasana territory

Our canoe at the headwaters of the Pira-paraná river in Tatuyo territory

amounts and qualities of vital energies, proceeding, in all essence, from cosmic *bogá*. These are liminal spots, sometimes tellingly designated as 'doors', where people can pass from one dimension of awareness to another, or where powers from 'other dimensions' (*gahí turíri*) can manifest themselves to human beings.

A characteristic feature of Tukanoan origin and migration myths is the list-ing of place-names. The linear development of the story, its chronology, is illus-trated step by step with descriptive names which refer to way-stations where cer-tain events took place during the progressive ascent of the rivers. This, then, is a lesson in geography and history, because these lists of power-laden 'houses' are quoted for didactic reasons and provide the hearer not only with a map on which he can follow the thread of a story, but also offer a time perspective of Tukanoan history, as perceived by the Indians themselves. The hundreds of place-names provide a grid of references to Tukanoan past and present, in the sense of clues to ecological considerations.[13]

So far, we have had before our eyes the river as a flow of water, descending from the mountains toward the plains. As we shall see now, Tukanoan river imagery is very rich and colourful, being based upon metaphors and analogues of a bedazzling variety. I shall arrange some of these images into an approximate order, from the simplest comparisons to the more elaborate ones.

One of the most common river analogues is the anaconda, the large aquatic snake of the Amazon rainforest. A few words about the natural history of this snake are in order here to clarify the facts. Anacondas can be seen swimming below the surface and, at greater depth, are traceable by chains of air bubbles that rise like strings of shiny beads. Anacondas can be up to eight metres long and can devour large mammals such as tapir, deer, peccary and paca. After killing their prey by constriction, most of the long bones having been broken in the process, the anaconda swallows its prey whole. The mouth of the snake expands greatly and the expansibility of the body is such that it can engorge even a bulky quarry. The snake's body will adopt a fusiform shape, and in this state can be seen lying on the riverbank digesting its prey for a number of days before vomiting it up again in the form of a foul-smelling bag of bones. During the mat-ing season swimming anacondas will lift about one third of their bodies almost vertically out of the water, and then slap it down again, making a loud noise to attract their mates. According to the Indians, the snakes rise out of the waters to watch the stars in the Milky Way, to find out if the time of fish-runs is near; in this context, the anaconda is called the 'mother of fish'. The Indians readily compare the swollen body of a digesting anaconda with a bulging-stemmed palm (*Iriartea ventricosa*) and with a pregnant woman; the vomiting-up of the digested matter, still enveloped in the skin of the prey animal, is compared to an abortion. The anaconda thus combines an uterine, life-preserving principle, with a strangling and aborting one.

The Indians believe that in deep pools at the foot of waterfalls, or in isolated

Negotiating the Pineapple Falls in Tatuyo territory

lagoons in the forest, monstrous anacondas are dwelling, which might occasionally 'devour' a lonely traveller—a quite effective threat to keep people away from spots shamans believe to be under the protection of *Vaí mahsë*. In another analogue, the Milky Way is an anaconda, or an anaconda skin. The yearly motions of the Milky Way are compared with the intertwining motions of two copulating anacondas, an image correlated with seasonal periods of insemination, germination and fertility. Since the river is a 'path' (*maa*), an anaconda is also conceived as a path, a trail winding through the forest. Evil shamans might transform themselves into a manioc squeezer, a snake-like woven cylinder, and float in the river near the port trying to attack bathing women to whom they appear in the shape of anacondas. A large log-drum is another analogue of an anaconda, and so is a canoe, or any dancing baton of hollow *Cecropia* wood. It all depends upon context. But even if we should say: 'In this context the meaning is such-and-such', we must keep in mind the many analogues and all their possible contexts. In sum, to identify the anaconda exclusively with an Amazonian river, or with the Milky Way of a tropical sky, may appeal to a Westerner's imagination, but it is—at best—only a partial picture; the dark side of the anaconda is just as compelling. The Indian who sees the coiling eddies of turbulent waters, or who perceives the slowly moving shapes of a drug-induced hallucination, will be reminded of anacondas and be made aware of dimensions which belong to the Master of Animals, the Master of Fish, and all the benefits and frustrations implied in daily subsistence and life-long adaptive strategies.

In one image, Tukanoan territory is seen as enclosed by six anacondas lying outstretched head to tail along the rivers Vaupés, Apaporis, Pira-paraná, Tiquié and others; there is no consensus concerning the exact limits, but in shamanic geography the image of a hexagonal territory prevails. A variant of this image speaks of pairs of anacondas lying parallel one to another, but each looking in the opposite direction. In most versions of the origin myth, the Tukanoans are said to have arrived in a canoe shaped like an anaconda (or inside an anaconda shaped like a canoe), the passengers being a group of agnatic brothers, the seating arrangement marking age and/or rank in terms of 'specialisation', i.e. chief, shaman, warrior and so on. In other versions of the same myth the arrangement is by tribal unit, exogamous group, phratry or by ranked sibs. It can be said that each Tukanoan phratry has its own anaconda myth, the reptile appearing as a primeval womb, an ambivalent mother image, a culture bearer or whatever the local tradition might see in it.

Segmentation is a fundamental theme in Tukanoan thought, and rivers provide obvious models, being segmented by rapids, meander loops, mythical way-stations, *Vaí mahsë*'s abodes, power spots, and by being divided into ecological zones. A river can be compared with the trunk of a palm tree on which leaf-scars mark segments, and these segments can be said to represent social segments, or individuals in a patriline. The segments, moreover, can be associated with the cylindrical mouthpieces of ritual trumpets which, in turn, are associated with certain animals, and so on and so forth. Any linear phenomenon in nature: river, snake, palm, seeds in a seed pod, fish skeleton (herring-bone pattern), intestinal tract, umbilical cord[14], forest trail, Milky Way, etc. can be seen in these terms; the river is the foremost model.

In one story we are told that, in the beginning of time, people cut down a large tree which, when falling to the ground, turned into a great river with many branches and affluents. In another story it is said that a river looks like a man standing with outstretched arms, his head at the sources and his feet at the river's mouth. The man shakes his long hair and out of it fall the leaves of a hallucinogenic vine which, while dropping, turn into all kinds of fish representing women. In still another story, a braided river system is just that, a tangle of hallucinogenic vines.

Shamans speak of the river as a path, man's trajectory on the way to transformation and purification in the headwaters. Men are imagined as travelling upstream, against the current, and river travel in myth and trance states are sometimes seen as an initiatory experience. To travel upriver is *mëríri*, to ascend, a verb which also means 'to relate to', 'to communicate with'. The headwaters are isolated regions lying beyond the rapids; the lower sections of a river are contact areas, with all their temptations and dangers. This recurrent theme is well summarised in the words of advice given by an old man: '*If you go to the river-mouth, you will become the owner of machetes; if you go the the headwaters, you will become the owner of feather-crowns.*'

Chapter V

TREES OF LIFE

The Eight Trees

We all have seen on film and television, in illustrated journals or in scientific books, the death of great trees in the tropical rainforest. We have heard the screeching of the chain-saws, have seen the first shuddering of the trunk, and then we have witnessed the slow sway followed by the crashing fall of the tree, tearing with it a tangled mass of vines and shrubs and undergrowth. A gap has been opened in the canopy, and we are looking now through a crack into the interior of an unsuspected world.

Tabebuia tree, Caruaasú, Brazil

But what exactly have we seen, or believe ourselves to have seen? Is it progressive governmental action opening up new horizons? Is it modern technology on the frontiers of untamed nature? Landless people trying to wrest a living from a hostile no-man's-land? We have seen the pictures and we have heard the politicians, the planners and ecologists discuss the same old clichés. And all the while the screeching of the chain-saws has continued.

In this chapter I shall discuss what really happens, what a nameless jungle tree (nameless to us, the television watchers) can mean to the Indians in whose land it grows. Let us choose then eight trees from the Vaupés territory, and list them first of all under their Linnean, vernacular, and native names.

Linnean	Vernacular	D	T	PT	U
1. *Tabebuia serratifolia*	*palo de arco*	*dohtógë*	*dohtógë*	*dohtóe*	*dohtöë*
2. *Monopteryx angustifolia*	*uacú*	*~semé*	*~simió*	*~simio*	*~simio*
3. *Erisma japura*	*japurá*	*barí*	*batí*	*batí*	*batí*
4. *Pouteria ucuqui*	*ucuquí*	*~poé*	*puhpía*	*puhpía*	*puhpía*
5. *Poraqueiba sericea*	*umarí*	*~mëë*	*~vamë*	*~vamë*	*~vamë*
6A. *Micrandra spruceana**	*seringa Arana*	*~vahsú*	*~vahsó*	*~vahsó*	*~vahsó*
6B. *Hevea rigidifolia**	——-	*~vahsúpë*	*vahpë*	*vahpë*	*vahpë*
7. *Socratea exorrhiza*	*paxiúba*	*buhpú*	*buhpú*	*buhpú*	*buhpú*
		~nyu	*~nyo*	*~nyo*	*~nyo*
8. *Iriartea ventricosa*	*paxiúba*	*buhu*	*vahta*	*vahta*	*vahta*
	barrigona	*beëgë*	*~nyo*	*~nyo*	*~nyo*

Micrandra spruceana and *Hevea rigidifolia* are considered the same species. Both are of the *Euphorbiaceae*.

The first tree we shall discuss is the bow wood tree or Tabebuia. It is called *ipé*, in lingua geral, and *palo de arco* or *pau d'arco*, in Spanish and Portuguese respectively, alluding to its wood being used in the manufacture of bows. *Tabebuia* is a medium-to-large tree (8 to 10 metres), of the Bignonia Family, which grows in mature rainforest areas of the *~nëngë* type. It is mentioned occasionally in botanical literature, mainly because its bark is believed to be of pharmacological importance in the treatment of malaria and cancer.[1] Because of its extremely hard wood Colombian peasants often mistake this tree for the pockwood tree (*Guaiacum officinalis*). It is also known as jacaranda (*Jacaranda copaia*). *Tabebuia* trees flower toward the end of the dry season (February) and the beginning of the rainy season (May, June). The Indians say that the pollen is similar to that of the *guamo* tree (*Inga sp.*) and that the yellow flowers attract the same insect pollinators (*nomé mera*/honey-beasts) to both trees. A flowering *Tabebuia* tree, with its dense mass of yellow efflorescences standing out from the otherwise monotonous green of the canopy, is a splendid sight, and European travellers will mention it as one of the most colourful manifestations of tropical nature. But otherwise there is little to say; the fruits are not edible; the wood is not available in commercial quantities, and belief in the bark's healing powers seems to have declined.

To the Indians, however, this tree is of major importance as a model, a kind of artificial memory. In order to understand this centrality in the natives' appreciation of the forest, we must remember that any meaning - or meanings - must be understood in the context of conceptual domains constituted by analogies. In Tukanoan terms, a *Tabebuia* tree does not just represent a narrowly circumscribed concept, but represents but one element in a chain or cluster. A *Tabebuia*, therefore, is 'like A, like B, like C', according to context. This means that if we know a number of contexts, we can deduce some general principle as to the meaning of a certain aspect and, in the case of the *Tabebuia* tree, we find that this tree means to the Indians: maleness, dominance, aggression, and procreative energy. It is a phallic tree. But why should the Indians say so? What would be the imagery in which they express these thoughts?

First of all a few descriptive notes are needed. One characteristic of the tree, which is immediately pointed out by the Indians, but which I did not find mentioned in the botanical literature I have consulted, is that *Tabebuia* trees are hardly ever associated with vines, creepers or epiphytes, but have rather bare trunks and branches. Another characteristic is the penetrating sweetish odour of the flowering trees, a scent one can perceive already at a distance, and which the Indians compare to the odour of anise, known to them from the Colombian anise-flavoured aguardiente. The large amount of flowers lying at the foot of the tree and which attract clouds of insects and other animals, contributes to the distinctiveness of this tree. After a long walk in the forest, the Indian's reaction to the sight of a *Tabebuia* tree is one of recognition, of wanting to say: '*So I have come to this section of the forest, the one where I shall meet this tree.*'

The large yellow flowers, high up in the canopy, open approximately in the middle of the dry season (middle of February) and continue in bloom to the middle of the rainy season (April). This is a time for hunting and fishing with fish-poisons, for gathering honey and caterpillars. But when the rainy season approaches, the Indians are wary because they say that *Tabebuia* belong to a category of trees likely to be struck by lightning, because of 'the attraction of its yellow blossoms'. The fruiting season is about three months later, from May to June, before the heaviest rains.

The first problem of interpretation arises when we take a look at the native name of the tree. It is called *dohtógë* (D T), the suffix *gë* being a classifier for trees, while *dohtó* is said to be related to the concept of 'bundle' or 'package', a term used when referring to units of objects, such as firewood, smoked fish, or flowers.[2] In a metaphorical sense, the same word is used to designate the male genitals and in this manner relates to the tree's 'male' image. The related verb, *dohtoári*, describes the act of making a bundle by bending something, and can

A *Uassai* (LG) palm in the Vaupés River near Yurupari-mirí

also be used to describe a crippled person, someone who is 'contracted', 'knot-ted'. The underlying idea, admittedly difficult to follow, is one of bending, deflecting, deviating, and was illustrated by the Indians in the following way: at certain times of the year, some stars or constellations (*nékamë*, *neká*) which appear in the Milky Way, announce the change of seasons in that they 'turn the corner' (*no'kéari*), changing the course of the yearly round and beginning a new season. According to the Indians, the name of the tree refers, then, to two con-cepts: firstly male potency (the 'package' image) and secondly the change of sea-sons, thunder marking the flowering of the tree and announcing the coming of the rainy season. In this change, the 'transforming' (*dohtesé*) force of the tree manifests itself. *Dohtógë* trees belong to a larger category called *buhpú gógë*, lit. 'thunder-flower-tree', a term with complex double meanings. On the one hand, it is believed that the soundwaves of a close thunderclap will make some trees suddenly shed all their flowers or all their pollen, while, on the other hand, it is said that *'thunder flowers in that tree'*. Thunder, in myths, dreams and hal-lucinations is a father figure, a powerful male, owner of women, owner of hal-lucinogenic snuff and of power objects such as the shaman's stick-rattle, the shining ear-pendants, brilliant rock crystals and other attributes, all of them of phallic or seminal nature.[3] The association of thunderclaps, pollination and ejac-ulation is found in many Tukano myths and other oral statements, and the *dohtógë* tree is thus a paternal symbol, a scatterer of pollen and yellow colours associated with life-giving, inseminating energies. The expression that *'thunder flowers in that tree'* refers directly to this imagery. The element *go*, in *buhpú-gógë*/thunder-flower-tree, derives from *góri*/blossoms; *goári*/flowers are a Tukanoan metaphor for the female sex organ (*~koré*), but the related word, *goro* means 'place' and is often used in shamanistic contexts, as 'place of origin', 'place of emergence', referring to a mythical vagina or womb. The 'energy' of lightning (in our terms, a discharge of electricity) is called *buhpú miarí*, lit. 'thunder to blink'. This verb, *miarí*, also means 'to flash' or 'to spark' and is related to *viarí*, a verb referring to the act of 'rendering something intimately', i.e. to give some leaf-wrapped fish to one's wife, an act of identification, of energy transmission, that only a husband can perform. In sum, we are speaking here of the tree image in terms of human sexual physiology; the tree represents a male, inseminating principle.

Flowering *Tabebuia* trees, besides attracting many insect pollinators to the canopy, allure certain rodents at ground level, a fact which is of interest to hunters. Pacas (*Coelogynis paca*) are nocturnal foragers which come to nibble at the flowers which have dropped to the ground, and during the daytime it is not uncommon to find cavi (*Myoprocta sp.*) near the trees. Both rodents have marked 'female' associations; the Indians designate them with kinship terms and speak of them as 'belonging to the household'. Their presence at the foot of *Tabebuia* trees is seen as one more model of cohabitation and fertilisation.

Underside of *Cecropia* leaf

Upper side of *Cecropia* leaf

Fruits of *yërë* (D), a cultivated
Poraqueiba sericea

A *babassü* (LG) palm
(*Maximiliane sp.*)

Another faunal association the Indians have observed is that of large macaws which often choose *dohtóge* trees for their noisy gatherings. These colourful birds have shamanistic connotations, being messengers and bringers of energies manifest in their yellow and orange-coloured feathers.

The wood of the *Tabebuia* tree is famous for its hardness. In the species *Tabebuia serratifolia* it is almost black, but in *Tabebuia Avellanedae* it is of a dark-red colour. From these woods, especially from the heartwood, Tukano Indians make their weapons: bows, arrow foreshafts, heavy clubs, and the mouthpiece of the blowgun, and next to these, some important ritual artefacts, such as the tubular log-mortar for preparing the mixture of powdered coca leaves, chieftains' staffs, stick-rattles, and large pronged cigar-holders. Let us anticipate that these eight artefacts are among the most important ones in Tukanoan material culture, and that all of them are imbued with a complex symbolism. The common denominator is the wood of the bow tree, and all its associations: maleness and its world of sex, drugs, and death.

It is impossible to go here into the details of how the aboriginal culture deals with these problems; we would have to digress too far into too many fields of Tukanoan ethnography. But we can summarise the main points. It is clear that bows and blowguns are instruments meant to kill, not only game animals but also people, enemies. The heavy clubs are weapons of war, and in times of peace are weapons of self-defence, and are also used to pound the hallucinogenic vines in trough-shaped wooden mortars; blowgun darts are coated with poison, another association with plant-derived chemical compounds. The fore-shaft of an arrow to be used for larger game must be made from very hard wood which is then inserted into the cane, while the other end of the fore-shaft is tipped with a bone or metal point, or simply sharpened to a pencil-shaped point. The long (1.5 metres) tubular mortar for coca preparation is essential for producing the very fine powder which is ritually consumed and produces vague sensations of euphoria or, if mixed with other narcotic ingredients and used as a ritual snuff, induces hallucinatory trance states. The stick-rattle, a thin, lance-shaped staff over two metres in length, one end of which is enlarged and forms a hollow chamber filled with seeds and pebbles, is a phallic shamanic power tool.

All these artefacts are manufactured of the hardest *Tabebuia* wood, and all of them (except the mortar) have phallic associations. Bow-propelled arrows are metaphors for male sexual aggression; blowguns and their darts the same. The stick-rattle is the phallic staff of the mythical Progenitor *Pamurí mahsë*, from which drops of semen fell into the womb of this earth, and the rattling noise it produces during collective ceremonies, when the shaman swings it in a wide circle, represents the 'scattering of the seed' with which it inseminates society and nature. The club, in its use as a pestle, produces a 'mixture', be it of mashed hallucinogenic vines or of ingredients pounded in a cup-shaped mortar, the act of 'pounding' being a metaphor for biological 'mixtures', for human sexuality

Poraqueiba sericea, Manaus, Brazil

which, in turn, is said to be closely related to hallucinatory experiences. Finely carved staffs are carried by headmen when they go out to welcome guests, and later on when they preside over ceremonial meetings with allies. The staffs are adorned with tassels made from the yellow tail-feathers of the Oropendola bird (*Icteridae*), called *umú*, a name related to *ëmë* meaning 'man', 'male', a name related to the seminal associations of this colour. Finally, the two-pronged cigar-holder, carved and decorated, is used during exchange rituals when a large cigar is inserted in the fork-shaped object which symbolises a sexual union, and which then goes from hand to hand, the men of two intermarrying groups alternatively smoking and reciting ritual texts. The *Tabebuia* tree also figures prominently in curing spells. For example, for puerperal or malarial fever and also for some cases of snakebite, shamans invoke 'black' (*nyidigë*), 'reddish' (*diabiridigë*) and 'clear' (*boredigë*) trees and their somewhat thickish leaves (*purí*) and 'extract' from them *gehsavereró ~ga*, lit. 'cold-emanation-a little', a refreshing and soothing essence. A shamanic spell pronounced to accelerate a difficult childbirth, invokes the *Tabebuia* tree, asking it to 'instill its red wood, its dark-red wood, into the 'blood' of the woman.[4]

All these ideas are incorporated in the bow tree, the *Tabebuia*. This flowering marvel of tropical nature has opened a door into dimensions of mind we hardly suspected when we first looked at this tree as just one of many that grow in the rainforest.

The second jungle tree we shall discuss in this chapter is called *uacú* (or *uaucú*) in lingua geral, a leguminous tree of the genus *Monopteryx*. In our case we are speaking of *Monopteryx uaucu* and *M. angustifolia*. This is a truly gigantic canopy tree of the *~nëngë* forest, which can reach a height of more than 30 metres and a trunk diameter of up to 1.5 metres. The most remarkable feature of this tree consists of its enormous table-shaped buttress roots which support the trunk. The trunk itself is usually free from creepers and epiphytes; the bark is coarse. The wood is of a yellowish colour and its biting smell (*oma sëriri*) is reminiscent of formic acid. Except for the inner core, it is not very hard and makes excellent firewood, giving off great heat. The inflorescences are small and of a yellow colour.

Uacú is mentioned in several place-names. Upriver from *Tipiaka*, a Uanano village on the middle Vaupés River, are the rapids of *Uacú-ravá* (LG), called *sëmé gumu*, lit. '*uacú*-beam' by the Desana, because the water cascades over a horizontal shelf, similar to a house-beam. Close to it is a high boulder, on the surface of which one can see a large and deep cleft of elliptical shape. This spot is mentioned in several origin myths and is said to mark the westernmost point of *Pamurí mahsë*'s, the Progenitor's advance, when his Anaconda Canoe crashed into this boulder. Others, less versed in mythology, see in it the outline of a vagina. Near the Desana village of Piramirí (LG), now called Teresita, on the lower Papurí River there is, on the Brazilian side of the river, a small peninsula called *sëmé nyoro* ('*uacú*-peninsula'). Near it are the rapids of *uacú-pinima* (LG), called *imika ëhtamu* ('small fish-rapids'), by the Desana. The region is known for its *uacú* trees and, like most rapids, is a mythological landmark. The long (ca. 20 cms.) flat pods (*paró*) contain two to four disk-shaped seeds, each of about 4 cms. in diameter and 1 cm. thick, which contain a yellowish edible kernel and a bitter-tasting oil. In the heat of the day the pods open with a cracking noise and the seeds are ejected (*paríri*) and scatter audibly over a large area surrounding the tree. The Tukanoan names of the *uacú* tree are: *~sëmé* (D), *~simió* (T, PT U), and *himió* (TT, BAR). The Indians classify *Monopteryx sp.* in the same category with *Eperua purpurea* (Leguminosae), called *diá sëmé* lit. 'river-sëmé' because of its riparian habitat; its flowers are purple-coloured and its fruits are not edible.[5]

Uacú seeds are an important food item. After boiling for several hours the softened pulses begin to release an oily substance (*ëye*), and are now kneaded by hand into a thick mass; occasionally this mass is pounded in a wooden mortar. The next step consists in preparing a storage pit inside the maloca or next to it, by excavating a hollow of about 60 cms. in depth and with a diameter of 30 cms. The walls of the pit are covered with layers of carefully placed leaves (*puri*) of the *miúge* tree, and in this manner the fermented mass can be preserved for weeks or even months.[6] Freshly boiled seeds or the fermented mass are con-

Vaupés River near Yurupari-Miri. *Mauritia flexuosa* palms in the foreground

sumed in varying proportions; sometimes as a main dish, at other times combined with manioc flour, as *chicha* or by toasting the seeds. Because of their high protein content, *uacú* seeds are an important food resource during the rainy season when there may be a shortage of animal proteins. As well as being a prominent wild-growing food resource, *uacú* seeds have two additional uses. In the first place, boiled seeds make an excellent bait for fishtraps, especially for large screens put up in a circle of about 5 metres diameter, with a small opening on one side. Moreover, large dry seeds are hollowed out through a cut in the edge and are used as buzz-disks. A looped string is passed through two small holes in the middle and, when 'winding up' the string and then stretching it, the disk rotates and produces a buzzing sound. We have seen this object used only by children.[7]

What we have said so far of the *uacú* tree sounds trivial enough: a buttress-rooted jungle tree producing some bitter-tasting seeds, apparently hardly more than an emergency foodstuff for a rainy day. But for the Tukano this tree holds a world of meanings. We must have another look at the tree and try to see it through their eyes. Buttress-roots always call the attention of the Indians; in the first place, from a practical point of view they offer concealment for a hunter or a hiding place for amorous adventures. They may provide shelter for a night, or asylum for a fugitive. On the other hand, the dark recesses between the roots might be dangerous; they may be the lair of a jaguar or there may be a poisonous hairy spider. Or there may be a forest spirit, some ghostly apparition. All these are considerations a man will keep in mind when approaching a tree with large buttress-roots. But on another, more significant level, a tree is perceived as a human body, most often as a female body, and buttress roots are compared to a human crotch. The sexual fantasies which men and women project upon prominent roots of forest trees, be they of the tabloid buttress type or stilt-roots[8], can be ambivalent. In most cases these roots will be interpreted as female limbs, as seductive women, or women about to give birth, but women will occasionally interpret them as male, with a phallus hidden in the forked roots. It depends upon context; it may be a myth, a dream or a personal experience.

In lingua geral table-shaped buttress-roots are called *bambas* or *sapomemas*, while the Tukanoan terms are *sáro* (D) or *saáro* (T). When nasalised, *~saáro* (D) or *~saro* (T) means 'receptacle for depositing something', with the implied meaning of 'a spot to be inseminated'. In the shamanic idiom these wordplays are common, and in any case, the Indians are quite plain-spoken about these sexual connotations. In many regions of the Northwest Amazon, people believe in the existence of strange human-like creatures called *bamberos* which derive their name from their close association with large table-rooted trees, especially *uacú*. Bamberos are called *~sáro paáge*, lit. 'receptacle-knockers', *paári*/to knock. If pronounced *páge* the word comes to mean 'father'. In discussing this terminology and the possibilities of intentional wordplay, it was added that *~sáro paáge* referred to '*the one who opens the receptacle, the door*'. This statement was followed by one of the many *bambero* tales in which these forest creatures were described as being in the habit of drumming on the table-roots and thus communicating over great distances. It was said that occasionally a bambero would violently throw a large quartz crystal against a table-root, the impact being strong enough to make the crystal penetrate the wood. There exist many hearsay accounts of bamberos having been seen at the foot of *uacú* trees. They are described as hairy little men, about 1.4 metres. tall, extremely shy and recognisable by their pungent odour. Among the Tukano, rock, crystals or any transparent quartz crystals have phallic-seminal associations and are common shamanic power objects. The act of 'throwing the crystal at the bamba' was interpreted by the Indians as a sexual act and it was mentioned that the electric eel (*Electrophorus sp.*) was called *~saa* (D, T, PT U) and that the electric charge was comparable to ejaculation. The idea underlying many bambero tales seems to be that these little creatures literally are thought to inseminate *uacú* trees.

Two other objects which are associated with the *saáro*/receptacle concept, are the trough for *chicha* preparation, and the hourglass-shaped pot-stand made from rigid palm ribs. The trough is called *peyáru saáro*/chicha-receptacle, and consists of a horizontal, hollowed-out log of *miratavá, puuri yoádigë* or *bohséru* wood.[9] The pot stand is conceptualised by the Indians as a spiral, a form related to Indian physiological imagery of copulation and gestation.[10] Related to this 'receptacle' concept is the following common practice. The Indians are very fond of palm grubs, the fat larvae of palm beetles (mainly *Rhynchophorus*) which can be eaten raw, boiled or smoked. In the vernacular these grubs are called *mojo-joi*, while in Desana they are called *pingara*. In order to provide breeding places for the beetles, the Indians will fell a *patabá* (LG) palm (*Oenocarpus sp.*) next to palms that attract pollinating beetles, and will then make a number of V-shaped cuts in the fallen trunk, to attract female beetles for oviposition. Such a trunk is then called *pingara ~saáro*, lit. 'grubs-deposit'. After 2-3 months, when touching one of these 'incubators' with a stick, one can hear a humming, grinding noise from the hundreds of larvae feeding on the pith, the one of *patabá* being said to produce especially well-seasoned grubs.[11]

Although buttress-root symbolism is an important part of the *uacú* image, the true focus of attention are the seeds. The flat disk-shaped seed has a slight depression on the edge, from which protrudes a tiny sprout. This basic outline of a circle with a small gap, a V-shaped incision through which emerges a protuberance, constitutes a fixed image or pattern the Indians see repeatedly in nature. It is a pattern which occurs on different scales and we must try to follow the chain of associations the Indians see, together with the underlying unifying concepts. What follows is, then, an exploration of the mind of the hunter, the forager, of basic observations of plant physiology, animal anatomy and behaviour, together with their multiple symbolic representations.

The Indians point out that many of the principal edible forest seeds have a bipartite structure; they consist of complementary halves, 'like male and female'. These seeds correspond to the following trees: *uacú (Monopteryx angustifolia), japurá (Erisma japura* Spruce ex Warming), ucuquí (*Pouteria ucuqui* Murça Pires et R.E. Schultes), *umarí (Poraqueiba serícea), caimo (Pourouma cecropiaefolia)* and *guamo (Inga sp.).* From the union of these two halves emerges a bud, called *~nyemé*, a word the Indians translate as 'small tongue', similar to an incipient flame, when starting a fire. This 'languette' eventually develops into a sprout or *~porá*, a term which can also refer to a male child, a son. Catholic missionaries, when preaching in Tukano, translate the Christian concept of 'soul' as *~sim-porá*, lit. 'that little flame'. A *uacú* seed, then, is seen as a model of sexual union and procreative energy.

This pattern is repeated in the imprint of a deer hoof. White-tailed deer (*Odocoileus virginianus*) are called *nyamá* (D T PT U). When in flight they spread the digits wide open, leaving a V-shaped imprint in which the Indians recognise the interdigital glands which leave a scent trail. Apart from comparing the imprint with a dry *uacú* seed, the Indians compare the V- shaped sign with a woman's spread legs or with the imprint of a woman's buttocks in the sand, and add that the deer's scent glands have the same odour as *uacú* seeds and as women's genitals. In another image, the Indians will compare a *uacú* seed with a vulva, and the bud (~*nyemé*) with the clitoris. A further comparison is made between a *uacú* seed and a deer liver, an organ called *nyeméro* (D T PT U), lit. 'bud-thing', or *nyemé turí*, lit. 'liver-dimension', the latter term referring to the lobular form of the organ. The points of comparison the Indians mention are three: 1) colour, said to be the same as that of deer, a vulva, and a colour concept designated as *bogë*, referring to edibility and palatability; 2) a spongy texture filled with blood, relating to tumescence and sexual arousal; 3) a combination of odour and flavour, with reference to the pungent smell of ammonia emanating from roasted deer liver. According to Tukanoan theories, conception takes place when sperm combines with 'pure' female blood produced in the liver of the woman. This 'blood' must be synchronised with the lunar phases, because the colour spectrum emanating from the moon is said to be related to that of the liver and of menstruation.

The pattern of V-shapes or of the gapped circle (as in the *uacú* seed) is also compared with two adjoining buttress roots of a *uacú* tree, and with this anatomical imagery we are approaching the field of ritual and the *uacú* tree's place in it.

It will have become clear by now that *uacú* trees represent aspects of human anatomy, physiology and procreative energies. Let us look at some details. Not only the overall exterior aspects of the tree—the roots, stem, branches and flowers—are anthropomorphised, but also the (ordinarily invisible) 'inside' of it. The tree bark is called *gahsíru*, the very same word one would use for dermis, hide. The wood is called *dií*/flesh, and its peculiar odour (*oma sëríri*) is compared to a pleasant body odour, while its yellowish colour implies seminal energies. The heartwood of the tree formed by much harder, heavier, wood has radial fissures (*toyóri*), and the entire core is said to smell of human excrement. This inner part is called *sëmegë gëra purídu*, lit. 'uacú-tree excrement-issue-forth-thing'.[12] Quite frequently these fissures form hollows which contain a yellowish liquid called *sëmegë dehkó*/uacú-tree water, *ohokaríri ohkó* (D) or *kahtisé ohkó* (T)/vital water, which the Indians believe to contain vitalising energies. Sometimes, when clearing a new field in the forest, the men will come upon a *uacú* tree and decide to fell it. They will then build a platform of poles around the tree, just above the buttress roots, and cut the trunk with their axes. When the cuts have reached a certain depth, a sudden spurt of water will form a metre-long jet and the men will hurry down and stand under this 'shower', attributing to it the power of muscular strength and sexual potency. The beneficent energies are conceptualised in terms of colours, odours, flavours and temperatures, as expressed in curing spells and other ritual practices. From what we have learned of this custom, the men are quite aware of the fact that the vivifying force was closely associated with the putrefying aspect of the tree interior.

Uacú seeds are a prominent food item during periodical exchange rituals between exogamous units. In the local Amazonian vernacular these ritual gatherings are called *dabucurí*, while the Desana call them *poóri*, a word referring to 'the scattering of seeds', a figure of speech which implies a range of images, from dehiscence and pollination to coitus and impregnation. *Uacú* seeds are also consumed in combination with other forest products (vegetable or game) during initiation rituals. When the fruiting season approaches, the Indians of neighbouring malocas will organise a dance which, in every respect, is a fertility ritual. The dance is called *yeheri* (D), *ye'resé* (T), a verb with the double meaning of 'to paint oneself' and 'to ejaculate'.[13] To this we might add that dancing and singing have almost always erotic connotations, the same as facial paint. The men dance slowly in a circle in the centre of which stands a woman of childbearing age, who from time to time utters a long-drawn cry: *ë ë ë ë*, as an answer to the men's chanting and swinging of their seed rattles. The chain of dancers forms a broken circle, the pattern of which we have already observed when speaking of the *uacú* seed/deer hoof/vulva sequence. Significantly, the circle of the dance is called *betó, petó* meaning 'funnel'. While the lead-dancer and pairs of men—hosts and allies—dance in front of the woman, imitating coital movements, her cry is said to imitate the mating call of a doe in heat. With this imagery we touch upon the theme of spiral or circular dance patterns, some of them related to the Tree of Life motif, to the ritual importance of the centre, and other similar motifs. Among the Tukano, the motif of encircling a tree in search of a life-giving fruit or seed appears in a number of shamanic texts which refer to the mythical origins of ritual.

Uacú trees flower at the end of the dry season (February) and the fruiting season comes just before the onset of the heaviest rains, in May and June. Although the trees are scattered, they do tend to form small clusters and people know where to go in order to gather the fallen seeds or pods. *Uacú* trees are difficult to climb and so all gathering has to be done on the ground, carefully selecting the seeds or pods which have not yet begun to sprout. Groups of men and women will visit the stands of trees and these excursions are usually accompanied by much erotic banter, hide-and-seek among the buttress roots, ending up in sexual promiscuity. This orgiastic aspect of *uacú* fruit gathering is said to have been much more ritualised in the past, and in connection with it the buzz-disk was mentioned. Among the Desana, a small flat tablet of wood swung in a circle on a string, like a bull-roarer, is at present hardly more than a plaything for children. It is called *nurame* (D), *nuree* (T), meaning 'horsefly', alluding to the buzzing flight pattern of that insect. The name was said to be related to *nurí* (T), penis, and the bull-roarer was associated with the hummingbird, a phallic bird that 'hums and pricks'[14]. The association of humming or buzzing noises, with sexual activities (or prohibitions) is mentioned in several ritual and mythi-cal contexts.[15] To this acoustic aspect of *uacú* seeds, in the form of buzz-disks, the Indians add an olfactory aspect related to their concepts of purity and dan-ger. There is great concern about the polluting influence of smells produced by singeing hair or toasting *uacú* seeds. Although smoked meat and toasted seeds are considered to be delicious, they are strictly reserved for adult, initiated males, and strict prohibitions are mentioned in many texts. It seems that this odour cat-egory is related to the oestrous smells which, for Tukanoans, are extremely impure and dangerous, especially for impuber boys and girls, or for adult men who are engaged in active hunting or in any ritual activity. A shamanic text recorded by us in the field, makes an explicit statement on this point, saying: '*Rutting deer smell of man. Uacú smells the same when roasted.*'[16]

In view of the many ritual and symbolic associations, it is not surprising that *uacú* trees should play an important part in Tukanoan myths and tales. In all these oral traditions the *uacú* tree represents a principle of procreation, insemi-nation and potent life-forces, frequently described in coarse language. Myth ver-sions published in late Victorian times treat this topic in romantic terms and tell of a chaste maiden who fell asleep under a *uacú* tree, only to awaken after a miraculous conception. Other texts are more outspoken. One myth tells that 'in the beginning', a group of young women living on the Vaupés River were child-less, because all male members of their community were old men. A shaman ordered the women to bathe in a lake, whereupon they became pregnant. Among their offspring was a beautiful girl who, when she reached puberty, rejected all pretenders. One day, when walking in the forest she came upon a *uacú* tree where a troop of monkeys were feeding on the seeds. On her request, the monkeys threw down some seeds which the girl greedily ate. Some of the juice flew down her body to her lap. She became pregnant and gave birth to a son, the future *Yurupari*.[17] In fact, the *uacú* tree is central to the *Yurupari* Complex in Amazonian mythology, a theme concerned with male initiation rit-uals in which cross-pollination seems to provide the model for exogamy.

In Desana the tree is called *sëmé*, a word that might be related to Desana *sëmeru*/umbilical cord, *sumúru*/umbilicus, *sëmea* in Tukano proper, and *semeno* in Pira-Tapuya and Uanano.[18] Whenever the Indians establish chains or fields of analogies, they often compare the pods of leguminous plants with genealogical lineages, with a sequence of 'seeds', an umbilical cord, or a group of agnatic brothers; a knotty vine or stalk would form part of such a semantic field. This idea of segmentation, of generations, a sequence of seeds, beads on a string, dancers in a row, always captures the Indians' attention and, more often than not, is interpreted by them in terms of social continuity. In this connection it is of inter-est to note that the name of paca (*Coelogynis paca*) is *semé* (D T PT U). Paca is a large rodent which can often be found at the foot of *uacú* trees, feeding on the seeds. Because of its stealthy nocturnal habits it is difficult to hunt, but it is one

Bactris gasipaes palms (peach palm) on the Vaupés river at Mandí

of the most persecuted game animals. In many ways, however, men's relationship to paca is one of kin; paca are 'like' women, in that they spend much time in their gardens or near the maloca, busying themselves with root crops. Paca hoard food by burying it (just like women do when storing in underground pits); they wash and peel the tubers before eating and—a trait always emphasised by hunters—they are very clean and have a pleasant body odour. It was also pointed out that paca's pelt marks represented *dobéri* spots alluding to its fecundity potential.

Uacú is undoubtedly one of the most significant trees in Northwest Amazonian Indian culture. Its fertility associations, iconic aspects, and metaphoric range overshadow its economic value as a food resource, and one might wonder whether these observations might not justify further research on the chemical composition of the seeds. From many oral traditions of neighbouring Amazonian tribes it would appear that the cultural importance of this tree goes far beyond the limits of the Tukanoan territory. The vernacular name *uacú* is most probably related to the word *oa* (T), *koá* (U), *goá* (D), meaning 'bone'. By this word is meant not only the connective tissue which forms the skeleton of vertebrates, but it also refers to the related concepts of scaffolding, of a general framework which supports a composite body. Related to this 'bone' image is that of the phallus, the ancestral procreator, the Father of the Tribe. This last image is expressed in the term 'bone-person': *goámë* (D), *oákë* (T), *koákë* (PT), *koá mahkë* (U), lit. 'bone-son', *goámara mahsá* (D), lit. 'bone-beings people'. The root ~*goa* (D), ~*oá* (T) ~*koá* (PT U) signifies 'basis', 'foundation', and in view of this meaning, Catholic and Protestant missionaries have occasionally used *goámë*, ~*oákë*, etc. as an adequate translation of 'God'. In the context of shamanic oral tradition, of myths and rituals, spells and metaphors, the phallic principle is far more evident than the concept of an abstract supporting and sustaining principle. It should be added here that there exists some confusion with regard to a similar root, but which refers to an uterine principle. The key icon in that case is the gourd (*Crescentia cujete*) called *koa* (D) or *oaká* (T PT U), and which is mentioned in many texts related to initiation rites and curing spells. Moreover, among the Baniwa Indians, a group of Arawak-speaking tribes who live north of the Tukano, mostly in Venezuela, the Northwest Amazonian *Yurupari* Complex is paralleled by the *Kuai* Complex which centres upon a mythical personage closely associated with the *uacú* tree. In fact, the tree is *Kuai*'s body and the seeds are his flesh. The Tukanoan and Arawakan versions interpenetrate and vary in many details, but the fact remains that *uacú* is truly a Tree of Life, of procreative energy and regeneration and, above all, a model of many aspects of cosmology, social organisation and ritual.

The third tree we shall describe is known in the Northwest Amazonian vernacular as *japurá* (which is also the Brazilian name of the Caquetá River), a genus of the Vochysiaceae identified as *Erisma japura* Spruce ex Warming.[19] The Desana Indians call it *barí*, while the Tukano proper and the Tatuyo call it *batí*.

Spanish-speaking colonos of the Caquetá and Putumayo Rivers call it *Flormorado* ('purple flower') or *Oreja de chimbe* ('bat's ear'). It is a tall (10 to 20 metres) tree that flowers in November in the ~*nëngë* forest, the fruiting season beginning early in the rainy season (April) and lasting through June. The fruit is a flat pod, about 15 cms. in length, which bursts with a loud crack, scattering the seeds all over the forest floor. The pods have wing-shaped calyx lobes which give rise to it 'bat's ear' comparison, and help in its seed dispersal. The seeds are flat disks, approximately 4x4 cms. in size.

The seeds are highly valued as a food item or, rather, as a seasoning. They can be eaten raw or toasted (much like *uacú* seeds), but most *japurá* seeds are cooked for several hours and then processed for storage in pits lined with Heliconia or *miúpu*, the leaves of the *miúgë* tree. After this preliminary cooking, the pericarp is removed and the seeds are cooked once more and then are washed in a basketry sieve, whereupon they are pressed through another sieve or pounded in a mortar. The soft mass can then be stored for several months, but the leaves must be periodically renewed. During the process of fermentation the mass acquires a pungent smell and flavour, rather like strong cheese. The Yorkshire botanist Richard Spruce called it a 'vile smell' and the Indians themselves will agree, but *barí*-butter or *yapurá*, as it is called for short, is a highly appreciated delicacy.[20]

Japurá is consumed mainly in the form of a culinary preparation consisting of small fish boiled in manioc starch (*verá*), peppers (*biá*) and *yapurá* butter, a concoction called *bahurí* (D), *vaí ~peéke* (T), *~peéni* (PT U) or *puné* (TT). This dish is signally declared to be a 'mixture' and Spanish-speaking Indians will call it *pescado revuelto* ('mixed fish'). If a small quantity of *barí* is added, the dish is rather liquid, but if a lot of *barí*-butter and no manioc starch are added, the consistence will be denser. People put much emphasis on the 'thickening' of the mixture, either by increasing the amount of *barí* or of starch. Moreover, it is emphasised that this dish must never be seasoned with salt, because, as the Indians say: '*It already contains japurá!*'

Here one begins to wonder why people should be so anxious to explain a simple recipe in all that detail, with so much emphasis. One should always pay attention to simple formulas and 'mixed fish' sounds too simple to be just that and nothing else. It turns out that the two conditions—the 'mixture' and the salt taboo—together constitute a net of metaphors we must disentangle if we want to understand the social meaning of the *japurá* tree. In the first place, it should be remembered that, metaphorically, fish are like women and women are like fish, an equation which recurs in myths and tales, spells and rites, dreams and visions. Fish-related aspects, such as culinary and olfactory components, fishruns, fish-baits, fish-traps, fish-poisons, etc., form a field parallel to many social-sexual aspects. In the second place, the act of cooking, metaphorically represents uterine gestation and transformation, another recurrent equation. It follows that the ingredients of culinary/uterine preparations must be carefully measured out and combined, especially in what concerns 'pure' and 'impure' components, that is, of observing the rules of what we can call 'exophagy'. Food intake should obey rules which parallel those of exogamy, of compatibility and complementarity, as understood by the Indians. Food, especially that which has been highly seasoned, should never 'arouse one's appetite', or else its consumption must be accompanied by lengthy shamanic spells aimed at purifying the food, as well as its consumer. It appears that we are dealing here not with vain superstitions or quaint primitive customs, but with sound advice, fundamentally concerned with aspects of health, birth control, and social cohesion.

Richard Spruce mentioned that *japurá* butter had a 'vile smell'. The Indians say that it has the smell of female sex organs, and that this is the reason why the *bahurí* dish should not contain any salt, because this would make it too stimulating. The dish contains the usual Amazonian condiment, Capsicum peppers, a basic seasoning of a stimulating nature, as the abundant salivation it causes is believed to be linked to abundant sperm; but then the addition of salt, another stimulant, would upset the composition and induce the consumer to uncontrolled (or uncontrollable) sexuality.

Some linguistic and semantic remarks are of interest in this context. The act of 'thickening' the fish broth is called *vaí bahurí*, in Desana, a word which, according to the Indians, is closely related to the Uanano noun *vahúri*, the plural of *vahúro*, a term referring to a small carrying bag, generally made of tree-bark or some other material. The same word—*vahúro*—is used to designate a bundle of Capsicum peppers (*biá vahúro*) (U) hung over the hearth fire for smoking. The little boxes made of plaited leaves, in which shamans keep their quartz crystals, symbolising sperm, are called *ëhtá vahúri* (U) and a tree-bark bag for carrying fish is called *vaí vahuró* (U). Going a step farther we find *~mënó vahuró* (U), as the name of the tobacco pouch, tobacco having marked seminal connotations on account of its fine *~marári*-like seeds. Next we have *~mëno vahuró* (U), a term of familiar usage referring to a man having large testicles, said to be associated with virility. From the Uanano perspective, the 'package' image is quite definitely a male concept. The Desana 'food' *bahurí* is 'thickened' with the addition of a potent male Uanano component. Moreover, the equivalent of the Desana verb *bahurí*/ 'to thicken', is *~peesé*, in Tukano proper. In Pira-Tapuya and Uanano the 'mixture' is called *~peéni, vaí ~peéke* in Tukano proper, and *puné* in Tatuyo. This group of words, on ground of their common root and significance, is said to be related to the Desana verb *penyarí* meaning 'to acquire allies', in a wider sense 'to achieve social cohesion' by 'condensing' (i.e. 'thickening') a relationship between two exogamous groups. Allies are called *~penyará* (D T), *~penyée* (U PT); *pe'nyame* is the term for 'wife's brother' in Desana.

In Tukanoan mental processes food and eating are closely paralleled by sexuality. One of the most common verbs for describing coitus is *barí*, 'to eat'; the sex act is described as 'to eat the women'. To designate the seed of *Erisma japura* as *barí*, refers to its being a food and a sexual metaphor. A culinary preparation from fish, the seeds of a jungle tree, manioc starch and some peppers can thus be read as a statement of social norms. None of this is in any way an undivulged knowledge, a hidden message; the encoded ideas are ever-present and the concept of 'mixtures' covers the fields of the culinary art, marriage rules, pharmacology, pottery-making; that is, many activities in which the precise measuring out of distinct components or ingredients is essential for obtaining specific results. In everyday life, this balancing of condiments allows for much erotic banter and some culinary experimentation. A dish of *bahurí*, well seasoned with *japurá*, when offered to an ally or shared with kinfolk, hints at these matters and there is nothing improper about these allusions. In any case, a common warning to a person who is seen eating, is: *mereké*! meaning, 'combine well!'.[21]

The fact that *japurá* seeds make a good fish-bait fits neatly into this overall imagery. The bait is prepared in the following way: the Indians extract from the inside of a thin stem of a *Cecropia* called *gahpí ~moáru* (*Cecropia sciadophylla* Martius) bits of a dry spongy matter, to serve as floats. They then prepare a mass consisting of macerated leaves of an ichthyotoxic plant (*Lonchocarpus sp.*) and mix it with *japurá* butter. Small quantities of this mass are stuck to the floats which are then thrown into quiet waters. Shortly after, stupefied fish rise to the surface and can easily be caught.

Images in which *japurá* symbolism is alluded to appear in many contexts. For example, the behaviour of tapir, when wallowing at a saltlick, is often described in highly erotic terms. A frequently used locution is: *vehkë barí torógë*, lit. 'tapir is sucking *japurá*'. The meaning of this expression is that tapir are meeting the females of the species.

Another rainforest tree is *ucuquí (Pouteria ucuqui* Murça Pires et R.E. Schultes), a member of the Sapotaceae. This is a tall tree, up to 30 metres in height, the fruits of which are much appreciated by the Indians, but which was hardly known to botanists until the middle of the present century.[22] A century and a half ago, the British naturalist Alfred Russel Wallace, when travelling in the Vaupés territory, mentions '*okokí*' as an edible fruit and comments on its acrid taste.[23] The abundant flowers are yellow and drop in profusion to the ground the same day they open. The fruiting season is in August and September, at the end of the rainy season. The large fruits are approximately pear-shaped and have a thick yellowish or orange-coloured skin when ripe. Tapir, peccary and paca are attracted by fallen fruits. *Ucuquí* (LG) is called *poé*, in Desana, and *puhpiá*, in Tukano proper, Pira-tapuya and Uanano.[24] The Spanish-speaking mestizos of the Caquetá River call it *yugo*, possibly a LG word.

The Indians say that *ucuquí* fruits make excellent fish-baits. In fact, ripe fruits that drop into quiet waters, from trees growing on the riverbanks, attract many fish and *ucuquí* fruit are used to bait hooks or traps of different kinds. It is here, in this observation that we find an immediate link with Tukanoan mythology. In a reversal of the myth of Eve tempting Adam with an apple, here we have the first Desana tempting a fish-woman with an *ucuquí* fruit. I first heard of this story when travelling by canoe on a small creek, an affluent of the Pira-paraná. We had been advancing slowly under the overhanging vegetation, when a thorny creeper touched my shoulder and tore my shirt. My Desana and Tukano companions burst out laughing and cried: '*ucuquí, ucuquí!*', joking and laughing at my embarrassment. They then told me the reason for their hilarity. In the beginning of time, the first Desana (or Tukano) had no woman. One day he went to gather *ucuquí* and climbed a tree that was growing on the riverbank. When he was throwing down some ripe fruits, a fish-woman (*boréka*) appeared in the river, attracted by the 'male' odour of the fruits. The man stealthily fashioned a line and hook from a nearby creeper, baited it with *ucuquí* and caught the woman. They were the first couple and ever since the Desana marry Fish-women, that is, Pira-tapuya or Uanano women. There exist many versions of this tale, of how the man (or men) planned this stratagem, how many fish-women there were, and how they reacted to their captor's ruse. But the basic plot was simple: the lonely forest dweller caught a fish-woman with a hooked creeper he had baited with ucuquí.[25] These five elements: forest dweller, fish-woman, hook, bait, ucuquí, form a constellation we shall find again. For the moment let me say that the creeper was a climbing palm (*Desmoncus polyacanthos* Martius)[26], the terminal part of the leaves of which having a spiny prolongation with a series of strong hooks.

So far so good. Let me first describe the fruit as the Indians see it. The edible endocarp is of a whitish colour and has a sweet flavour when cooked; the Indians see in it a seminal substance, sperm, and emphasise that it acquires this quality only after being boiled. It is a fact that the juicy fruits are extremely acid[27] and that boiling eliminates this sharp taste, but the important point is that, according to the Indians, the act of boiling represents a transformation by which the 'acid semen' of the forest achieves compatibility with the 'sweet' and 'female' riverine element represented by the spherical seed of *ucuquí*.

This whole fruit, when ripe, is of *boge* colour, a dark orange-brown which indicates edibility, palatability and healthfulness. The purse-shaped fruit (both a uterus and a scrotum) combines in its form, structure, colour, odour and flavour all the elements which, in Tukanoan thought, constitute a model of healthy plant-growth and embryonic development. *Ucuquí* is prepared in the following way: after peeling off the skin, the fleshy mesocarp is discarded and the endocarp is put on a large basketry sieve[28] where it is squeezed out by hand, separating the seed kernels from the soft mass. The abundant juice is collected in a vessel standing below the sieve and now water is added, together with the juice (*manicuera*) from freshly grated manioc. After boiling this mixture for several hours, it is served cold and has a very pleasant sweetish taste.

A creek in Taibano territory

The next question is concerned with linguistic and metaphoric matters. In Desana, *ucuquí* is called *poé*. However, if pronounced *poé* with a short e, the word means 'field', 'garden', or *chagra*, in the Northwest Amazonian vernacular. From this is derived *poéka*, a term used to designate all kinds of cultivated fruits. Now if nasalised and pronounced ~*poé*, the word becomes a kinship term which is used by Desana women to address their Tukano, Pira-tapuya or Uanano husbands' sisters.

These, in turn, call their brothers' wives ~*sío* or ~*siogal'sio*-thing, a word which in their languages is used to designate a short wooden hook, originally an elbow-handled adze, which the Desana call *yohóka*. In other words, while Desana women address their sisters-in-law as '*ucuquí*', the three other categories of women correspond by saying 'hook'.

Let me explain this in more detail. Hook symbolism is quite common in the language of foragers, fishermen and hunters. A long tapering rod, with a natural hook on its thicker end, similar to a fishing rod but sturdier, is an essential tool in the forest, and one can find longer or shorter hooked sticks in any maloca. Such sticks serve to shake fruits from the branches of trees, to tear down wasps' nests, to pull down vines, or to retrieve dead or wounded birds or monkeys which, after having been hit by an arrow or blowgun dart, became entangled in branches. Hooked sticks are useful in climbing trees and then for grappling neighbouring trees or vines and pulling them close. A hooked stick is not an artefact in the strict sense of the word, but it is an efficient tool in many circumstances; one grasps with it, gets hold of something and then pulls the desired object toward oneself. It is a practical prolongation of one's arm and hand; just as one catches fish with a hooked line, so one hooks one's prey in the forest.

A hooked rod is called ~*vahséro*, in Desana, ~*seró* meaning 'crotch' or 'fork'.[29] The word *vahsú* means 'branch' (pl. *vahsúri*); it also is the name of a large forest tree of the Euphorbiaceae (*Micrandra spruceana*), which bears edible fruits the Indians are very fond of. The fruits are tripartite, symbolising three intermarrying phratries, and the edible mesocarp is white and viscous, being compared with sperm. *Vahsú* trees figure prominently in fertility rituals, in myths, spells and curing rites. The very name (*vahsú*) is probably synonymous with *mahse*/man, male, and expresses a fundamental procreative principle represented in the viscous fruits and the white latex of the stem. The Desana term for cross-cousins is *bahsúri* (sing. *bahsuríge*), cf. *vahsúri*/branches, and with this the hook metaphor becomes clear. Cross-cousins are the branching-out, the ramifications of the family unit.

Going back to the terminology of *ucuquí*-hook, the associations are now clear; the fruits are being shaken down with a hooked stick, the first Fish-Woman was caught with a hooked vine baited with *ucuquí*, and in everyday life *ucuquí* is used as a fish-bait. At this point of discussion the Indians mentioned that the two categories of women who exchanged the terms ~*poé* and ~*sío*, were 'baits'. They were the representatives of their respective exogamic units; they were the lure, the baited trap. One category said to the other: 'You are the object, bait, ucuquí, fish', and the other replied: 'You are the tool, hook, hooked rod, hooked creeper'. In further discussions the Indians mentioned the multiple meanings of the word for 'bait'/~moá. This is a word with three alternative, but interrelated meanings: 1) salt, 2) pollen, 3) fish-bait. Of salt, we know already that the Indians believe it to be a sexual stimulant, while pollen is said to be equivalent to human sperm, and to represent cross-fertilisation in general. The bait, then, is the female element offered by the allies. It is worth repeating here that, metaphorically, a cultivated field is a fertile women, a recurrent theme in myths and tales.

I have said that, while in Desana ucuquí is called poé, in Tukano, Pira-Tapuya and Uanano it is called puhpí. This word is closely related to the Tukano verb puhpisé, meaning 'to dehisce' and describes the action of a seed vessel bursting open. This is a significant image in Tukanoan thought; dehiscence is compared to ejaculation, lightning, the scattering of any seminal matter, and is related to ritual gift exchange, the exchange of food items which are imbued with seminal or otherwise genital reproductive meanings. Exogamy is cross-pollination; it is controlled dehiscence. Ucuquí gifts, then, are of foremost symbolical significance during exchange rituals celebrated between exogamous groups. Moreover, I have mentioned that the Indians believe that loud noises can precipitate dehiscence, and that a sudden thunderclap is correlated with the abrupt dropping of flowers from a tree. Thunder is called buhpú (D), ëhpó (T PT U), words that are related to puhpisé/to dehisce, in view of thunder's image as a celestial ejaculator of seminal quartz crystals. In this context it is not far-fetched to mention that the word for spider is bëhpë (D T PT U), a word which, in view of the frequent exchangeability of ë/u, in Tukanoan languages, seems to be related with the thunder-dehiscence image. Large black and hairy spiders of the rainforest can be extremely poisonous, and are mentioned in mythological and shamanic spells as dangerous sex organs, mainly of a female nature. In sum, to call ucucquí 'dehiscence-related', would be another indication of the close association between this forest fruit and social/sexual relationships.

One last observation. Shamanic spells mention an ucuquí Banisteriopsis and distinguish 'green, red, and white vines'. These spells refer to Uanano women. Near Yavareté, on the left (Brazilian) bank of the lower Vaupés River, is a place called poé-pë/ucuquí-rock. In Uanano this would be puhpía-pa/dehiscence-rock. The spell says of the hallucinogenic potion: *This is the potion of the Fish People*', referring to the Uanano and Pira-Tapuya.

Our next concern is *umarí*, a tree known all over the Western Amazon under its LG name, and often mentioned in travel accounts, ethnography, folklore, but less frequently in botanical treatises.[30] The Linnean term is *Poraqueiba sericea*, while the Indians call it *mëë* (D) or ~*uamë* (T PT U). Wallace mentions it as *oomarie*.[31] Schultes and Raffauf believe it to be a cultigen and say that modern botanists '... *have not found it in a truly wild state*'.[32] I myself have seen *umarí* trees not only on ancient habitation sites, in regions which at present are uninhabited, but also, on several occasions, my Indian companions on the Piraparaná or the lower Vaupés pointed out to me what they said were wild-growing trees and which did not seem to have any recognisable associations with former human activities. The fruits were small and the edible portion was poorly developed.

Umarí trees are about 8 to 12 metres high; they flower in the rainy season and bear fruits nine months after, in the dry season. The flowers are yellow and the oblong fruits are about the size of an orange and, when ripe, are of a yellow-to-orange colour. Among the sweet-tasting forest fruits, *umarí* is the Indians' favourite. They prepare an appetising, slightly fermented beer from its fresh fruits, and they also use the boiled fruits, much in the same manner as *uacú* (*Monopteryx angustifolia*) or *Japurá* (*Erisma japura*), in preparing a dish of *bahurí* ('mixed fish'), by adding manioc starch.

The conversational topic of *umarí* is treated with relish by the Indians. It is always associated with the mythological Tapir, the Master of *Umarí*,[33] and with the tricks and ruses the Tukanoan ancestors invented in order to abduct these *Umarí* women. *Umarí* symbolises Tukanoan victory over Tapir, that is, over the Arawakans. This is a recurrent theme in oral tradition, and the myths, tales, and spells in which *umarí* is mentioned, frequently are elaborated with details which are difficult to understand as long as one is not well acquainted with the wider context of *umarí* lore and imagery.

Two facts are outstanding and are emphasised by the Indians: on the one hand, the fruits are very sweet and have a very special odour and flavour; on the other hand, *umarí* trees are monoecious, i.e. they have separate male and female flowers on the same plant. Monoecy occurs in many other plants the Indians make use of in one way or another, but the interpretation of this biological fact varies. *Umarí*, as the Indians see it, is a very special case, perhaps because it is so closely related to tapir imagery.

Tapir people were endogamous, they say, and so is *umarí*. Doesn't it fertilise itself? Or is there cross-pollination? This theme is elaborated in a number of tales in which sleeping arrangements are mentioned, a matter which is important in Tukanoan spatial, social and sexual orderings. Inside a maloca, hammocks should be strung so that the man's hammock is above that of his spouse's, and the same order should be observed when a group of people, both men and women, are camping overnight in the forest. A recurrent plot refers to this occasion: some people go into the forest to gather *umarí*, an activity often associated with institutionalised promiscuity. At nightfall, the women insist that the men put up their hammocks at ground-level, while they themselves go to occupy a higher level, the model being a reversal of the arrangement of male inflorescences and female flowers. The result of this co-habitation are 'sterile seeds'. I have recorded a number of texts dealing with these discussions, in which the *umarí* harvest becomes a focus of debate on exogamy, cross-pollination, the position of women in Tukanoan society and other equally emotional problems. At the same time, *umarí* fruits being Tapir's womenfolk, the imagery links these particular fruits with maternal descent.

To give an example of *umarí* imagery in relationship to the formation of alliances in mythological times, the following excerpt from a Barasana text is of interest. It says: *'This happened on the Umarí river where the Umarí Fish are, where the Pira-Tapuya are. The Umarí Fish went to where Tapir had left his excrement...This is why Umarí Fish are People; they eat what people eat. This is how the descendants of Boreka Fish and Umarí Fish became allies.'* By Tapir's excrement are meant his abandoned habitation sites: *boréka*, as we remember, was the Fish Woman the first Desana caught with a hooked creeper, and the Umarí Fish are Tapir's women. The sight of an *umarí* tree, then, evokes all these images: Tapir and his desirable women, monoecy and cross-fertilisation, sleeping arrangements and their consequences, a delicious beverage and, last not least, the prospects of a Saturnalian harvest somewhere in the forest or on the riverbanks.

I shall next refer to two trees of the Euphorbiaceae. One is *Micandra spruceana*, called *vahsú* in Desana and *vahsó* in the other three Tukanoan languages, while the other is *Hevea rigidifolia*, called *vahsúpë* (D) and *vahpë* or *vahpë pahkasé* (i.e. big *vahpë*) (T). The vernacular term for the first tree is *seringa Arana* and alludes to its being collected for its latex during the rubber boom of the ill-famed Casa Arana, in the early years of this century.[34]

The importance of these trees lies in their edible fruits. *Vahsú* fruit is tripartite and the mass that envelops the edible seed is of a whitish colour and a gelatinous texture. It contains toxic cyanogenic glycosides similar to those present in bitter manioc (*Manihot esculenta*), which must be eliminated before the kernel becomes edible. I can begin by saying that these two characteristics imply two metaphors: the seed's tripartition represents three intermarrying phratries (i.e. Desana, Pira-Tapuya, Tukano proper), while the edible mass is compared to sperm. From these metaphors it is obvious that this tree plays a major part in the symbolic relationships between the forest and social organisation.[35]

There exist several ways of preparing *vahsú* and *vahsúpë* to make them fit for consumption. After peeling off the gelatinous mass, the olive-sized, ground-nut-like kernel is grated on a large manioc grater, water is added, and the mass is boiled. This boiling process is called *tuúri*, lit., 'to temper', a verb used to describe the drawing of a bowstring, or the boiling of a liquid to the precise point where a 'transformation' takes place, in this case, when the poison is eliminated. Women say that they can recognise this instant by a sudden change in odour; while still raw, the grated mass has an astringent smell of something herbaceous and green, but as soon as the poison began to 'separate', the mass takes on a quite different odour. As a matter of fact, the smell was described as of 'something cooked'.

So we find ourselves enmeshed in the binary opposition of the raw and the cooked, in itself simple enough, but new each time in its embroidered or concealed form. Let me explain this briefly from the Tukano perspective. Professor Claude Lévi-Strauss had hardly published his book on *Le cru et le cuit* (1964) when I travelled in the Vaupés and recurrently overheard conversations referring to my Indian companions as to whether they were the one or the other. Wherever we arrived, they were questioned whether they were 'raw' or 'cooked', i.e. whether they were marriageable or not. The men who asked these questions were dead serious, but in the background there usually were some giggling girls who eyed my boatmen and seemed to have little concern for these culinary distinctions. Later on, of course, I met this situation on many other occasions; Tukanoan food concepts and restrictions were paralleled by rules of mate selection in terms of compatibility which implied the concepts of edibility, toxicity, and transformation from a raw state into a purified cooked one. Among other occasions, the topic would turn up in a cycle of narratives dealing with a spirit-being called *vahtí*. A notorious seducer, this forest kobold, when coming across a lone woman in the forest or near a maloca would call out teasingly: ~*kasëri* ~*kasëri* ~*kasëri* / 'raw raw raw', alluding to the cultural restrictions which forbade him to have sexual contacts with her.[36] Now if we apply this to the *vahsú* case, the situation is as follows: raw *vahsú*, although it represents marriageable people ('brothers' and 'sisters') is forbidden as an illicit affair, but is sanctioned as soon as it has been 'cooked'. Once the grated mass has been boiled and detoxified, it can be mixed with boiled fish, but must never receive the additional condiment of *Capsicum* peppers or salt, because this would produce a sexually exciting mixture. Another way of preparing *vahsú* is similar to that employed in the processing of *uacú* (*Monopteryx angustifolia*) and *barí* (*Erisma japura*) seeds. The grated and boiled *vahsú* is buried in leaf-lined pits where it ferments in anaerobic conditions and turns into a sweetish condiment. This can be added in small quantities to boiled manioc juice (*manicuera*, in LG) or to manioc flour, but again must never be mixed with peppers or salt, being thought to be too aphrodisiac. Occasionally, *vahsú* can be soaked for a few days in water, then grated, and pressed out by hand through a basketry sieve, but this procedure is considered to be a less appropriate way of preparing it, than by fermentation in underground pits.

Dabucurí rituals are frequently based on *vahsú* or *vahsúpë*, the raw seeds being exchanged for other forest seeds such as *ucuquí* (*Pouteria ucuquí* Murça Pires et R.E. Schultes). In many myths, narratives and songs, *vahsú* exchange rituals are mentioned in detail, and the emotional quality of this forest product is equal, or even superior, to that of *umarí* (*Poraqueiba sericea*), *vahsú* being a

Mauritiella cataractarum palms

male element, while *umarí* has female connotations. *Vahsú* is also mentioned in many shamanic spells, among others as a gift meant to appease evil spirit-beings of a phallic character.[37]

In practice and in imagery, *vahsú*, like *uacú* and *barí*, is used in the ritual balancing of sexuality, as expressed in food exchange between exogamous phratries, and in customary dietary restrictions, interrupted seasonally by a short licentious period.[38]

The rich palm flora of the Vaupés offers a valuable food resource to the Indians. Their importance as economic plants has produced copious literature on species such as *pupunha (Bactris gasipaes)*, *patabá (Jessenia pataua)*, *mirití (Mauritia flexuosa)* and others, palms which produce an abundance of edible fruits rich in oils, proteins, and other nutrients. This emphasis on economic uses has overshadowed the many other qualities the Indians associate with palms, notably with those which do not produce edible fruits. In the pages that follow I shall concern myself with two species which are, probably, the most important palms as concerns the role they play in imagery and ritual.

The palms I am referring to are *Socratea exorrhiza* and *Iriartea ventricosa*.[39] Although botanically the two belong to different genera, the Indians classify them as closely related, but separated by other criteria we shall examine later on. These palms reach heights from 20 to 30 metres, the diameter of their stems being about 30 cms. The most outstanding characteristic both palms have in common are their stilt-roots which form a cone-shaped structure, up to two metres in height, of many individual straight roots of a reddish colour. *Iriartea ventricosa* is furthermore distinguished by a huge fusiform swelling near the middle of the stem, reaching a maximum diameter of up to one metre. In both palms the cylindrical leaf-stalk is dark-green and notably swollen at its base. The Indians say that the geographical-ecological distribution of the two palms is different, a supposition which, as we shall see, is significant in view of their symbolic associations; *Socratea exorrhiza* is said to belong to the dense forest, while *Iriartea ventricosa* is associated with the riverine environment.[40] Wallace, who studied these palms during his travels in the Vaupés almost a century and a half ago, calls *Socratea exorrhiza* a 'beautiful tree' and refers to *Iriartea ventricosa* as 'the most majestic of the genus'[41], but otherwise descriptive data are sparse and sober. Both palms are monoecious, having unisexual male and female flowers on the same plant. The fruits are not edible.

Palms and palm fruits are mentioned casually in conversation, and baskets full with *mirití* or *pupunha* are a daily sight, be it in the kitchen area or soaking in the creek. When spoken of, they are referred to by their proper names: *mirití* is *~nee*, *pupunha* is *ërí*, and so on. It is, then, conspicuous to hear *Socratea* and *Iriartea* referred to as *iri ~nyú* (D) or *ti ~nyo* (T), meaning 'that palm'. The same expression occurs in shamanic texts and spells, in descriptions of ritual, in songs, and it soon becomes clear that this refers to a wide spectrum of palm symbolism focused on these two species. With the expression 'that palm', we approach a conceptual domain of things or rather one 'thing', that is not being referred to by name. That palm is 'it', something known to all, but unmentionable.

We must, then, try to look as these palms from the Indians' perspective. In Tukanoan terms, these palms consists of two distinct, significant parts: the lowest, or what we would call the 'foot' of the tree, and the upper part formed by the crown. In between is the long and slender stem of the palm, which connects the two extremes. The stilt-roots of these palms occupy a very special place in Tukanoan empirical observation and imagery. These roots form a particular ecosystem which hosts many different animal species according to local and seasonal conditions. In the interstices and hollows between the roots there may be snakes and toads, spiders and scorpions; small rodents can be found to hide there and during the rainy season, when the riverbanks or adjacent parts of the forest are flooded, small fish and crabs will inhabit this dark and humid tangle of spiny roots. This, then, is a place of teeming but silent life. The Indians see in this basal portion of the palms a place of origins, of offshoots; in their imagination this is a genital region, a region of groins, male or female, of anatomical bifurcations of an essentially sexual nature. This part is called *saáro*, a word used to designate 'a place for depositing something', derived from the verb *saári*/to deposit, to hide. It is a receptacle, a place of transformation and birth.

The upper part of these palms is complementary in many ways. In the first place, the frondage, too, constitutes a very special biotope, noisy and colourful, inhabited by squirrels and birds, tree crickets and bees, an altogether different faunal combination, but one dominated by the sexual dimorphism of the palm and its spectacular pollination process. The central vein of the palm fronds (~*pu*) is called ~*goá*/bone, with the overt connotation of being a kind of *baculum*, the supporting part of a penis. The shoot of the palm is called ~*porá*, lit. 'sons'. With this part, the concept of 'offshoot' is related, together with a phallic image, with the concept of 'segmentation', because of the segmented (internodal) structure of the stem of the palm, and with the image of a spiralling funnel, because of the twisted shape of the overlapping young leaves of the leaf-stalk.

We must now turn to a fundamental myth in which palm symbolism plays a major role. It is a long story of which there exist many versions, and I shall summarise only the most relevant parts.

There once was a man who had an adolescent son and two adolescent daughters. Preoccupied with his son's impending sexual initiation and ensuing affirmation of continued male dominance in the household, the father ordered him to rise early and go to the port where he would find a hidden 'thing' at the foot of a palm tree, in other words, where he would be sexually initiated. The girls overheard this conversation and hurried to the port, while their brother continued to sleep. While sitting at the port and 'eating ants' (the erotic connotation of which we know already), the girls looked at a palm that was growing there, and noticed something strange. Something was swaying back and forth, it was 'shining', and 'the starch was inseminating'. *'That palm is pretty!'* cried the girls, and back they went to the maloca. What the girls had seen was the process of dehiscence of the anthers, near the 'pregnant' swelling of the palm. Before we continue we must analyse some details of palm terminology:

(Linnean)	(D)	(T PT U)
Socratea exorrhiza	*buhpu ~nyu*	*buhpu ~nyo*
	buhu ~nyu	*këhsá*
Iriartea ventricosa	*buhu bëge*	*vahta ~nyo*

The word *buhpú* (D) means 'thunder'; *bëhpó* (T), *ëhpó* (PT U). The girls at the port saw that '...there was thunder at that palm' (*~na inyore ~ke bëhpó ti ~nyo-pë nitohapáro*). Thunder, in Tukanoan imagery, is an analogue of the Father as the owner and eventual giver of women, of active sexuality, of fertility (rain), of plant growth (dehiscence and pollination) and of tobacco (pollen-like tiny seeds). The girls also saw that 'it was shining, shining, and the starch was inseminating' (*boréyu ~nukú-paro boréyu ~nukú vehtá varésaharo ~mëha*). The expression 'to be shining', 'to be resplendent' is a metaphor for sexual arousal and erection, and 'starch insemination' refers to pollination-ejaculation.

The alternative Tukano term *këhsa* enlarges the field of palm symbolism by relating it to port symbolism. To bathe in the river at dawn is called *kuhsáye* (PT), *kusáa* (U), *uasé* (T), *guarí* (D), words related to *këhsa* through the *u/ë* and *r/s* shifts. We have already spoken of the ritual/erotic atmosphere which prevails at the port, the landing-place of a maloca. The concept of 'bathing' has little to do with washing or swimming as such, but is understood rather as an immersion in a state of sexual arousal and expectancy, the palm being the icon of these dimensions of behaviour. It is of interest to note that the Desana verb *guarí*/to bathe, if pronounced *guarí*, comes to mean 'to become enraged, strong', with the implicit meaning of sexual excitement. The same term is used to describe the strong sexual attraction a woman might exercise over a reluctant male.

Turning now to *Iriartea ventricosa*, its Desana name is *buhu bege*, the first part most probably being an abbreviated form of *buhpú*/thunder. The word *bëgë* presents certain difficulties. This is a masculine form, the feminine being *bero*, and the two words can be, tentatively, translated as 'oldster' and 'old woman' or 'hag'. The masculine form can be applied to animals of the dense forest, or to ritual musical instruments associated with them, and has the approximate meaning of 'old thing', expressing ambivalent feelings of reverential awe paired with disgust. If I understand this right, the term *bëgë* does not designate a fixed, given state, but a potentially evil power. The root *be* might be related to *behpó* (T)/thunder, *buhpú* (D)/thunder, *bëhpë* (D)/poisonous spider, and to the *eh*-group of terms, words, all of which (thunder, spider, and their analogues) desig-

Socratea exorrhiza, Cachimbo, Brazil

nate ambivalent concepts.

The last palm term is *vahtá ~nyo*. In casual conversation *Iriartea ventricosa* can be referred to as *vahtá ~nyo* (T PT U). To say *ko vahtá* (T) with reference to a woman, alludes to her fertility potential, and *ti koró vahtá* (PT) means 'that reproductive female', an expression used in erotic banter. The expression *si ko vahtá* (T), used by young men when flirting with the girls, has the double meaning of 'What a palm!' and 'What a female!'. The term *vahtero* (T PT U) refers to the genital functions of the human crotch, while *dia vahtero* is an expression used to designate the riverine zone where the forest is said to 'inseminate' the river *(dia)*.

So we return to botanical facts. Pollination of palm trees is accompanied by an interrelated complex of sensorial phenomena which form part of the sexual physiology of these plants.[42] In the first place, one can observe several changes of form: while the female buds begin to swell and open, the male stamens rapidly elongate and become erect. When dehiscence has taken place and the pollen has been discharged, detumescence sets in and the rod-shaped stems assume a pendulous position. Another notable change consists in a marked rise in temperature of the sexual organs of the plant; a temperature elevation of more than 10°C has been observed in pollen and flowers, in relation to the surrounding air temperature. Finally, when the buds open, and during the process of pollination, a strong and peculiar odour can be perceived near the palms.[43] I myself have seen large patches of the forest floor covered with odorous whitish or yellowish palm pollen.

The girls said: '*Father, down there we saw a pretty palm; bring us a piece of wood to make a rod for squeezing out grated manioc.*'[44] To explain the meaning of these words, I must illustrate them with a description of the technological process. In the course of manioc preparation most Tukanoan tribes use a simple device which consists of a tall tripod formed of three strong poles of equal length, about 1.8 metres long, tied together at the top, while three shorter, horizontal rods form a triangle at about one metre's distance from the floor.[45] This triangular frame serves to support a large circular basketry sieve on which a woman squeezes out by hand the previously grated mass of manioc tubers. Two of the rods are permanently tied to the upright poles, but the third one is joined only at one of its ends, the other end being left free and movable. This freedom of movement is necessary in order to introduce or withdraw the sieve which, when full with humid, grated manioc, is quite heavy. For this reason, the movable rod has to be made of very hard and resistant wood, because it is being handled all the time, and has to carry the weight of the full sieve when this is being withdrawn; the other two can be made of any wood. What the girls wanted was this movable rod; they had seen the 'female', pregnant body of an *Iriartea ventricosa*, penetrated by a straight, pollen-splattered shaft, and that was what had called their attention. The sexual homology is obvious.

The myth of which this opening scene forms part is fundamental to an under-standing of Tukanoan social organisation, marriage rules, male initiation ritu-als, palm symbolism, and many other aspects.[46] Of course, there exists no text but there are many local versions in which emphasis and details may vary. The initial scene, however, already contains the key elements of this important Amazonian myth cycle: the indolent son, the demanding young women, the problems of controlling sexuality, and of maintaining a patrilineal system and male dominance. This is the myth of *Yuruparí*, perhaps the most important rit-ual complex of the Amazon.[47]

The girls' demand greatly troubled their father who was already much upset by his son's failure to act responsibly. The old man went to the port and brought a short piece from the stem of the palm; but the girls angrily refused it and said: '*We saw something different.*'

We must connect botanical facts with social organisation and founding myth. Monoecious trees could not (or should not) pollinate themselves; from the father's point of view this would have been a model of endogamy. Since he was determined upon exogamy, i.e. cross-fertilisation, it was necessary to establish a difference between the two palms; the riverine palm *Iriartea ventricosa* was to be the female palm while the male palm was the selvatic *Socratea exorrhiza*.

The girls had said that they wanted a rod for squeezing out manioc. The father had brought them a rod of *Iriartea ventricosa* wood which, as all Indians know, is not strong enough; the rod has to be of *Socratea exorrhiza* wood. It was a short rod of this wood he had hidden at the port for his son, but that was a male privilege. This rod has well-known phallic associations, and the act of 'squeezing out starch' is being talked about by women in quite unmistakably erotic terms. This brings us to the feminine domain of manioc processing, a daily task in which most women and girls of a maloca are engaged during much of the day. Seen as a semantic field, manioc processing is paralleled by many others, such as exogamy, sexuality, hunting and fishing, culinary practices, technology, forest imagery and so on, interrelating and branching out into many aspects of motivations, needs and goals. In view of this broad spectrum, it is necessary to summarise and to concentrate on a few selected aspects which are specifically related to palm symbolism:

1. The three upright poles of the tripod represent three intermarrying phra-tries.
2. In the four Tukanoan languages I am using, the tripod is called *nyamá*/deer; according to the Indians what is meant here is White-tailed deer (*Odocoileus virginianus*). The similarity between deer and the tripod con-sists in the following image: in order to establish scent posts for pheromonal communication, deer will occasionally adopt a tripodal position; while standing on three spread legs, the animal will lift up horizontally a hindleg

and rub its metatarsal glands over the preorbital glands which then are rubbed against trees.[48] The deer image is closely associated with that of women, and the tripod—be it as a manioc-pressing device or as a smoking grid—carries the connotation of gestation and transformation.

3. When a woman presses out (*sirúri*) the cyanogenic glucoside on the sieve, the poisonous liquid (*~nyohká*)[49] drips down into a vessel standing under the tripod. After about 15 minutes the liquid separates into white starch (*verá*)[50] which sinks to the bottom, and a turbid, yellowish liquid, properly called *~nyohká*. Initially the starch is liquid, but after approximately one hour it coagulates and turns into an elastic, curd-like substance. The imagery surrounding this part of the process of manioc preparation is based upon the model of a biological, procreative act, followed by embryonic evolution and, in an abstract sense, on perceptual and mental processes of visualization and conceptualization. The key term is *~nyohká*[51], from the verb *~nyohkaári*, meaning 'to harden', 'to be or to become elastic or tough' (i.e. residual starch, tough meat or manioc tubers, *vahsú* wood). In a biological context the word can be glossed as embryogenesis and foetal development. Moreover, in the context of altered states of consciousness, for example in a drug-induced trance, a person will visualise culturally pre-established forms in irregular, coloured blots or shapes, or upon entering a forest or any other multisensorial space, will 'hear' and 'see' abstract energies or eidetic images and events; these phenomena, too, can be referred to as *~nyohkaári*.

It is, then, within this configuration of images that we must try to understand the girls' demand for '*a rod to squeeze out starch*'.

The episodes and plots which, after the initial scene, follow in the context of the *Yuruparí* cycle, refer to the struggle for male supremacy. In this endeavour, the possession of certain sexual icons in the form of ritual musical instruments, constitutes the central theme. The two palm trees play a key role, exemplifying, at different points, the two sexes or, occasionally representing both in the same tree. The central icon is 'it', the unspoken.

The problems Tukanoan culture depicts, analyses, and tries to resolve in myth and ritual are, to a large degree, of an ecological nature; ecological in the sense of being an organised intellectual effort to establish peaceable, sustainable interactions with the social and natural environment.

A few final observations on the significance of certain food restrictions are due before we turn to the wider scene of the forests and its many dimensions. As we have seen in the foregoing pages, a number of wild forest fruits are closely associated in the Indians' minds with human sexuality. Many of these fruits or seeds contain an oily substance and all of them are believed to be very nutritious, but to arouse improper sexual desires. The consumption of these items is therefore controlled. As a matter of fact, young unmarried people approaching the height of their libidinal energy are strictly forbidden to consume these foods which, according to their elders, are harmful to the young. The Tukanoans believe that the procreative potency of young people constitutes a kind of non-renewable resource of society, a valuable asset each phratry should carefully economise. In their understanding, sexual and food taboos for adolescents aim at preserving their procreative energy which should not be squandered within one's own phratry, because this would diminish the exchange value of marriage partners.

These are sobering thoughts. It seems that food and sex restrictions are not necessarily related with ideas of birth control, wildlife preservation or sanitary norms.

Chapter VI

THE FOREST OUTSIDE

To enter the Forest

The relationship between people and the forest is structurally and operationally analogous to that prevailing between two exogamous units, and is, therefore, the source and focus of strong emotions. It is a matter of give-and-take, a relationship based upon principles of reciprocity according to which concessions must be made in exchange for benefits. This form of interaction is satisfying because it is not based upon an artificial nature/culture dichotomy, but integrates the environment and social organisation into a common model, ruled by common mental processes. The approach between the two partners is similar in its anxieties and expectancies, in its courtship behaviour and metaphorical language. The partners speak different but mutually intelligible languages; they communicate through sensorial codes and shared semantic domains, codes pervaded with botanical, zoological and otherwise biological analogues applied to mate selection, sexuality, and family life, as seen within the context of exogamous exchange patterns.

Cultural norms establish the limits of what can be obtained from the forest-alliance and what must be given in exchange. At the simplest level, the forest provides food, and the allies provide women. The forest offers protection, and so do the allies. On a more complex level, the forest is a dimension replete with stimulations (and stimulants) just like women and sexuality, and at the same time it harbours perils, poisons, uncertainties. The forest smells of woman (*oma seríri mahsó*). To obtain its benefits—game, fruits, medicines, narcotics—men have to observe a multitude of prescriptive rules which aim at conserving this bountiful environment. The prohibitions of overhunting and overharvesting—whatever it be—are clearly formulated by shamans, elders, and most adult people. The many sexual restrictions are to be understood as mechanisms of population control which, together with the use of effective anticonceptive plants, constitute adaptive norms of importance. With these premises in mind we now can approach our stated field of research.

Cosmic energy, as conceived by the Indians in the form of *bogá*, is imagined as acting vertically upon the earth, the forest, the river, and the entire biosphere. It is said that these energies 'descend and make things come alive'.[1] Shamanistic wisdom and everyday knowledge of this impact, this energy flow, is said to be essential for leading a satisfactory life, free of disease, with a close-knit family, and trustworthy allies. To acquire this knowledge from one's elders is a person's fundamental responsibility.

This cosmic influence upon the Tukanoan world is conceptualised as an interaction, as a vertical impregnation in the sense that the *bogá* energy complex inseminates nature and man, being then diffused horizontally through the physical environment. While the vertical energies consist mainly of undifferentiated *bogá*, the horizontal diffusion consists of derived energies conceived as colours, odours, flavours and temperatures. Many of these horizontally diffused energies are said to be transmitted by pollen; as a matter of fact, the forest is described as a pollen-charged environment.

Cosmic energies constitute man's vital force and man expends these energies in the course of his lifespan. The forest, however, is a depository, a vast storage place of vital forces upon which man can draw according to certain, culturally determined, rules. It follows that to destroy the forest or to misuse it would be equivalent to the destruction of a vital source of energy; even to ignore the forest would be man's loss.

The principal energies man has in common with the forest are formulated in sensorial terms, but there are others which deeply influence his states of mind. They all are essential to man's well-being; as soon as they diminish in the individual, they can be retrieved from the forest, in order to revitalize the person. This can be done by establishing a personal contact with the forest environment and its different components, or with the help of a shaman who pronounces spells or performs a curing ritual. For example, in some cases where energy loss in a person is believed to lead to a state of illness, the shaman will first pass a crystal over the patient's body and determine the precise kind of energy his organism has lost. He then will drink a hallucinogenic potion and visit in his trance a number of power-spots the patient has recently gone to, in order to discover at which particular spot lies the cause of the dysfunction. Once the shaman has finished this repeated scanning process, he will pronounce the necessary curing spells, accompanied by admonitions referring to operational ecological rules.

In Tukanoan theories of disease, the underlying idea is that the patient must be reborn into a state of good health. This implies the patient's symbolic return to the womb where he passes through a sequence of embryonic-foetal evolution, followed by his rebirth. In all these phases, shamans pronounce spells in which they invoke a sequence of phenomena observable in plant-growth, that is, dehiscence, pollination, germination, seed leaves, axillary buds, stems, flowers and fruits. They all are called upon, usually in a wide colour spectrum combined with temperatures, odours and other qualities. The imaginary breaking ('gnawing') of the placenta is brought about by invoking a number of rodents, such as squirrels, paca and agouti. In many cases people are said to be able to cure themselves from minor physical illnesses by going into the forest while concentrating upon sounds, colours and odours, upon any sign they might interpret as warnings or advice, encouragement or demand. In this endeavour they are greatly assisted by their habitual use of analogies, of seeing in the forest a memory device in which all sensorial perceptions are registered and trigger associations, awaken memories which help to solve personal conflicts. Sometimes a person who feels ill will go alone into the forest to restore his health. A syndrome of physical fatigue combined with claustrophobic agitation is compared with a tightly woven basket the patient wears over his head, and sometimes the entire maloca is compared with such a basket. When leaving the maloca ('a small basket') and entering the forest ('a huge basket full of everything') the patient will soon recover.

Energy flow in the rainforest is recognised by the Indians as the complex process it is, but it is seen in terms of their theory of colour energies and their respective associations. In the first place, the quantity and quality of energies is said to depend upon the age of the trees and associated plants, as well as on the altitude, because the Indians are very much aware of the horizontal layering of biological phenomena. In the overall structure of the mature rainforest they will recognise three levels: 1) the lower part of the tree trunk, 2) the upper part of the trunk, and 3) the canopy and upper part of the crown. All three levels have their associations of creepers, mosses, epiphytes, parasitic plants, pollinators, predators and defenders.

The uppermost level (level 3) may be at 20 to 30 metres from the ground, and is said to be characterised by 'heat' (*ahsiró*) and the periodic flowering of trees. This implies a variety of shapes, colours, odours and textures, observable mainly in the development of male and female flowers and—most importantly to the Indians—the presence of multi-coloured and multi-odoured pollen (*poréri*) which is said to move horizontally within a given tree, or between trees of the same species. The pollen of this level is said to be at the ~*marári* or *noméri* stage of inseminating energy. The second or intermediate level is said to maintain a medium temperature (*doberó ahsiró*) in which flowers bloom under the influence of *dobéri* energies. On the lower portion of the forest, the most important part of the flora is represented by medicinal herbs which grow at the foot of large or median forest trees. The temperature is 'low' and propitious for maintaining their therapeutic properties. The associated flora of lianas, parasites, mushrooms and lichens contain energies which are quite different from those of the host tree.

Sunlight, heat and rain penetrate at different rates depending upon many local variants, so that energy compositions and concentrations vary greatly from place to place and from level to level. In the rainforest some plants flower in the dry season (*bohori*), while others flower in the rainy season (*dehkó në*, lit. 'water-period'). The Indians single out certain trees which they consider to be important in their ecological theories as sources of food, as icons and metaphors, or because of many other associations. These trees flower in the middle of the dry season and the middle of the rainy season.

Temperatures vary from one level to another, and each level has its particular combination of energies; these do not diminish from top to bottom, but contain specific energies, according to their temperatures. Women are said to be the specialists on medicinal plants growing on the different levels; level 1, for patients from birth to three years, level 2, from three to seven, and level 3, for patients above seven years. These levels are correlated with dietary norms, and in this manner a walk in the forest is, to a large degree, a medicinal, pharmacological experience. In all three levels exists an atmosphere called 'heat-incubator'[2], a specific warmth which induces plant growth, quite independent from solar heat. The Indians say: '*Solar heat cannot hatch a bird's egg, but a bird's body heat can*'.[3]

All sounds in the forest are coded and are thought to transmit precise messages. The principal and most permanent sounds are those made by insects. The quantity and variety of insects depend, to a large degree, upon the seasons, and the flowering season of canopy trees, especially those of yellow efflorescences, which will attract thousands of insects quite different from those found at ground level during the fruiting season. The continuous buzzing and whizzing of cicadas is interpreted by the Indians as a chant *dári dári dári nyiiiiii*; while others sing: *dári dári dari yoooooooo*, referring to *dári* energies, and the verb *yorí*/to carry, to be charged with. '*The insects sing to the energies*', say the Indians, and add that by this are meant all the pollinators, the bees, wasps and coleoptera.[4] In describing the impact this insect song makes upon the person, the verb ~*menyahári* was mentioned as an apt portrayal of a state of mind. The verb is used to describe the act of jumping from a tree into a pool; in a modified form of *pe nyahári* it means 'to listen and to enter', with the added explanation of 'to follow the sound to its source'. The underlying idea is that of changing from one dimension to another, and 'to be or to become penetrated' and totally absorbed by the energies of the forest, as understood by the Indians. To jump from a tree into a pool is indeed a multi-level penetration.

Sound messages are especially eloquent and powerful near stands of fruit trees, such as *uacú* (*Monopteryx angustifolia*), *patabá* palms (*Jessenia pataua*), *umarí* (*Poraqueiba sericea*) when growing on abandoned garden sites. The messages will vary in accordance with the intruder's phase of sexual activity; prepubertal and pubertal youth will receive messages different in intensity and significance from those a newly married couple or an old woman will be exposed to.

The interpretation of the message will vary with the person's capacity for establishing significant associations. For example, a married woman, when going to her garden, will perceive sound messages referring to childbirth (which takes place in the garden), to her mother's lineage, her sisters-in-law. An abandoned site or any spot with secondary growth (*viadó*) is associated with the concepts of 'fermentation' and 'recuperation'; '*It is like an unmarried woman of child-bearing age*' (*piárisamo* T), as the Indians say. This potential of a 'deposit' is expressed in sounds, mainly of insects, i.e. of pollinators.

Another category of sounds which actively communicate important messages are the voices of birds. Amazonian Indians are famous for their colourful feather ornaments made in different forms and combinations. Among the Tukanoans, the symbolism of these feather-crowns is complex, expressing a range of colour energies corresponding to their wearer, and thus indicating hierarchies. The feathers are taken from brightly-coloured birds such as macaws, parrots, toucans, caciques, orioles, egrets, hummingbirds, harpy eagles and others, and, in the Indians' view, these birds are the 'owners' of these feathers; they are mediators in the energy flow and have loaned the feathers to the men. The birds, then, will watch the wearers of feather-ornaments and will openly express their criticism of their behaviour, not only when they actually wear the ornaments, but the men's merits in relationship to the public display of their colour energies. Men will closely listen to the voices of birds which, occasionally, will accuse a person of being unworthy of wearing a certain ornament or colour combination. The forest invites self-criticism, it seems.

Insects attract birds and so, during the flowering season, there will be regional bird migrations. One can recognise endemic species (~*ariri mahsá*) and migratory species (*aríri mahsá*), two terms used to distinguish autochthonous peoples and animals (emphatically, tapir) from passers-by-people, animals, with missionaries forming a category apart. The voices of mammals, most of them game animals, are of course well known and a hunter will be able to distinguish males from females, juvenile specimens from adult ones, and can, in any case, imitate their calls.

The particular odours of the forest constitute a complicated code of identification which is of prime importance to the hunter and forager. When penetrating into the forest, especially when travelling in a little-known region, the Indians will always carefully sniff the air, not only to identify and locate animals and fruits, but also people, intruders. Whenever they discover a human scent, the immediate question arises: *mári mahsá* or *gahí mahsá*, 'our people' or 'other people'. This is never to be taken lightly; the presence of strangers in the vastness of the forest cannot be ignored, and human body odours identify personal differences in great detail. The Tukano believe that, in the first place, humans have a general surface body odour (*sëríri*) that is shared by all members of a phratry. To give an example: the Desana, Pira-tapuya and Tukano proper inter-

An old man passing by in Barasana territory

marry exogamously and have the same *sëríri*. In the second place, it is said that there exist personal odours (*oma sëríri*), lit. 'carry-odour', which are closely related to one's habitual food intake. This leads to a stereotyped image of 'hunters', 'fishermen' and 'horticulturalists', the Desana being classified as forest-dwelling hunters/gatherers, the Pira-tapuya, Bará and Uanano, as riverine fishermen, and the Tukano proper, as riverine horticulturalists. There is some truth in this food/odour association, notably if the observation is based upon digestive processes and flatulence, matters which are closely observed and discussed in the intimacy of maloca life, but to establish tribal categories is unrealistic because all groups participate in a variety of resources, with only slight seasonal changes. In the third place, people of both sexes are said to emit odour signals in periodic cycles which correspond to physiological stages in the life-span of the person: prepubertal, pubertal, intensity of sexual activity, pregnancy, menstruation, lactation, menopause, illness and old age. These odours are called *poré surí* and refer mainly to the person's fertility potential. The name is derived from *poré*, suggesting dehiscence, pollination, insemination, and *suurí*, literally, 'to combine', here used with the meaning of 'to copulate'. The quality of *poré surí* is described as similar to the perfume of ripe fruit, sweet roots or aromatic herbs, and changes gradually with age.

The same odour classification is applied to all animals. Tapir, deer, peccary, monkey, the rodents and other mammals have their species odours (*sëríri*), but carnivores, fish-eaters and herbivores have their particular digestive odours (*oma sëríri*).

There are many reasons for going into the forest other than hunting. People will go to harvest palm fruits or the seasonal fruits of other forest trees; they go to collect edible ants, grubs, and honey, or they go in search of raw materials, woods and vines, pieces of bark or reeds for basketry making. They will carefully choose a tree for boat-making, another for making a *chicha* trough, a mortar or some strong paddles. All these are practical needs which can readily be fulfilled in the forest. Frequently, depending on the season, whole families spend days or even weeks in the forest, building temporary shelters. Some people will go in search of medicinal plants, and shamans—forever observing and exploring—will go to find new varieties of psychotropic plants.

The Desana word for rainforest is ~*nëngë*, a term which is related, or, rather, identical, to *nu'gú*, a word meaning 'root', both in the botanical and genealogical sense. This is the so-called 'Dimension of Trees', where the Tree People are, the ancestral spirits which are incorporated in the vegetation. Their shapes, odours and sounds, ever-present in the noon-day swelter and the evening darkness, transmit a steady flow of signals that people must be alerted to and receptive to as soon as they approach the forest. In each micro-environment a person has to be in full control of his or her actions, and has to know the protective spells which are necessary for certain localities and activities. The Tree People are not identified with individual trees or species, but represent the forest as a whole. They do not belong to one's family, but they are 'like' one's kinfolk in that, when looking at the forest one makes personal associations which are triggered by odours, the flavours of fruits, the sounds of the insects, the whole impact of the tree's multiple energies perceived in a chromatic scale, an olfactory scale, a scale of temperatures. The occupants of each maloca have their particular relationships with the Tree People of the neighbouring forests, absorbing and assimilating their beneficent energies. Wild animals do not participate in this energy flow; they have their own *bogá*-derived energies, but their animal existence remains outside the great circuit.

When we think of Amazonian Indians, we imagine them living in the forest or somewhere close to it, on the riverbanks. We have seen films and photographs of Indian hunters and of women and children trudging along a forest path, carrying baskets and firewood. We rightly think that these people belong to the forest. But now we must try to go beyond this sober, but narrow, conception of, what to *us*, is their reality, and attempt to see the forest from the Indian's perspective. And here, once more, we have to explore dimensions of meaning which appear strange to our minds. Let me quote a few statements an old man made when I discussed with him the forest: '*The forest has many roots; the forest is like one single huge tree. The forest is a wide expanse, similar to a perceptive human head'.*[5] In reading these words, we can understand the 'root' metaphor and the 'tree' metonymy; the 'perceptive head', however is an image we have difficulties in interpreting. So I shall go on with more descriptive details and attempt to reconstruct a context.

The Indians will say that most Tukanoan tribes—Desana, Barasana and, of course, the linguistically isolated Makú—'belong' to the forest, that they originated in the forest. In elaborating this theme, reference will be made once more to sensorial associations. It is said that *'forest women smell like the forest'*, but it is added that the forest does not have a 'female' odour which could be associated with women, but a diffused odour of fertility which consists of a blend of the perfume of flowers, the odour of pollen, the acrid smell of ants and the sweetish odour of ripe fruits, all this combined with the musky stench of rutting animals, rotting fruits and decaying leaves.

This odour, then, is described as a very peculiar one, restricted to a forest environment and quite different from that of a riverine environment. 'River women' (Uanano, Pira-Tapuya, Bará and others) are said to smell of fish; not of water, but of what water produces; a river smells only of that and of the adjacent soils, the energies of which are diluted in its waters. These olfactory associations between the forest and women are expressed in the words: *nomé moa yearí*, lit. 'woman-salt-conserve', meaning that women conserve the procreative capacity the Indians see in the teeming life of the rainforest.

The act of 'entering' the forest is accompanied by feelings of anxiety mixed with expectancy. The specific verb describing this act is *su'ári* (D), with the distinct meaning of 'to penetrate', 'to thrust into'. When used in an anatomical-physiological context, this verb refers to copulation, and this analogy introduces us into a key concept in Tukanoan relationships between man and the forest.[6]

There can be no doubt about the erotic significance of the verb *su'ári* and its equivalents in other Tukanoan languages. To enter the forest, metaphorically, is a sexual act and there is only one other fundamental experience in Tukanoan existence: drug-induced hallucination. We thus have a triangle of dimensions: the forest, coitus and trance. Minor, but nevertheless related states, would be dreams, near-drowning in a river, drunkenness from alcoholic beverages, prolonged music, a high fever. According to the Indians, it is in these states or dimensions (*turi*) where the individual finds himself facing a plurality of sensorial stimulations he has to identify, interpret and obey. The forest presents this situation.

The man/forest relationship is verbalised in the following way. A Bará shaman said: *'The shamans search for life in the forest; the life of the people is there'.*[7] The word for 'life' has markedly erotic connotations; the Desana word *ohokáriro*, means 'life' in the sense of sexual satisfaction and reproduction. The word for cooking plantain is *ohó*, but it is also an obscene term for penis, because of the shape of the fruit; ~karíri means 'to sleep', but it also means 'to sleep with', alluding to sexual intercourse. The word ohokáriro, translated as 'life' (ohokaríri)/to live) has, therefore, several meanings. The least common one corresponds, more or less, to our 'state of active metabolism', life being seen as a result, which is followed by a biological, developmental cycle. The more usual interpretation, however, refers to sexual union, in the sense of 'to live with'. It may sound a bit baffling, but should we ask a Tukanoan Indian: 'Where do you live?', what he understands is: 'Where do you copulate?', a question which, in a virilocal, exogamous society, makes a lot of sense. The concept of 'union', carnal or spiritual, is extended to man's relationship with the forest, and can therefore be applied to an abstract communion the person enters into when changing into a trance-like state of penetration into gahí turí, that is, another dimension. This is the state the Bará shaman was referring to when he used the Tukano proper term for 'life', which is kahtiró (kahtisé/to live). This word has the same multiple meanings as in Desana. Shamans say that they share with flowering plants the same energies, and that they establish a sexual relationship with them on that basis; the shaman appears as a pollinator. Both shamans and flowers contain ~sëríri bogá/odour-energy, in this case the energy of plant-growth.

The problem is further complicated by the following observations. The Desana word ohokáriro/life, can be interpreted as 'to sleep the penis', that is, as referring to the sexual aspect of the life concept. By changing the pronunciation and nasalising the last part of the word - oho ~kariro - the meaning is modified, not changed but extended to an unsuspected field, that of fishing. The term oho ~kariro now refers to a place, or a stretch on the river where people go fishing with dragnets at low water level. These nightly outings of small groups of men are characterised by a very special atmosphere. While wading in the shallow waters or resting near a fire on a sandbank, the talk will be of women, of one's allies, and there is emphasis on close bonding, on the excursion being aimed at obtaining food for kin and allies alike, on the analogy of fish and women, and of this special way of fishing being a demonstration of good will. The entire attitude toward fishing, stalking a nocturnal rodent, indeed toward each other, is quite different from that observed during the daytime, and this difference is expressed in a particular way of referring to the men's mood; they call it: mári ~naitiaroga, lit. 'our-darkness-little'. This mood, then, is closely related to the Indian's attitude toward the forest. The expression ~nëngë naitiari/forest-darkness, is emotion-charged; it contains a component of fear, but the overall feeling is said to be one of joy and affection and, as some people expressed it, of expectancy.

This feeling is justified, because when dawn is approaching and the men return with their catch, they will arrive at the port and meet there the young men who are taking their morning bath. And soon the girls will furtively come down from the maloca. This meeting between people returning after a night of fishing

A Barasana Indian making a mouthpiece of *Tabebuia* wood for his blowgun

and hunting, with bathing youths and the nubile girls on their first amorous appointments, is not a casual matter, but implies institutionalised, even ritualised, aspects. The 'drumming' on the water, the highly patterned laughter, and the shrill notes of an occasional pan-pipe, tend to form the atmosphere of a loosely structured fertility rite. Adults and elders listen to the sounds coming from the port; they will comment on the new generations, on their children and grandchildren, on their following the old-accustomed ways at that liminal spot which is the port, and at that critical time which is dawn.

There are spots in the forest where a single tree will stand in a circular open space almost free of undergrowth. Such a spot is called *sorogóro*, and the tree is referred to as *sorogorógë*. The Indians are aware of the fact that the absence of vegetation is not caused by human agencies, and so have developed their own theories about, what we would call an allelopathic phenomenon. They believe that these spots are charged with energies, specifically with energies imagined as whirlpools, whirlwinds, funnel-shaped presences with sucking and regurgitating motions. The verb *soroári* means 'to gyrate', and *soróri bero* is an expression used to describe a boys' game which consists in swinging in wide circles (*bero*) from a long vine hanging from a tree. The term *goró* means 'place', 'spot', and is frequently used to refer to a 'place of origin', in an anatomical, genital sense. *Sorogóro* sites are located at crossroads somewhere halfway between malocas belonging to different patrilineages; there may be two or three in the neighbourhood, known to all. Lovers and young people meet there for privacy, and adults will be joined there by small parties of allies who come for an informal gift exchange. *Sorogóro* spots are trysting places which have an important function in the maintenance of informal contacts with one's neighbours and allies. The idea of a high energy charge may be related to the presence of large numbers of tiny ants which are attracted to these solitary trees; they are called *moa koára*, lit. 'bait-carriers', because, according to the Indians, they can be seen carrying pollen.

The initial sensorial impact a person receives upon entering the forest depends on his or her biological stage in the reproductive cycle, and on the capacity to interpret the sights and signs. That, of course, is a matter of the person's age, knowledge of traditions, intellectual perceptiveness and psychological sensibility, and, last but not least, it depends upon the particular occasion on which a person enters the forest.

In the case of a hunter, before going into the forest, he will have to prepare himself in many ways; first of all, for at least a day or two he will have to avoid all sexual contacts except with his wife, and even dreams with an erotic content would be not only a bad omen but an affront to the game animals. Second, he will observe a diet of unseasoned cooked food, devoid of oils and fats; above all, he should avoid roasted food and anything that would smell of singed hair. Third, the morning before the hunt, he will drink a large amount of liquid peppers, absorb some of it through his nostrils, and thus will purify himself. The hunt is a courtship.[8] Having eliminated all body odours by absorbing peppers and carrying tucked under his belt some aromatic herbs—the same ones he would use during a dance—the hunter must make himself attractive to the wild animals.

He has painted his face with specific design motifs expressing potency and fertility. In the case of large game, such as tapir, deer, peccary or paca, the kill is compared to a sex act, and is discussed by hunters in these terms. These erotic aspects of hunting find their expression in dreams, drug-induced hallucinations, and in almost daily conversational references made during the evening hours when groups of men discuss current events, such as tracks, sightings, kills, and similar matters. In view of the conditions under which the hunter enters the forest, it is obvious that our image of the easy-going native huntsman is inaccurate. The truth is that he acts under many cultural constraints which, although irrational to a large degree, constitute a control system of notable adaptive value.

The relationship between the hunter and his prey is characterised by a tenuous balance of concessions, similar to the mutual compromises made between exogamous parties. This situation is worth exploring in more detail, not only because it is likely to help destroy some stereotypes of predatory hunting, but because of its theoretical interest. I shall return to this point later on. I have said that the hunter approaches the game (principally tapir, deer, peccary and paca) as if courting it. Using peppers and aromatic herbs to mask his body odours and to make himself seductive, he will spend days or weeks during the dry season—sometimes alone, at other times in the company of a few others—stalking deer, tracking tapir, or setting traps for some minor game. During the rut he will watch deer from a stand in a tree from where he can see pairs of fighting bucks, and does giving their mating calls. In all these forms of behaviour he will see human parallels, an imagery which will accompany him wherever he goes.

In the first place, deer are said to have a very feminine nature; they are very clean, sweet-odoured and soft-eyed, and move with exquisite precision, altogether an idealised picture of female seductiveness. In Tukanoan mythology, deer are Tapir's womenfolk whom the gruff old beast did not want to share with the newcomers to the Vaupés. There are countless stories of how the Tukanoans tricked Tapir into giving them some of his women who, it must be said, were not altogether averse to running away with their Tukanoan suitors. Deer are notoriously fond of sweet *umarí* fruits, a forest tree that became identified with Tapir's domain. Tapir became the mythical Master of Umarí, thus exercising mastership over deer. This theme is so frequent in Tukanoan oral tradition that it pervades the hunter's thought wherever he goes in the forest.

Deer/women relationships are expressed in many standard images. Deer mark their territories with chemical signals by rubbing their preorbital glands on scent posts, and by urinating around their territory. Women, too, are territorial in that they urinate on the periphery of their gardens. To dream of women, of their laughter, and of watching them walk, is a sure sign that the hunter will find deer on his next foray into the forest. To dream is ~keri; when discussing this word, in the context of dream symbolism and hunting, the verb ~keári was mentioned as being related to ~keri. Now ~keári is a term which describes the fighting of two bucks over a female, the rattling of the antlers, the two animals hooking and pushing. At first, this looks like a gratuitous digression, but soon it turns out to be of immediate interest. The Indians say that the friction and rubbing together of deer antlers produce an odour called *poa sëríri*, lit. 'hair-odour', a smell which is similar to that of roasted *uacú* seeds. In Tukanoan culture, this particular smell represents the essence of impurity; it is among others, the smell of menstrual blood, an element which is abominable because it is the denial of all procreative energies. It simply signifies sterility.

And once more, as happens so often with Tukanoan thought processes, a wordplay, a slight change in pronunciation, introduces a new perspective. The word *poa* means 'hair' or 'feather', but following the frequent *p/m* shift, we have the word ~*moa* which has the alternative meanings of 'salt' or 'bait'. As to salt, what is referred to here is a salty-tasting residue obtained from burning a podostemmoaceous plant (*Mourera fluviatilis*) which grows on submerged boulders at falls or rapids in black-water rivers. Tapirs visit these spots to lick the plants and even to dive at considerable risk to gnaw at plants growing below the water level. This 'salt' is said to smell like menstrual blood. In its meaning of 'bait', in the present context, the word ~*moa* refers to the same range of ideas. A menstruating woman is like a 'fake', she is a deviant, 'she is not edible', as the Indians say. If a menstruating woman should go into the forest, wild animals like jaguars, anacondas, anteaters, tapir and deer, would attack her, because, by her very condition, she would be asserting a principle of sterility, quite out of place in the forest's atmosphere of reproduction and growth.

The territoriality of deer is reaffirmed in other ways. Tapir is always eager to lick salt, and so he will follow the urine trail of deer and thus retrace the territory of 'his women'. On the other hand, the word for antler is *saáro* which, if nasalised and pronounced ~*saáro*, means 'place where something can be deposited', an expression with overt sexual connotations, as we have seen when speaking of buttress-rooted trees. This 'place', then, is deer territory, metonymically represented by antlers.

Immediately after killing tapir or deer, the hunter will cut out the tongue and bury it. This is done so the spirit-stuff of the animals won't talk and tell the others of their kind. The tongue is called *nedu*, *du* being a classifier, while the root of the name is related to the verb ~*neréri*/to lick; a salt-lick is called ~*nerédu*. Discussing this and related terms, conversation turns to salt-licks. These are lonely spots frequented by tapir in search of salty-tasting plants or briny soils, and Tukanoan hunters will observe them from a stand, high up on a tree. Deer, too, will visit these sites, and this meeting between 'old man Tapir' and his Deer Women is the subject of many myths and erotic fantasies. Symbolically and emotionally, salt-licks are similar to ports. Courtship and preening, sniffing and licking allow for many analogies, and salt-lick scenes are frequently mentioned in myths, hunters' tales, dreams, and hallucinations.[9] Sometimes the hunter, perched on his stand for hours, hungry and somnolent, will imagine that the animals turn into people. Odours, noises, or the latency of drug-induced trance states will suddenly trigger images of Deer Women going to the river to fill their pitchers, of tapir youths splashing in the muddy water; there will be mating calls, the snorting of deer or the whistling sound made by tapir. The drowsy hunter will find himself in another world. Salt-licks are liminal spots, they are thresholds, as the shamans say, and some hunters will cross them and become transformed into tapirs, never to return to their families.

Chapter VII

BETWEEN ARCADIA AND THE WASTELAND

The Collective Experience

It was the forest which regaled the Indians with what they consider its greatest gift, the narcotic vine which connects this world with the wondrous expanse of illusion. The story of the mythical origin of this drug, with its dionysiac touch and harsh dramatization, is told by shamans and old men, and never fails to leave the audience spellbound and disquieted. A mere summary of this myth cannot convey to the reader the uncanny quality of the scenery, nor the immediacy of the actions; the shamanic idiom is a powerful mode of expression which loses its impact when translated into plain English, but summarise we must.

In the beginning of time a group of men had assembled in the first maloca, deep in the forest. They all were Tukanoans, and there was one man of each phratry: a Tukano, a Desana, a Pira-Tapuya, a Uanano, and the rest. There were no women then. The men were in a state of great expectancy; they knew that they were to receive a precious gift, a faculty of mind, illuminating insights. They were in anxious suspense, almost in fear.

It was then when, looking out of the door of the maloca, they saw a woman emerging from the dark of the forest, carrying in her arms an infant. She walked with halting steps and crossed the line separating the forest from the open space surrounding the maloca. The men were aghast when she entered the door and walked to the centre of the maloca. The child in her arms was blood-red, shining red, and she cleansed it with a green leaf. The umbilical cord was trailing. The men were overwhelmed by the sight, they were delirious and began to talk loudly among themselves.

The woman was standing in the centre of the maloca and said: '*Who is the father of this child?*' At first, the men did not understand her. But then one man stood up and, seizing the child's right arm, cried out: '*I am his father!*' Then another one rose and cried: '*I am his father!*' And then they all rose and each one cried: '*I am his father; we all are his fathers!*' And they took hold of the child and tore it to bits. They tore off his arms and his legs, and they tore off the umbilical cord and distributed bits of it among them. And this was how the Indians obtained the narcotic vine. The Tukano, the Desana, the Pira-Tapuya, each one received his own vine, and they have kept it ever since.[1]

The myth continues and there are many variants of it, but the central theme is the same: the unknown women who emerged from the forest, the newborn child, the sparagmos scene, and the visionary quality of the entire setting.

We must briefly turn to botany, pharmacology and neurophysiology. The hallucinogenic vine the myth refers to belongs to the genus *Banisteriopsis*, first described by the British botanist Richard Spruce who collected it in 1853 in the Vaupés territory, and brought it to the Royal Botanic Gardens at Kew.[2] In more recent years Professor Richard Evans Schultes, of Harvard's Botanical Museum, has published or co-authored many botanical and pharmacological treatises on *Banisteriopsis* and other narcotic plants of the Colombian Northwest Amazon, and at present there exists an abundant bibliography on this hallucinogen.[3] *Banisteriopsis caapi*, the species most commonly used by the Tukanoans, contains beta-carboline alcaloids which produce colourful visions. Combined with tryptamines contained in leaves of *Psychotria viridis*, a plant of the madden family known in the vernacular as *chacruna*, or with *Diplopterys cabrerana*, the hallucinations are intensified and changes in colour vision are produced. The Indians use innumerable plant additives in the preparation of their hallucinogenic potions, the botany, pharmacology and phytochemistry of which continue to offer a wide field for research.

The hallucinogenic potion is prepared in the following way. Several bundles of fresh, finger-thick stems of *Banisteriopsis* vines are macerated with a heavy pestle in a wooden trough, and cold water is poured over the shredded mass. Next, the liquid is sifted through a large circular basketry sieve into a special vessel decorated with abstract designs which are painted on its globular body with white, yellow, and red mineral pigments.

Tukanoan Indians might take a *Banisteriopsis* infusion for several reasons; they might drink it during a night-long collective ceremonial, celebrated with the purpose of entering a mythical dimension in which the participants become witnesses to the Creation. They might prepare the potion to be consumed during a ritual meeting between allies, that is, between two complementary exogamous phratries when there is a gift exchange accompanied by drinking bouts, dances and songs. Other occasions would be initiation rituals, or certain hunting or harvesting rituals. On some occasions only the shamans take the narcotic, or a shaman and a patient whose illness he tries to diagnose and cure.

As well as this range of situations, there exists a wide choice as to how to refer to the specific 'kind' of *Banisteriopsis*. I say 'kind' quite advisedly, because I am not referring to a species in Linnean terms. The Linnean system classifies according to form, to morphology, and flowers are of prime importance for identifying a species. To the Indians, the important thing is what the plant does to the human organism, and this effect depends upon the spot where the plant grows, upon the soil conditions, upon the age of the plant, and upon all the plant and animal associations of its immediate environment.

Richard Spruce had called the species he had discovered *Banisteriopsis caapi*, taking this word from a Tukanoan language, as understood by him. *Banisteriopsis* is called *gahpí* (D), *kahpí* (T PT U), *kahí* (TT TB BA BS). In discussing this word with the Indians, the suggestion was made that it was related to the Desana words *gahsíru*, meaning canoe, *gahsiró*/bark, and *gahsíro*/cutis.[4] According to Desana traditions, in former times canoes were made from large pieces of tree bark, and among many mythical and other shamanistic contexts in which the Anaconda-canoe is mentioned, the analogies include canoe, womb, and placenta. *Gahpí* and its synonyms were said to refer to a placental concept; placenta is *gahsíro*/cutis, skin, and the vascular organ within which embryonic-foetal development takes place.[5] *Gahpí* (i.e. *Banisteriopsis*) and its synonyms were said to refer to a placenta the person had to enter when taking the hallucinogenic potion. The process of 'entering' this abstract dimension is called *yaheári* (D), *yaheáse* (T), meaning 'to come out of oneself', 'to ascend', 'to levitate'. The word *yahé*, erroneously believed to be of LG origin, is used all over the Colombian Northwest Amazon to designate the hallucinogen prepared from *Banisteriopsis* vines. Toward the Caquetá and Putumayo Rivers, this term is replaced by the word *ayahuasca*, a Quechua term.

During ceremonial occasions, *Banisteriopsis* is consumed only by adult men, who sit in a semi-circle facing the interior of the maloca, while the women are gathered in the dark rear of the building. In the course of the night, some eight or ten small cups of the potion are distributed, while the men dance, sing, and play a number of different musical instruments, such as flutes, pan-pipes and horns, accompanied by the sounds of seed and gourd rattles. At times the women will emerge from the darkness and take part in a dance, only to disappear again after a while. Their shrill ritual laughter, however, can be heard occasionally when they encourage their menfolk to drink more and more of the narcotic potion. The entire scene is far from being a frenetic orgy; quite on the contrary, it is extremely formalised and solemn. The rhythm of the dance becomes more and more coordinated, and dance-steps and gestures reach a precision that makes the group appear to be one single organism moving in a highly controlled and precise way. Song and dance become completely fused.

Banisteriopsis visions are very colourful. After the first few cups, and after an initial tremor and the sensation of rushing winds, the drug produces a state of drowsiness during which the person concentrates with half-closed eyes on the luminous flashes and streaks which appear in his visual field. This first stage is characterised by the appearance of small, star-shaped or flower-shaped elements

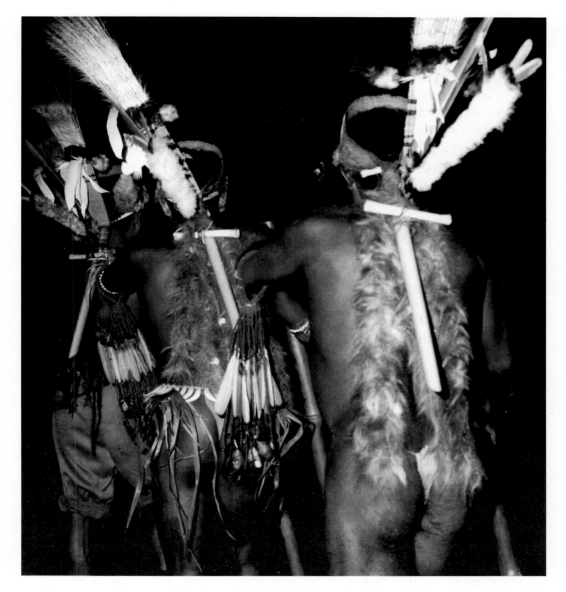

Barasana and Bará Indians dancing

which flicker and float brilliantly against a dark background, in kaleidoscopic patterns. There is a marked bilateral symmetry to these luminous perceptions, which sometimes appear as clusters of fruits or feathery leaves. Grid patterns, hexagons, zigzag lines and undulating lines, rapidly vibrating lines, eye-shaped motifs, many-coloured concentric circles or chains of dots slowly float by, combining and recombining in ever new patterns and changing colours. The visions appear in horizontal bands or stripes, slightly vibrating and approaching or receding. After a while, the symmetry and the overall geometrical aspect of these perceptions disappears and a second stage sets in. This is after four or five cups. Now large blots of colour will be seen moving like thunder-clouds, and from them emerge diffuse shapes looking like people or animals, or unknown creatures. The Indians interpret these shapes as mythological scenes peopled by ancestors and spirit-beings; visions which, to them, bear proof of the essential truth of their cosmogonic and religious beliefs. This is a highly emotion-charged stage, and people gesticulate while talking and singing, but generally look at the floor before them. Eventually all these images disappear; there will be soft music and shapes like wandering clouds, and the men sit silently in a state of blissful serenity.

While the second stage marks the onset of true hallucinations, the first stage is a trance-like interval during which the person, while not divorced from reality, visualises elements that appear in external objective space as geometrical patterns, clearly outlined and brilliantly coloured, but which cannot be designated as true hallucinations. The Indians themselves recognise that there is a difference between the two stages. Stage one is an inner, subjective dimension; they call these luminous sensations with terms that can be translated as 'threads, sprigs, little flowers' or 'clusters', and think of them as a pleasant experience, but quite different from the emotion-charged images of the second stage.

The literature on native hallucinatory content abounds with descriptions on the weird imagery produced by advanced *Banisteriopsis* intoxication.[6] It should be kept in mind here that the sphere of hallucinations is one of interpretations in which the person projects a set of pre-established, stored material upon the screen of shapes and colours. Understandably, the mythical scenes seen by the Tukanoans during the second stage of the drug experience can be seen only by members of their society. They see the anaconda, the stick-rattle of the Sun Father, the First Maloca, First Woman, First Dance, and so on. To the native viewer the interpretation of the floating shapes of the second stage is far more difficult than that of the geometrical patterns seen in the first one; after all, some of them could be identified as pre-existing models in nature, for example spirals, hexagons, concentric circles or diamonds. But now consensus as to meaning has to be achieved by the viewer in communication with others, especially with shamans and other experienced men. The individual hallucinations hardly ever constitute a private world, an intimate and almost secret experience; they are freely discussed, and anyone will ask questions. During a *Banisteriopsis* ceremony, shamans will ask individual participants about aspects of their hallucinations, and then will explain to them a wide range of shapes, colours, and motions, in terms of mythological scenes or forest spirits, ancestral beings, Tree People, game animal, spirits and others. In this manner a process of imprinting is brought into play, and any individual who is acquainted with the basic significance of colour symbolism, of ritual paraphernalia, mythological themes, and

Tatuyo Indians dancing

animal behaviour will soon be able to identify—by establishing analogies—a number of images each time they appear in his visions.

The second stage of the drug experience is interpreted, in essence, as a return to the maternal womb. It is a visit to the place of Creation, the *fons et origo* of everything that exists, and the viewer thus becomes an eyewitness and participant in the Creation story and the moral concepts it contains. The vessel which contains the hallucinogenic potion is said to be a female body, the maternal body, and by drinking its contents the individual is enabled to enter it through the 'door', the vagina one often sees depicted at the base of the container. At first, the consumer struggles with the vessel; addressing the vessel standing on the floor before them, the men will chant: '*I shall drink your contents and then I shall fill you with dirt*! or they will threaten to kick the vessel or to defecate into it. The men pretend to be afraid of the vessel, but in a ritual dialogue they challenge the danger.

The 'danger' is that of incest. The return to the maternal womb is imagined as consisting of two steps: first the individual enters the vessel's vagina as a phallus, and then he assumes an embryonic state which eventually leads to his rebirth. In other words, he commits incest and then, becoming his own progenitor, is reborn. There exists, then, a strong sexual component in the drug experience of the Tukanoans. The narcotic intoxication is often compared to an orgiastic rapture, a state of 'drowning'. The return to the womb implies the direct and intentional modification of time. When the individual becomes an embryo, it is a reversal of time, but—it is said—'*when one drinks (Banisteriopsis), one dies*', and this means an acceleration of time. Return and rebirth take place outside the normal biological time scale, and this state of standing outside the empirical universe is produced by the drug.

The Indians say that during a common *Banisteriopsis* session they never have visions of strange beings, monsters or alien landscapes; there is nothing new, so to speak. They see the land, peopled by their recognizable ancestors, the well-known animals, the familiar trees and rivers. The difference from ordinary reality is that the dead now speak and admonish, teach dances and songs, spells and cures. As a matter of fact, everything we would designate as *art*: instrumental music; song and dance; pictorial representations; rhetoric; poetic structure in oral literature; is said to have its origin in hallucinatory vision. Plants and animals tell the visionary how they want to be treated and protected so they can better serve him; how they suffer from carelessness, overhunting, the cutting down of trees, the abuse of fish-poisons, the destructiveness of firearms. Seen from this perspective we must admit that a *Banisteriopsis* trance, manipulated by shamans, is a lesson in ecology, in the sense that it gives nature a chance to voice its complaints and demands in unmistakable terms. Since everything seen and heard in the trance state is already known from traditional shamanic teachings, the trance only proves that shamans had been right all the time when they

A Tatuyo youth with ritual adornments

Tatuyo youths dancing with stamping tubes

said that the ancestors, the plants and animals, the forest and the river, were a living presence. Their voices offer and withhold, give and demand, acting and reacting as if they were one great unit, complementary to mankind, neither friend nor foe, hospitable only as long as man keeps the rules and controls his greed and aggression. These trances, then, are of social-ecological importance. The shaman-controlled drug experience is a technique of behavioural modification, and its latent phosphenes continue to influence behaviour in normal states of awareness.

Other trance states, induced by other *Banisteriopsis* admixtures and leading into other dimensions of awareness, are of significance for the individual. They are said to awaken memories of long-forgotten episodes, and may be helpful in solving personal conflicts. The *pemahsíri mahsá*, the 'listen-think people' will find the 'way' (*máa*) in the process of individuation. On the dionysiac level, the

A Barasana shaman drawing his visions in the sand

visionary will find compensation for the harsh rules which control his sexuality.

It would be mistaken to think that *Banisteriopsis* provides the Indians with an easy escape into an artificial paradise of intra-uterine security, sex, and male dominance. One is struck by the absence of hedonistic aspects in the ceremonial, and by the solemnity and seriousness of the atmosphere. And once more we must remember that the perceptive universe is not to be understood in so many patterns of one-to-one relationships, but in analogies which spread and ramify until they cover everything. An old Desana shaman was dictating some formal texts on *Banisteriopsis* visions, speaking in the ritual idiom of metaphors and cryptic allusions. When he had finished I asked him to summarise and explain to me the essential points of his long discourse. This is what he said.

'The vessel is like a human head. The vessel is like the placenta of Yajé Woman when she carried that infant. The vessel is like the celestial vault. When

people fail to understand this, they believe the vessel is their enemy.'[7]

Before venturing any further into these recondite dimensions of *Banisteriopsis* trances, I must briefly return to the first stage of the drug experience, the one in which small geometrical patterns appear in the visual field. From a neurophysiological point of view, these visions are entirely different from the hallucinations of the second stage. They are technically known as phosphenes, being subjective images which originate in the eye and the brain, and which are common to all people. Occasionally, phosphenes can appear quite spontaneously, especially when the person has been deprived for a certain time of visual stimuli, such as would be the case in prolonged darkness, or when exposed to unvaried sights such as a cloudless sky, a wide river, or rain in open country. They can also be produced by external stimulation: by pressure on the eyeballs, a sudden shock, or by looking into the darkness when waking up at night. In all these cases the eye may perceive sensations which vary from tiny dots to intricate moiré patterns, and from fan-shaped rays to glowing circles, all in different hues, generally blue, green, orange and yellow.[8]

Phosphenes can be induced by a number of chemical agents. Hallucinogenic drugs such as LSD, mushrooms (Psilocybin), mescaline, bufotein and harmaline are known to produce phosphenes of abstract patterns, and frequently the afterimages can be observed for several months after the initial experience. Laboratory experiments with thousands of people of different age groups and cultural backgrounds have made it possible to define at least twenty phosphenes which are found to be inbuilt in the human brain structure. It so happens that most of these cross-cultural phosphenes coincide with the Tukanoan patterns. I had given a choice of coloured pencils to the Indians, and had asked them to draw their *Banisteriopsis* visions. Now, when looking at a large collection of drawings of patterns seen during stage one, I noticed certain motifs that immediately reminded me of the ornamental patterns found on some Indian artefacts. There were scrolls and diamonds, rosettes and chain motifs that I had seen before, most often in painted form, and in this manner the colour designs began to fit into the general style of decoration as practised by the Tukanoans.

In the Vaupés area the usual decorative medium is composed of vegetable dyes. The basic colours—red and blue—are obtained from plant sources; the red dye is extracted from the leaves of *Bignonia chica* or from the seeds of a shrub (*Bixa orellana*), while the blue or blackish dye, a resistant tannin, is obtained from the fruit of a forest tree (*Genipa americana*). The nearest object to be decorated is one's body, and I have mentioned body paint as an important code of communication. Little wooden stools used exclusively by men are decorated with painted designs, and so are barkcloth aprons, the stamping tubes of light cecropia wood which are used to accompany their dances, pottery vessels, and gourd rattles. The most outstanding examples are the paintings executed on the front walls of the malocas, made of large pieces of flattened bark. It can be said that the entire style of what we would call the applied art of the Tukanoans, was based on drug-induced phosphenes. Moreover, further study of phosphenes and decorative designs showed that these luminous sensations and their graphic representations in ornamentation were coded in terms of Tukanoan colour symbolism and iconographic parallels. There was a large number of design elements on the significance of which people agreed. Certain motifs stood for specific concepts; a bifid form of divergent scrolls represents the male genitals, while a U-shaped element represents a vagina, a 'door', a labyrinth. A spiral was said to represent incest, alluding to the twisted body of a ritual trumpet used during initiation rituals, while a double-C scroll was said to signify fish traps put back to back. Phosphene by phosphene, decorative pattern by decorative pattern, all referred to male and female, union and disunion, preferential or forbidden marriage, seminal matters, ritual alliances and other, related ideas. The phosphene-derived geometrical patterns acquire a practical function in that they have become graphic symbols, or signs, which express the major tenets of Tukanoan society. The graphic symbols which are their 'decorative art' remind them, day by day, of cultural rules and norms. They are a system of communication which reminds the receptor, the user, the mere onlooker, to practice moderation in hunting and fishing, in eating, in needlessly destroying the environment, in fighting, in population increase, in sexual licence, in interpersonal strife.[9]

Animals and plants, when seen during a narcotic trance, will communicate with the visionary: they will speak to him in a language he can understand and will explain to him the rules by which they must be treated in ordinary reality, if they are to be of use. These contacts in the hallucinatory dimension are of great importance; shamans are well aware that the manipulation of trance states provides them with a means of control, not only of overhunting and overharvesting, but also to channel aggressive interpersonal relationships and a variety of other stress situations which might eventually manifest themselves in illness or other disruptive states. In speaking of this topic, they always emphasise that '...when drinking Banisteriopsis we see our maloca, our gardens; we see our forests and we see the fish and we see the game animals.'[10] Another shaman said: '...with Banisteriopsis we see the abodes of the game animals, of peccary, deer, curassow, we see all of them.'[11]

But Banisteriopsis visions go far beyond the everyday imagery of hunting and fishing. A Barasana Indian said: 'When we drink Banisteriopsis we see the concomitance of our (spiritual) life and our (animate) existence.'[12] I mentioned already that shamans say that a deep Banisteriopsis trance can reveal unsuspected, long-forgotten memories, not only of a person's infancy, but of experiences in ancestral generations glimpsed in the course of prolonged visions. This is said to occur when tobacco intake is combined with certain Banisteriopsis varieties, and when perceptions and feelings converge, bringing past experiences to the surface. It is also said that mind-reading and thought transference are common in these states. Much of this is irrational, but the *Banisteriopsis* ceremony seems to provide people with an important catharsis, not accessible in other states.

To understand the above, I must recapitulate at this point. I have mentioned that *Banisteriopsis* trance, produced by the contents of the ritual vessel, was compared by shamans with a womb, a brain, the Milk Lake of human creation, and the celestial vault. Within this micro-to-macrocosmic scale of comparisons shamans mention other analogues, notably in the context of spells. One refers to human testes, the structure of gonadic lobes apparently being known to shamans. Other comparisons are astonishing in that they refer not to concrete objects but, rather, to states of mind: underwater imagery, music, and the sex act. Deep pools in the river, rapids, and foam-flecked eddies are emotion-charged sights to the Indians; they are natural danger spots, and are models and metaphors associated with devouring and birth-giving fantasies. Diving or near-drowning are liminal states, between air and water, light and darkness, life and death. The underwater dimension, then, is full of perils, but it is also replete with fantasies about the life of Fish People, Otter People, Dolphin People, or anacondas, of revival (after a near-fatal accident) and rebirth. The dimension of music can be appreciated only if we realise its influence upon specific states of awareness. The perception of music, instrumental or sung, is greatly enhanced by *Banisteriopsis*, and individual instruments or tunes trigger specific associations and hallucinatory images. Shamans are masters in orchestrating the many different sensorial components of collective ceremonies, with emphasis upon auditory stimuli, interspersed with sudden silences or noisy episodes. The sex act, with its associations of *dári, ~nariri, noméri* and *dobéri* energies, is interpreted similarly as an overwhelming, total experience.

And then there is the forest, the home of *Banisteriopsis*. It was from the forest that the unknown woman appeared carrying the shining infant, and the hallucinogenic vine is the sign and symbol of the forest. To enter its darkness is to enter a womb, a brain, an orchestration of sounds, a universe which protects and nourishes, teaches and admonishes, and satisfies all desires.

Once, when walking in the forest with the Indians, I commented on the silence. There had been hardly a sound, no bird calls, no monkeys in the tree tops, no breeze in what to me was an oppressive quiet. Now my companions were astonished. '*The forest is not silent*', they said; '*You speak of silence because you are ignorant. You don't know how to listen!*' I had wanted to reply, but I was cut short. '*Silence is ignorance*', I was told peremptorily; '*Some people don't know how to listen.*'

Vines, creepers, and epiphytes are among the most common plants of the rainforest. Some of them hang vertically from the highest branches of tall trees, others twist around their trunks and sometimes cover them like a web, a network. Others tie trees together at the canopy level, while some form thickets in the undergrowth. Vines are an essential, structural, dynamic part of the forest. And now that we know of their powers, of their multiple symbolic associations, we can understand what vines can mean to the Indians. In looking at them they think of Yajé Woman, of the infant's umbilical cord, of an undulating snake, a braided river system, the Milky Way, a trail in the forest, perhaps the trail of tapir, of deer.

In Desana, the nonspecific term for vine is *~singá*, and Yajé Woman is called *~Singa mahsó*. In the other three Tukanoan languages, however, the word for vine is *~mihsí*, related to the verb *vihsíri*/to deviate, with the implied meaning of culturally improper deviation. At puberty, a young girl who develops hysterical fits will be called *vihsíri nomé*/distracted woman, and adolescent boys can be said to be *biá vihsíri*, lit. 'pepper-deviated', sexually aroused. It follows that the tangle of vines seen in the forest often evokes unsettling images of otherworldly bliss and fatal seduction. Shamans will carefully pull down the vines, examine them closely, sniffing and chewing stems or bits of bark, pondering odours and flavours. The forest is bountiful, but it can also be a great tempter.

In Desana, *~Singa mahsó* takes her name from *singaári*/to crawl. Undulating vines and creepers are often compared to snakes and to the distinct tracks left by a snake on a sandy beach, during the dry season. These sinuous furrows call people's attention. Could this have been a poisonous snake, they wonder? Or was it, perhaps, the spirit of that mythological Snake Person who seduced bathing women? We remember that sandy beaches, especially the port near the maloca, are mental scenarios charged with desires and anxieties. The sign of the snake, with all its ambivalence, triggers off new associations. In conversation it was said that these tracks made one think of 'a fertile, crawling state of heat'; in other words, the presence of an energy.[13]

And even if the Indian should go into the forest simply to gather some vines for practical uses, such as repairing a roof or making a sturdy carrying basket, he will see in these lianas not what we call a 'raw material', but something alive and replete with energies.

Let me explain this. The common, all-purpose carrying basket of Tukanoan women is a deep, round-bottomed, bag-shaped container measuring about 50 cms. in height by some 40 cms. in diameter. These baskets are woven from the aerial roots of an aroid, classed by the Tukanoans as 'vines' (*~singá*). They are very resistant and flexible, and can be found in almost all Indian households where they are the characteristic burden baskets of women. Undecorated and sturdy, these baskets go unnoticed by the occasional passer-by, but are significant items among the Indians. In the first place, these baskets are not manufactured by the Tukanoans themselves, but are made by the Makú, the nomadic hunters of the interfluvial zones who trade them to the Tukanoans in exchange for horticultural products. The baskets symbolise a female element, and Tukanoan women use them mainly to carry female-related matters, such as man-

The Bará shaman Kikítu at a *Banisteriopsis* ritual in a Barasana maloca

A Bará shaman taking a dose of narcotic snuff

ioc tubers, *Monopteryx* seeds, and potter's clay. In the second place, this type of basket is called *puíbu*, the broad carrying strap tied to it is called *puíkaro*, and the tree from the inner bark of which the strap is made, is called *puíkaroge*. While the element *pui* conveys the image of abundance, of plenty, *bu* is a classifier, meaning 'thing'. Moreover, *puiró* (or *puibugë*) is the name of a rainy season (late March), evoking the image of fishruns and baskets full of fruits, good hunting and ant-collecting, the suffix *ro* being an augmentative. The same sense of abundance is attached to the basket's name in Tukano proper (*pii*) and Pira-Tapuya/Uanano (*pee*), and the Indians elaborate on this point; the basket contains 'everything', it is a cornucopia replete with field fruits, tree fruits, smoked ants, fish, anything a woman will harvest and hoard and then distribute freely in her home. No wonder, then, that the *puíbu* basket should appear in many contexts as a symbol of plenty and of women's productiveness.[14] In some mythological texts gift baskets are described as being 'as large as the celestial vault', while of a man who possesses great knowledge of spells and ritual procedures, it will be said: 'he is like a basket', in the sense of being a 'fountain of wisdom'.[15] In other contexts, such as migration stories, dreams or hallucinations, *puíbu* baskets are compared with a womb, a garden, a maloca. In any case, the basket has female associations and these are based, to a large degree, on olfactory qualities. The peculiar combination of odours emanating from the aroid, the carrying strap, and the yellowish exudations they emit, is said to have an enticing smell in which the deep forest, womanhood, and the abundance of fruits are linked together.

There are other types of baskets quite as humble and, apparently, as insignificant as the *puíbu*. There is the *mehperi* basket, also a symbolic trade item metaphorically representing food and sex taboos; there is the *teremú* basket, the symbolism of which expands these conceptual domains, to include in them hexagon-related metaphors, body paint, and the music of flutes. I could go on and on, discussing the entire range of what we so superficially refer to as material culture, and point out its coded meanings which speak over and over of man's interrelationships with his forest environment. These artefacts (a clumsy term) are made from raw materials (another clumsy term, as seen from a Tukanoan perspective) extracted from the forest: wood, stone, clay, bone, pigments, all of which contain 'energies', in terms of colours, smells, textures, temperatures. Are these, then, artefacts? They are part of nature and, however transformed, they continue to be part of nature. Their code of communication is that of nature: food, sex, growth, decay, balance and renewal, and their daily use is a constant reminder of this link and of the need to preserve the sources of these vital elements. Many things in Tukanoan life are made from vines gathered in the forest, and vines are perhaps the most common plant material brought back from the forest. People are familiar with vines; they are essential in the construction of malocas or temporary shelters; in tying together the different elements used in manioc processing; in building fishtraps, manufacturing baskets, or making an improvised roast. Their pliable strength is ever-present, and the fact that it is a vine which provides the link with *gahí turí*, the other dimension, is just one of its many uses.

The Individual Dimension

The Indians' understanding of the forest as threshold and transformer is a sphere which is yet little explored and less appreciated. To introduce the reader into this dimension of space and time enfolding personal destiny, I shall quote an abbreviated version of a shamanic tale I tape-recorded in the Vaupés in its original Desana version.

'There once was a man whose wife did not love him. He decided to leave his maloca and to lose himself in the forest. When he was thus wandering in the forest he met a stranger. The stranger asked: '*What are you doing here?*' The man answered: '*My wife does not love me and I want to get lost in the forest.*'[16] The stranger asked: '*Where is she now?*' '*Over there, at the maloca*', said the man. '*I shall bring her back to you*', said the stranger and left.

The stranger had been carrying a bag and in that bag he had a jaguar garment[17]. The man had seen it. The stranger now put on the jaguar garment and, while the man was watching from a hideout, the stranger went to lie in ambush on the trail that led from the maloca to the river. After a while the woman came out carrying a pitcher and went down to the port. But on the way the Jaguar Man seized her, hit her with his adze, threw her down and raped her. There was blood everywhere. He then carried the woman back to where the man, her husband, had been watching. '*Is that the one who does not love you?*' asked the Jaguar Man. '*Yes, it's her,*' said her husband.

The stranger had put away his jaguar garment and said: '*I am going to visit my people at the headwaters of the river. Come with me.*' So the three went walking in the deep forest and it was a very dark forest and they walked for a long time, far away. They spent the nights around a fire, the man and his wife sleeping in a hammock, while the stranger lay down on the ground.

One night the man awoke. By the dim light of the fire he looked at where the stranger was lying, but what he saw was a huge jaguar. He looked and looked, and the sleeping jaguar was moving his ears as if listening. The man whispered to his wife: '*Look!*' but the jaguar woke up and said: '*What are you talking about?*'

The next morning they went on. The stranger said: '*Now we are quite close*' and so it was. They came out at a clearing and there was a beautiful maloca, large and well painted, full of Jaguar People wearing their best weapons and adornments. The stranger had changed into his jaguar garment and said to the

couple: '*You stay close to me and hold on to my tail; nobody will harm you.*'
The Jaguar People welcomed the Jaguar Man, who was their chief. He was a
black jaguar[18] from the rivermouth. They danced and sang for many days.

After a long time the stranger said to them: '*Now go home, the two of you.
Don't tell anybody of what has happened; if you do, I shall have to come for you
and fetch you.*' The two returned to their maloca. It was a long way to go but
finally they arrived and greeted their kinsmen. '*Where have you been?*' people
asked the man. '*I had a walk,*' he said. But people asked again and again and
finally the man told them. That very same night he died.'

The motif of a man going into the forest to 'get lost' appears in narratives
and informal conversations. In most cases the man's motivations are conjugal
tensions, a wife's adultery, or a forbidden love affair. The Indians explain that
a man who decides to lose himself in the forest for what we would call romantic reasons, '*walks as if he knew the trails but doesn't really know them; he walks
as if he knew where he was going. But in truth he is lost.*' It is all an illusion, they
add; he walks as if he had taken a drug. The 'danger' is that he might meet his
own shadow, or that he might be led astray by *vearí mahsá*, those beings of the
forest twilight who appear in the form of forbidden relatives and try to seduce
him. Some men, however, might go into the forest simply to meditate; not out of
despair, but trying to find solutions to some personal problem of a more simple
nature, perhaps an angry exchange of words with a kinsman, a son's disobedi-
ence, a problem of prestige behaviour. But 'to lose oneself in the forest' is a serious matter to the person concerned. Women who find themselves in a similar situation, being unloved, abandoned, or mistreated, do not go into the forest; they
escape by canoe and are 'lost' on the river where they eventually turn up in the
maloca of kinsfolk or of a lover. Such an escapade may have wider consequences, because when a woman abandons her husband's home, an alliance is
broken and with it a vital network of reciprocity behaviour is dissolved. But men
choose the forest; they break not only with their allies but with society. Men in
the forest, if they are not lost in it forever, are thought to enter a thicket, an
almost impenetrable thorny shrubbery where they hide and from where, if discovered, they refuse to emerge.[19] Or so the stories go. The 'thicket' is a standard
image in some states of mind, and is mentioned in a whole range of contexts,
from mythical to commonplace. In other states, the image is that of a wasteland
the errant wanderer comes upon when roving in the deep forest. It is described
as a wild—we would say, romantic—landscape of silent woods, towering cliffs,
slow-moving rivers with islands and coves, a landscape uninhabited by man or
beast. At other times this no-man's-land is described as almost devoid of vegetation, or as having been abandoned a long time ago by an unknown people;
overgrown gardens, ruined malocas, and trails leading nowhere form a ghostly
maze from which the wanderer, once he has arrived there, cannot escape.

A tape-recorded Desana text, spoken by a shaman, tells of a man who left his

Ritual vessel for *Banisteriopsis* preparation

family in anger and now enters the forest. After several days '... *he closed his eyes and in closing his eyes, a different dimension appeared... large lakes, lakes like coves; there were rivers with inlets... 'Where did I come from?' he thought, but he could not remember... there were abandoned clearings, large lakes and rocky promontories; there were no people; large trees were floating in the rivers ... It can't be! There he wept, there he wept. He had no fire either; the fire had been left behind... There was nothing he could do. ... he went up and darkness fell. He wept all night ... there were no people, no people; old clearings, old house sites, that was all... That is what he thought, sleepless, while dawn was coming.'*

The reaction to personal conflicts may be one to despair and depression, but in some cases it is one of rage and hatred against those who are held responsible for the emotional shock suffered. Often enough the solution to these personal conflict situations is sought in the imaginary sphere. A man will go into the forest under the influence of a hallucinogenic drug, and will believe he turns into a jaguar.[20] In his trance state he will act out his hostility by imagining that he is mauling or decapitating his enemies, raping women, and committing the most outrageous acts of violence, after which he will recover his normal state, feeling relieved of his tensions and aggressive thoughts. The story of the man who met the Jaguar Person, i.e. himself, belongs to this complex, and there are others which are variants of this recurrent theme. Jaguar transformation is a motif widespread in the American tropics, going back to prehistoric times, and playing an important role in shamanistic beliefs and practices, and the Tukanoan case provides a new perspective of these thought patterns. But these are extreme cases. To turn into a jaguar, get entangled in a thicket, or find oneself in a wasteland, are individual situations, known to exist, but of infrequent occurrence.

There exists a special relationship between the forest and old people. The old cease to receive energies from the forest and the flow is now reversed; it is they who, in the course of their lives have accumulated a great amount of energies they now can give back to the forest. This is called *duhári*/to restore, to return something. The forest finds nourishment in this restitution of vital forces which are absorbed by the three layers of vegetation, from undergrowth to canopy. It is clear that a person's continuous contacts with the forest are not one-sided, not exclusively exploitative, but involve interaction.

These images, then, form part of the forest, of what the forest can come to mean to the Indians. In the last resort, they represent the atavistic horrors of death, annihilation, nothingness, and in this sense they are the necessary counterpart to the image of life and growth the Indians see in their forest environment.

The foregoing descriptions and textual quotations open up dimensions of human experience which are rarely mentioned in the literature on Amazonian Indians. They show us that the rainforest, far from being only a source of food, medicinal plants, and raw materials for all kinds of artefacts, also provides a screen upon which people project their hopes and fears, with which they can identify, where they can find company in their loneliness, solutions in their intimate conflicts and, last not least, where they experience a sense of beauty and of wonder. Why should we have denied the Indians' capacity to see the forest from this perspective? Why should we have ignored it for so long?

In the course of my inquiry I have been led occasionally into the darker aspects of forest imagery, into the sombre side of the human predicament, brought into focus and projected upon the forest, its shapes and textures, its smells and sounds, and its innumerable associations. There can be no doubt that this is an important aspect of Indian life, but it cannot be said to be the predominant mood. The forest is always more of a home than a wilderness. Many people—shamans, above all—know only too well that the forest is a mirror and that its feral image is man's own reflection of states of mind he must and can control by introspection. His awareness of the deeper meanings of the forest will give him security. When a hunter has to spend the night in a solitary section of the forest where jaguars, real or imaginary, are known to roam, before lighting a fire he will say a spell. The words of this incantatory formula identify the hunter with a bright flame, and his thoughts with the radiance of the fire. Jaguars and forest demons will see the fire, but not the hunter. *'His power of mind will protect him against all harm'*, it was said.

In speaking of jaguar transformation I have touched a major theme, not only of the shamanic understanding of man's aggressive tendencies, but of a much broader field of human experience. I have mentioned the verb *~menyahári* when speaking of the auditory impact the insects' 'song' is said to make upon people in the forest, and now I have quoted the same word in the context of jaguar transformation. It is necessary, then, to analyse this verb in more detail and explain its meanings in several contexts, because it provides the key to a wide range of images which are fundamental to our understanding of the Tukanoan worldview.

The verb *~menyahári* is related to *nyaári*/to be transformed, to develop, and *me*, a prefix expressing force, impact. As a noun, *nyaári* means 'shape', 'form', as in speaking of a technological process (canoe-making, pottery, etc.): *'It's taking shape'*; or of an idea: *'it is taking shape in my mind'*. The expression *mahsá nyaári*/ 'people-to shape' refers to the effects of a shaman's teachings. The essential meaning of *~menyahári* is that of powerful transformation. The contexts are many and can be listed in a sequence of, more or less, increasing complexity:

a) *~ehó ~menyahári* means 'to catch a cold', i.e. when entering a maloca where many of its inhabitants are lying in their hammocks suffering from severe and highly contagious 'grippe'.

b) *~vihó ~menyahári*; to smell and absorb a hallucinogenic snuff (*vihó*), and experience altered states of awareness.

c) *buhpú turári ~menyahári*, lit. 'thunder-force-to penetrate', an expression describing the belief in invisible thorns a shaman carries in his forearms and hurls against his enemies, the thorns possessing pathogenic powers.

d) *yee ~menyahári*, to turn into a jaguar.

e) *diagë ~menyahári*, lit. 'river-in to penetrate'; to playfully jump from a tree into the river; metaphorically, to penetrate several levels of awareness.

f) *Vaí mahsë turí ~menyahári*, lit. 'Master of Game-dimension-to be penetrated by'; i.e. to receive the energies of wildlife.

g) *vahtí ~menyahári*; to be exposed to the ambivalent influence of a forest demon's suggestions; i.e., to confront a choice of action, with reference to sexual-social norms.

We now return to the insects' song in the forest. The humming and buzzing sounds are made by innumerable insects and are said to make a strong impact upon the hunter, a sensation described with the word ~*menyahári*. When asked for a more precise definition of this impact, it was described as *yeéa guári ~menyahári*, lit. 'jaguars-fierce-penetrate', an unexpected and cryptic expression. The word *guári* expresses fierceness, anger, a threatening attitude. A jaguar or dog's growl is described as *guári*, and so is an ill-tempered woman's scowl. The key to the meaning lies in metaphor and pronunciation. The word for jaguar is *yeé*, the same as for shaman; it is related to *yeéri*/to copulate, *yeéru*/penis, and *yeégë*, the phallic staff of the mythical Procreator *Pamurí mahse*. The word *guári*/fierce, if pronounced *guarí*, means 'to bathe', with the implied meaning of 'to harden', referring to sexual arousal. The insect song has turned into a jaguar's growl, and thence into nature's fertility.

Many shamanistic curing spells invoke the help of animals. Some spells begin with the words: '*In the House of the Hills they live like people. They are people like us*'; others begin saying: '*Deer are like people*', while other spells enumerate all kinds of monkeys, birds, fish, or forest fruits and seeds. The spells explain how shamans deal with the Master of Animals, how they 'feed him' with seminal substances: starch, manioc flour, groundnuts, toasted ants, *vahsú*, in order to appease him, 'make him sleep'. In a metaphorical sense, the shaman's relationship with the Master of Animals has a strong sexual component, in that the shaman provides the Master with procreative energies which in turn produce the wildlife upon which people depend for their sustenance. The shaman's animal helpers are called upon for their odours and colours, and for certain behavioural characteristics, such as sharp teeth, claws, rapid movements, etc., but all this so-called animal symbolism is of a sexual nature and expresses genital, generative concepts. In other spells, shamans will 'prepare the trails' of game animals so, when leaving the Master's abodes, the forest will appear attractive. He will trace for them straight trails leading toward the malocas, trails marked with yellow clay (*mata bahsí*) and perfumed with the odours of forest fruits and seeds. He will do the same for fish in the river. In his spells he will make game 'descend' (*buaríri*) from the hills, and fish 'ascend' (*mëeríri*) from the rivers.

The image the Indians themselves make of the local fauna and flora is a key to many behavioural patterns, not only of the hunter, fisherman and forager, but of society at large. When speaking of vertebrates the Indians will say that, in spite of the many differences in form, the similarities outweigh all other considerations; their feeding strategies, reproductive behaviour, sleeping habits, social life, sounds and movements, are very much like those of human beings. At the same time, animals have much in common with plants; anteaters smell like certain trees, deer have the same colour as dry Heliconia leaves, paca has pelt marks like necrotic fungal spots on leaves and its meat is as juicy as a ripe fruit. And plants are like people; their anatomy and sexual physiology, their textures and

Barasana shaman wearing in his necklace a cylinder of white quartz and other insignia of his rank

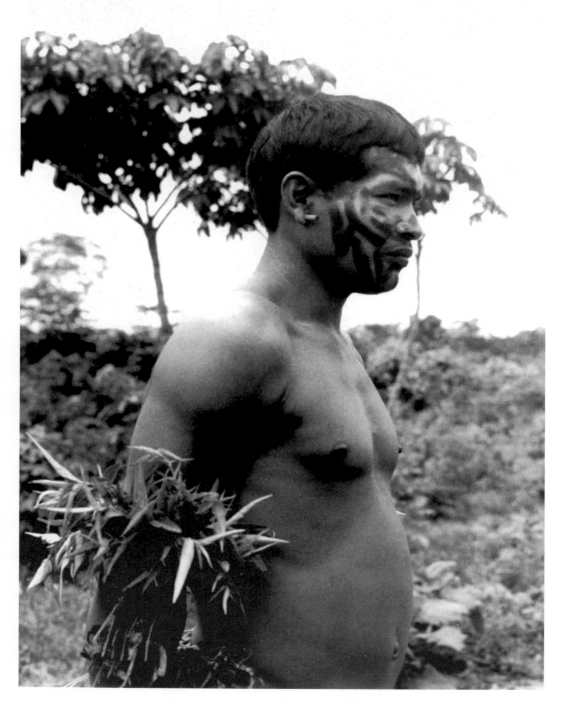

A Taibano Indian with aromatic *bayá-pia* leaves around his arms

A Barasana shaman dances in a trance during a *Banisteriopsis* ritual

colours, odours and flavours have much in common with those of human beings. These are not idle comparisons; they refer to principles of energy, energy relationships and balance, the equilibrium of the Indians' sensorial universe. In their own words these comparisons refer to ~*nuguri*, the roots (cf. *nëngë*/forest), in the sense of a common energetic origin. The Indians communicate, individually or through their shamans, with animals and plants; this communication is not meant to be with zoological or botanical species, but with energies the Indians believe to be inherent in wildlife. Daily shamanistic and personal practices and understandings link people's health, food, sex, social interaction and metaphysical experiences into a coherent belief system in which man is inseparably joined to nature.

This linkage is best exemplified by three aspects of the environment which by now should be familiar to the reader: the forest, the game, and the garden. Man's relationship to these three fundamental aspects of life is *like* the one he must hold in mind with his allies. The forest is the bountiful basket, a brain, a vision, a woman. Game animals are like people, like allies, like women. The garden is a loaded table that the forest and women offer to men.

APPENDIX

A Note on Protein Availabilities

The topic of protein resources has caused much discussion among Amazonian scholars. Some anthropologists have advanced the theory that proteins are scarce and that this constitutes a limiting factor in cultural developments, while others have doubted this deterministic approach.[1] I agree with the latter, having observed no shortage of protein resources, and being well acquainted with the Indians' acute awareness of the importance of this substance in their food intake.

In the Vaupés territory, where serious flooding of the forest does not occur, hunting provides proteins during the entire year; even during the height of the rainy season the hunter can find ground-dwelling mammals and does not depend on arboreal species alone. Fish are a major source of proteins and may be difficult to catch in the main rivers at high water level, but can always be caught in flooded inlets and smaller streams. Most authors will refer to game and fish as principal protein resources, and tend to ignore or underestimate the importance of other sources of supply, a failure which easily leads to doubtful theoretical formulations referring to economic stability, social organisation, and cultural development in general. In the following I shall mention some protein availabilities of the rainforest, which deserve to be taken into account.

Edible frogs are an important food item. There are two kinds in the Vaupés area: one is called ~omá (D T PT U), a large tree frog, and the other is ~nya'pá (D T PT U), a good-sized ground-dwelling species.[2] ~Omá frogs announce their breeding time by loud croaking for several nights and days, when thousands of them gather in small ponds formed by the first rains of March and April. The Indians then dig pits in the forest floor, called ~omá gobe/frog holes, about two metres wide and up to two or three metres deep, which promptly attract frogs in search of spawning sites. Once the animals have jumped down into the water, they cannot escape because the vertical walls of the pit have been smoothed, and now the men will climb down on a pole and collect by hand large numbers of them, stringing them up on a thin vine, through the mouths and mandibles, a process called ~omá piúri.[3] Next, water is boiled in a large vessel and the frogs are thrown in; this is thought to neutralise a certain odour clinging to the skin of the animals. The next step consists in putting the frogs on wooden spits, and smoking them on a tripod grid for three or four hours. Then the smoked frogs are taken off the spits and are pounded in a wooden mortar[4] until they are converted into a brownish, powdery mass. This powder is packed into leaf-lined[5] baskets, made in a three-strand lattice technique with hexagonal spaces, called teremú[6], which are then kept on a shelf over the hearth. If carefully preserved in a dry, moderately smoke-filled place, the frog meal can be kept for eight to ten months. The entire process, from collection to packing into baskets, is done by men, except for one significant phase: that of boiling, which is done by women.

Frog meal is consumed by both sexes, especially during the rainy season. The meal is first washed, after which the water is thrown away and the damp mass is now boiled in water and seasoned with peppers and salt; it should never be mixed with starch, nor with 'mixed fish' (*bahurí*), because this would arouse too much sexual activity among the participants.

I have mentioned that the boiling of the frogs is meant to eliminate or neutralise a certain odour, and this aspect explains the name of the frog; *~omá* is related to the verb *~omári* (D) meaning 'to carry', 'to be tainted', 'to be saturated with something'. The frog is the 'carrier' of *~oma sëriri*, the peculiar odour. The Indians explain this by saying: '*It has the same odour as ~nya'pá frogs*'. Now this frog is said to have a sexually arousing, but at the same time repellent, smell. The name *~nya'pá* means clitoris: *nyapá* (D), *yahpé* (PT U). It is the same odour category as *sëmé* (*Monopteryx angustifolia*), *barí* (*Erisma japura*), and *vahsú* (*Micrandra spruceana*), the three forest seeds from which the Indians prepare the protein-rich 'seasoning' I have discussed when speaking of the eight trees and their extraordinary symbolic value.

The five edible components of this olfactory complex must be boiled by women before the seeds and frogs can be safely consumed. This process of boiling constitutes a multiple transformation: it eliminates the rank odour, it purifies the substance, and it is equivalent to uterine gestation, three points which were made clear by all informants. This, then, is the reason why the only female activity in frog processing is the boiling.

Another process of protein conservation is the following. The Apaporis River which forms the western limit of Tukanoan territory is interrupted near the middle of its course by the great Jirijirimo Falls. At a short distance below the falls, the river narrows and begins to flow through a labyrinth of tunnel-like chasms closed in by vertical walls of stone. During most of the year these tunnels are invisible, lying below the water level, but during the dry season they emerge. It is then when certain migratory birds called *sióra* (D T PT U) arrive and fill the crevices of this chasm. At about 6 a.m. many hundreds of them leave the tunnels, spiralling in dense, reverberating clouds, to return at about 4 p.m. for the night. Inside the tunnels the birds are so crowded together that the local Indians can catch them with nets and baskets by the hundreds. After plucking and gutting them, they smoke the birds for several hours and then press them between wooden boards or flat stones. They then pack the smoked birds in leaf-lined baskets which can be kept for many months if stored above the hearth-fires[7]. I had read about this practice in Spix and Martius's travel account of almost two centuries ago, where a description of it is given from the Caquetá River, only 150 kms. to the southwest of the Jirijirimo Falls. The account speaks of the abundance of birds in these parts and says that, during the months of December to February (i.e. during the dry season) the Indians killed thousands of birds, smoked them, pressed them between palm leaves, and in this preserved form kept them 'under the roof', that is, in the smoke-filled dwelling.

The preservation of food stuffs containing quality proteins, by smoking and storing them for many months, is not limited to frogs and birds. Among the Tukanoans, at least a dozen species of fish, some of them quite large, are either smoked and then preserved whole, or are pounded after smoking, and the coarse meal is kept in leaf-lined baskets.[8] Eels (*Synbranchus sp.*) are rolled into individual spirals, and large fish such as *pirahiba* (LG) (*Brachyplatystoma sp.*) are cut into slices before smoking. Juvenile specimens of South American caiman, *jacaré tinga* (LG) (*Caiman sclerops*), *diaké* (D), *ehsó* (T PT U), are gutted and smoked, and then are pressed between pieces of wood. If kept in leaf-lined *teremú* baskets in a smoke-filled room, they can be preserved for at least three months. Whole specimens of paca and agouti are sometimes treated in the same manner, although their meat tends to become very tough after a few months.

Insects foods are of some importance in the Vaupés territory.[9] Those most frequently mentioned in the literature are *mojojoi* (LG), the larvae of beetles of the genus

Rhynochophorus, and ants, mainly of the genus *Atta*. I shall first refer to the larvae. These beetles are among the most important pollinators of palm trees, a fact well known to the Indians who relate it to the imagery of social cross-fertilisation. The larvae are about the size of a little finger, and develop in the piths of palm trunks that are decaying on the forest floor. Since these larvae are a highly desirable food item, the Indians will occasionally fell a palm[10] to let its stem serve as a breeding place for beetles. With an axe a series of V-shaped cuts are made in the thick and hard bark, so that the scent of the pith will attract female coleoptera for oviposition. After three or four months, when knocking on the log, one can hear a humming noise from its interior, and when touching the bark, one can feel a notable rise in temperature.[11] This, then, is an established way of *cultivating* larvae. Otherwise, the Indians will look for decaying trunks while hunting in the forest, or will fell some old specimens of palm trees as food reserves for later use.

Mojojoi larvae can be consumed raw, boiled, or smoke-dried, and are considered an aphrodisiac delicacy. Like all protein-rich, oily, and fat-containing food items, larvae are associated with many beliefs referring to social-sexual matters. The key to these questions is to be found in the names of the beetle and the larvae.

The palm borer, a large black beetle with a pointed proboscis, is called *mimidóro*, from *mimíri*/to suck[12], and *dóri*, a small funnel, like those made of a twisted green leaf and used for absorbing liquid peppers through the nostrils, or medicines orally; in many contexts, the image of a small funnel is that of a vagina. Of the palm borer it is said: '*That beetle inseminates the palm; it procreates larvae.*' In other languages the name of the beetle is different, but the meaning is similar: *do'taeno* (T PT U), from *do'tasé* (T), *do'táye* (PT), *do'táa* (U)/inebriating '*like the odour of pollen; like Banisteriopsis, Virola, alcohol*'. Next, the larva is called *~pingarámë*, an ambivalent term which appears in a male form (*~më*), but seems to allude to an embryonic concept based on the doubled-up shape of the grub, and the womb-like trunk in which it develops.

Palm grubs and dry-toasted ants are not just occasional snacks, but are emotion-charged because of their 'fat' and olfactory associations. Their imagery is often mentioned in myths and spells, in the course of exchange rituals[14] or as occasional metaphors in casual conversation; indeed, Tukanoan everyday life would be difficult to understand without taking into account these allusions. Both insect foods can be preserved for a short time without spoiling, and their nutritional value seems to be high. Other insect foods are termites and caterpillars, the latter being called *~ii* or *nihtía* (D). They are seasonal and are collected mainly in February and March, when they are smoked and then pounded in a mortar to be kept in storage baskets. The mealy powder can be mixed with fish soup, or is simply boiled in water. Caterpillars can also be eaten raw or dry-toasted on a cassava griddle.

NOTES AND REFERENCES

CHAPTER I

1   On the basic ethnography of the Tukanoan Indians of the Colombian Northwest Amazon, see, among others: Århem, K., 1981; Bidou, P., 1976; Bruzzi, A., 1962; Goldman, I., 1963; Hugh-Jones, C., 1979; Hugh-Jones, S., 1979; Jackson, J., 1983; Koch-Grünberg, Th. 1909-10; Reichel- Dolmatoff, G., 1971. On Tukanoan mythology, see Amorim, A., 1928; Bidou, P., 1985; Fulop, M., 1956; Reichel-Dolmatoff, G., 1989; Stradelli, E., 1890; Trupp, F., 1977. Recent studies of Brazilian Tukanoan Indians along the Rio Negro describe acculturational situations which differ from those encountered in the Colombian Vaupés. Some examples are: Buchillet (1989), Chernela (1989-1992), Meira (1989), Ribeiro (1989), Ricardo (1991). Popular introductions to Tukanoan ethnobotany are by Schultes, R. E., 1988; Schultes, R.E. and R.F. Raffauf, 1992. Bibliographical references to specific aspects of research are given in the text, and in the Notes and References corresponding to the different Chapters.

2   *yeegë*/stick-rattle; from *yee*/shaman, jaguar; cf. *yeéri*/to copulate; a phallic staff used by shamans in many ritual contexts. For details, see RD., 1989, Index, p.547.

3   On hexagonal space and rock crystals, see RD., 1979b.

CHAPTER II

1   The concept of 'cosmos' is called *pepíri turí*, lit. 'thought dimension' or 'abstract dimension'. The term *turí* has various meanings which range from that of a spatial dimension to intellectual and psychological spheres. The root element of *bogá (bo, bu, po, pu, mo, mu)* can be found in a number of words which refer, literally or metaphorically, to a conceptual field concerned with procreation, insemination, and impregnation. Some examples are: *boo*/manioc starch, an element with seminal associations; *bogë*/ritually pure food; *borá*/phallus; *po'gá*/manioc flour or dehiscence of pollen, especially of palms. Otherwise, this term is used to refer to a leaf-wrapped bundle which might contain either smoked ants or palm grubs, or smoked hot peppers, delicacies which are said to be aphrodisiac. The same word can be used to designate a funnel-shaped quiver containing poisoned blowgun darts, a common phallic symbol. Moreover, we have *poé*/cultivated field, metaphorically a fertile woman; *poeka*/field fruits; *poóri*/to scatter, to dehisce, to inseminate; *porá*/son, sapling, shoot; *~porá*/generation; *~poré*/clitoris; *poréri*/to germinate, to recuperate or reproduce periodically; *poreru*/penis; *poyarí*/to become transformed; *puíbu*/women's basket with uterine associations; *~moá*/salt, metaphorically, sperm.

2   In Tukano proper, the sun is called *muhipë*, a word related to *muhipu*, derived from *muhí*, a palm (*Mauritiella cataractarum*) and *pu*/leaf. These leaves are used for roof thatch and, metaphorically, represent a shamanic concept of protection and guardianship. In PT and U, the sun is called *ahsë*/heat.

3 'Heat force'/*ahsë turári.*

4 For example, in the shamanic idiom there will be mention of *boréri bogá, bo'ré bogá, diári bogá,* i.e. white, yellow and red energies. The sun's 'whiteness' is referred to as *turári uáro boréri bogá,* lit. 'force-good-white-energy'.

5 Colour intensities are expressed in the following manner: 'white brilliant reflection' (*boré gohsé siriro*), 'yellow brilliant reflection' (*bo're gohse siriro*), 'red strong reflection' (*diabíri gohsé siriro*). On colour energies, see RD, 1978.

6 On phosphenes, see RD, 1975a; 1978f; 1989, Index, p. 548. These publications contain numerous bibliographical references.

7 *savéri-da*; cf. *savéri*/incipient; *saveóri*/to reach the age for being carried straddling on the hip; *savéori*/to have budding breasts. *yëbëri-da*; cf. *yëbëri*/ripeness (fruits, first stage of pregnancy); *yëbëari*/to make a lump of something (clay, soap, washing).

8 This common vine is called *too* (D) and figures prominently in Tukanoan shamanism. The chemistry of this plant is unknown, but might be of interest because it is occasionally used as an admixture to hallucinogenic potions. See also Schultes and Raffauf, 1990, pp. 399-400.

9 For example, shamanic spells will invoke 'yellow male light' (*gohsé borégë arimi*), 'rosy female light' (*gohsé diabiririgo*), 'black light' (*gohsé nyígo*), 'crepuscular light' (*nyípíro*). The same shaman who spoke of these spells summarised his theories in the following statement: *'The origin of all energies is the sun. The sun transmits them to people and to their hallucinations. On our earth these energies manifest themselves in yajé visions, in the colours one sees in the rock crystal, and in the sex act.'*

10 For more data on colour energies as understood by the Tukanoan Indians, see RD, 1971, Index, p. 283: Energy, concept of.

11 On *ëmëkóri mahsá* (Beings of Day), see RD, 1971, Index, p. 283; *ëmëkóri -mahse*; idem, 1989, Index, p. 545: Mythical people, tribes.

12 For details on the Master of Animals, see Chapter IV.

13 The 'white cloud level' is called *boréri bogá,* lit. white energy; the rain cloud level is *dehkó bogá*/water level.

14 On jaguar/shaman identification, see RD, 1975.

CHAPTER III

1 On maloca structure, use, and symbolism, see Hugh-Jones, C., 1979, 40ff; Hugh-Jones, S., 1979, *passim*; Koch-Grunberg, 1909, II, 69ff; RD, 1971, Index, p. 285: Maloca.

2 A sample list of plant specimens cultivated near a maloca would contain the following: peach palm (*Bactris gasipaes*), an *umarí* tree (*Poraqueiba sericea*), guamo trees (*Inga sp.*), imbaúba (LG) (*Pourouma cecropiaefolia*), some aroids (*Xanthosoma sp.*), a pokeweed (*Phytolacca riveroides*) for its green leaves. Genipa (*Genipa americana*) and *carayurú* (LG) (*Bignonia chica*) are used to prepare black and red body paint, respectively. A liana is cultivated to be used in dying fishing nets a dark colour (*vaí nyimuri*/fish-to blacken), so that they will be less visible to fish. Another liana is used to dye the fibres for string-hammocks (*punge nyimuri da*) or split canes for basketry trays. Among narcotics we find coca (*Erythrochylon coca*), tobacco (*Nicotiana tabacum*) and *Banisteriopsis sp.*

3 For a complete mythological text, see RD, 1989, 184ff; on the *kuru kuru* see p. 198, note 13.

4 Wallace, 1972, p.178.

5 *vearí* (D), *veasé* (T), *veáye* (PT), *veáa* (UA), all of them meaning 'to abduct, to seize'. This faculty of 'seizing' the intentions of a person is attributed to certain shamans. If it is related to soul-loss or soul-theft, is not clear; these concepts do not seem to exist among the Tukano. It was mentioned that, apart from not casting a shadow, *vearí mahsá* can be recognised by their habit of pressing with a finger upon their umbilicus. The meaning of this gesture remained unexplained. On *vearí mahsá*, see also, RD, 1971, Index, p. 289: *Vearí mahsá*; *idem*, 1989, p. 127.

6 Saliva is a symbolic equivalent of semen and is frequently mentioned in this sense in Tukanoan myths, spells, and ritual practices. See, for example, RD, 1989, pp. 159-160, 204, 256. The digging-stick pertains to the same imagery; it is called *púdigë*; from *púri*/to prick, stab, copulate.

7 The Linnean terms are: bitter manioc (*Manihot esculenta* Crantz), Aroids (*Xanthosoma sp.* or *Colocasia sp.*), Dioscoreas (*Dioscorea alata*), cooking plantain (*Musa paradisiaca*), sugar-cane (*Saccharum officinarum*), peppers (*Capsicum sp.*), groundnuts (*Arachis hypogea*), maize (*Zea mais*), pineapple (*Ananas comosus*), Pokeweed (*Phytolacca rivinoides*), guamo (*Inga edulis*), *cucúra* (LG) (*Pourouma cecropiaefolia*), cashew (*Anarcadium occidentale*), *cubijú* (LG), (*Solanum topiro*), coca (*Erythroxylum coca*).

8 The verb 'to select' is *behsesé* (T), *behséye* (PT), *behséa* (U), *beyéri* (D). The words for 'garden' are *vehséri* (T PT), *vehséaa*(U), *poé* (D).

9 The Indians establish various categories of trees which they group together because they are said to share characteristics of wood, ashes, i.e. of 'energies', as defined by the natives. Three categories include trees of the forest (*~nëngë*) environment, and one category refers to trees found mainly in secondary growth (*via'do*). All tree names are quoted in Desana, each name being followed by the classifier *ge*.

Category A
i *sëmége* (*Monopteryx angostifolia*), *uacu* (LG). The ashes are of a yellowish colour. For additional details on the cultural context, see Chapter V.

ii *vabepúngë*, unidentified, *loiro* (in Creole Vaupés vernacular). The Indians distinguish three varieties: 'yellow', 'dark yellow' and 'red'. The heartwood is very hard; the wood is used for canoe-making and carpentry. The ashes are of a yellow colour.

iii *poé (Pouteria ucuqui* Murça Pires et R.E. Schultes), *ucuquí* (LG). The wood is hard and the ashes are yellow.

iv *savídige*, unidentified, *miratavá* (LG). Very hard wood and yellow ashes; used for canoe-making.

v *diakégë*, unidentified, *marupá* (LG). The Desana name is derived from *diake (Caiman sclerops)*, *jacaré tinga* (LG), the bark of the tree being similar to the skin of this cayman species. The wood is white and very hard, being used for canoe-making and carpentry; the ashes are white and reddish.

vi *bohségë*, unidentified. Three varieties are distinguished by the Indians: 'yellow', 'dark yellow' and 'red'. The tall straight trunk is covered with a red bark by which the tree can be recognised at a distance. The colour of the bark is said to be like anatta (*Bixa orellana*), called *mohsá*, giving origin to the tree's name. The wood is very hard and is used in carpentry; the ashes are white and are highly valued.

vii *~mëë (Poraqueiba sericea)*, *umarí* (LG). Wood and ashes similar to the aforegoing. Edible fruits. For cultural details, see Chapter V.

viii *~karé (Pourouma cecropiaefolia)*, *caimo* (Creole Vaupés vernacular). Wood and ashes similar to above. Edible fruits.

Category B
i *barígë (Erisma japura)*, *yapurá* (LG). Two varieties are mentioned by the Indians: one pertaining to the forest (*~nëngë*), the other to the riverbanks (*dia dehkopë*). The wood is whitish and resinous, producing ashes of a dark reddish colour. Being rather soft, the wood has no practical uses. For cultural data, see Chapter V.

ii *vahsúgë (Hevea pauciflora* var. coriacea*)*. The wood is white and resinous; ashes are reddish or purple-coloured.

iii *oá*, unidentified, *vivapichuna* (LG). The ashes are yellow.

Category C
i *dohtógë (Tabebuia serratifolia)*, *palo de arco* (Spanish vernacular). The very hard heartwood is used for many artefacts; the ashes are reddish to dark red. For cultural details, see Chapter V.

ii *karé (Hymenaea courbaril)*, the *algarrobo* (SP).

Category D
i *~meré (Inga edulis)*, *guamo* (Spanish vernacular). The ashes are white and are said to be of poor quality, similar to that of cecropia species.

10 The expression the Indians use in this context is *kunyu ~poréri*, derived from *kunyúri*, a verb that implies the meanings of 'to soften', 'to let ferment', used mainly when referring to certain birds (toucan, guan, cock-of-the-rock) which keep seeds in their crop and then regurgitate them in the process of seed dispersal. The verb *~poréri* means 'to scatter the seed' and can be applied to plants or to human procreation.

11 The Smoke People are called ~*emëo mahsá*; this demands a more detailed discussion. The concept of Smoke People is related to a far-extending image of fertility. Gardens are fired during the last days of the dry season, and shortly afterwards whole families go to camp near streams and creeks where *unyú (Serrasalmus sp.)*, *varí (Cichlidae)*, *mëhá (Crenichichla sexatilis)*, *mengasiba* and *saí* fish are found in hollows between stones and roots, ready to swim to their spawning-beds with the first rains. This is an almost festive occasion on which people catch these small to medium-sized fish, smoke them, and pack them into leaf-lined baskets. These fish are referred to a ~*emëo vaí* ('smoke-fish') or, in a ritual-familiar way, as *emea mahsá vaí* ('smoke-people-fish'). The word ~*emëo* means 'smoke' in T PT U; *imika* (D). However, the image of smoke is not limited to that of clouds produced by fire, but includes the images of pollen, tobacco seed, sand, swarms of tiny fish, and similar elements, all of which form a concept of insemination. The first rains are called ~*emëo puéro* (PT), *puíro* (D); *puéro* (T PT U) is the name of a large carrying basket called *puíbu*, in Desana, and these baskets symbolise abundance, fertility, productiveness. If translated literally, ~*emëo puéro* is 'smoke-basket', but the meaning is 'abundance of fertility', which is the name of this part of the rainy season. The Desana call these fish, before they leave for their spawning-beds, *mëë vaí* or *mëë mahsá vaí*, '*umarí*-fish' or '*umarí*-people-fish', alluding to the yellow fruits of the *umarí* tree (*Poraqueiba sericea*), and their marked fertility associations. In sum, the imagery of 'Smoke People', as mentioned in discussing Tukanoan gardening practices, combines the smoke of firing the plot, with the 'cloud-like' schools of tiny fish, with the process of smoking fish over the camp fires, and the overall atmosphere of a change of seasons and of the promise of fertile soils, trees, fish, and women.

12 On Desana colour symbolism see RD, 1978d.

13 This refers to a 'kind' of *Inga* the Indians call *peyó meré*/tortoise-*Inga*, in Desana. It is characterised by very short (5 cms.) pods.

14 Reference is made to paca (*Coelogynis paca*), a medium-sized rodent of nocturnal habits. The Indians compare its pelt marks, which form rows of whitish dots, with fertility-charged *dobéri* dots.

15 Linares, 1976.

16 Unpublished myth fragment recorded on the upper Vaupés River by the author. The word *kerámepeoro*/garbage, is composed of the verbs *kerári*/to weed, and *mepeóri*/to throw away. It occurs in shamanic curing spells in the sense of obstacles which have to be eliminated before a cure can be made effective. In the present context, the garbage concept seems to refer to a similar obstruction, but the meaning remained unclear. The prohibition to urinate at certain spots or at certain times is mentioned in several mythical contexts, with the implied meaning of sexual prohibition.

17 This is the typical alarm communication of this rodent.

18 *puri* is the Desana name of a fruit called *uiki* (LG), mentioned by Henry Walter Bates (1975, pp. 267-268). Bates writes: 'The most singular of all these fruits is the *Uikí*,

which is of oblong shape, and grows apparently crosswise on the end of its stalk. When ripe, the thick green rind opens by a natural cleft across the middle, and discloses an oval seed the size of a Damascene plum, but of a vivid crimson colour. This bright hue belongs to a thin coating of pulp, which, when the seeds are mixed in a plate of stewed bananas, gives to the mess a pleasant rosy tint, and a rich creamy taste and consistence.'

19 It seems that this plant (*Phytolacca rivinoides*) apparently springs up in new clearings without being planted. In Desana it is called *nyamá pu*/deer-leaf, because deer are attracted by it.

20 Cavies (*Myoprocta*) are common household pets among the Indians. Inside a maloca, they often hide in an empty, sleeve-like manioc press that might be lying in some dark corner.

21 The concept of 'returning' the garden to the forest, so it can regenerate, is related to the concept of *gaméri*, 'to act reciprocally', following the model of exogamy. Although the land belongs to the man, the horticultural produce is the woman's, and she represents the allies. On some of these aspects, see also RD, 1990.

CHAPTER IV

1 On the concept of a 'Master of Animals' or 'Master of Game', see, above all, Zerries, 1954. On *Vaí mahsë*, see RD, 1971, Index, p. 289: *Vaí-mahsë*; idem, 1989, Index, p. 543: Master of Animals.

2 Some comparisons which might be of relevance are as follows: *ëhtá* (D)/rock crystal, transparent quartz crystal as used by shamans. In curing spells and incantations, these crystals are compared with semen. The minerals are thought to be 'excretions' of a stony matrix; *ë'tá* (T)/excretion; *ë'htayé* (D)/excretion, stone (of the soil); cf. *ë'hëri* (D)/to burn, to transform; *ë'hë'sé* (T)/to burn, to transform. To this, the following comments were made: '*Quartz makes one think of Vaí mahsë's hills*'; '*Inside the hills there is fire, there is energy*'. Cf. *ë'asé* (T)/to desire, to love; *ë"tesé* (T)/to toast (manioc flour, coca leaves, edible ants). The concept of *ë'ye* (D), *ë"sé* (T), lit. 'fat', 'lard', refers to an 'impure' seminal element, and is feared in the form of fatty or oily substances in fish, meat, forest seeds, or insect foods. This impurity or unwanted sexual arousal is thought to be highly pathogenic. Its essence is said to saturate the hills which is one of the reasons why young people should avoid them, lest they become too excited and disobey all restrictive rules.

3 The odoriferous and sexually 'dangerous' atmosphere of the hills is mentioned on many occasions. It is said, for example, that young girls, when approaching a rocky hill, will feel aroused by aromatic odours, cool airs, the water dripping from the stony surfaces. Women will put flowers in their hair when they go there, to counteract seductive odours. It is said that some people cannot recognise the odours for what they really mean; they will find them seducing and will be deceived by them and follow them '*as if it were the scent trail left by a game animal*', and then they will be 'lost'.

4 On the symbolic significance of this lizard, see Köster and Bohme, 1975.

5 For more data on this topic, see RD, 1987, p.9. On the almost vertical walls of many of *Vaí mahsë's* hill houses one can observe pictographs painted in ochre, showing game animals, fish, fruit-laden trees, and anthropomorphic figures, some of them ithyphallic and carrying adze-shaped or spear-shaped objects. So-called X-ray representations of deer are present; jaguar representations are prominent. Phosphene-like geometrical patterns, such as zigzag lines, crenellated lines, dotted lines, spirals, concentric circles, etc. are interspersed with figurative representations. The Chiribiquete hills, at the headwaters of the Apaporis, with their hundreds of spectacular pictographs, seem to have been a major sanctuary. (I owe this information to Professor Thomas van der Hammen and Carlos Castaño, members of the Colombian Chiribiquete Expedition, 1992). Although this rock art was undoubtedly executed by a hunting culture, it is impossible to attribute it to a specific linguistic cultural tradition such as the Arawak, Caribs, or Tukano.

6 The term *~ehkará* (D), translated here as 'breed', is related to the verb *ehóri* (D), *ehkasé* (T), meaning 'to give to eat'. For example, a litter of animals (dogs) or a flock of chicken will be called *~ehóra*. Metaphorically, the expression 'to give to eat', 'to feed', is used in an erotic sense and refers to copulation. In this sense, the expression *ehóri* is related to *~inyarí* (D), a verb that literally means 'to look', but metaphorically refers to the communication between two exogamous groups; *~inyarí mahsá* are the 'look at-people', the people one confronts and with whom one establishes a reciprocal relationship. In such a relationship one 'gives to eat', i.e. one exchanges women, food items, and artifacts which symbolise this reciprocity. In this context it is revealing that the expression 'to give to eat' is *~nuúye* (PT), *nuúa* (U), and that the related *nurisé* (T), *nurínye* (PT), *nuria* (U) means 'to become erect'.

7 The following list correlates the restricted game animals and fish with their food intake, and its respective *ëye* content. The quantity of *ëye* is indicated by the number of crosses (+).

GAME	FEEDS ON	ëye CONTENT
Tapir	*Monopteryx angustifolia*	+ + +
	Erisma japura	+ +
	Jessenia pataua	+ +
	Mauritia flexuosa	+ +
Collared Peccary	*Hevea pauciflora* var. *coriacea*	+ +
	Pouteria ucuquí Pires et Sch.	+ +
	toá (D), indet.	+ +
	Poraqueiba sericea	+
Deer	*Monopteryx angustifolia*	+ + +
	Pouteria ucuquí Pires et Sch.	+ +
	toá (D), indet.	+ +
Monkeys		
Lagothrix lagotricha ssp.	*Monopteryx angustifolia*	+ + +
	Jessenia pataua	+ +
Cacajao melanocephalus	*Euterpe oleracea*	+ +
Alouatta seniculus		

Callicebus torquatus
Rodents

Coelogynis paca	*Jessenia pataua*	+ +
	Euterpe oleracea	+ +
Dasyprocta agouti	*Hevea pauciflora* var. *coriacea*	+ +
Mioprocta	*Poraqueiba sericea*	+
Fish		
Brachyplatystoma spp.	*miúpu vaí* (indet.)	+ + +
Doras dorsalis	*soó* (indet.)	+ + +
	yuandoáro (indet.)	+ + +
Leporinus copelandi		+

NOTE: It is remarkable that the sloth (*Bradypus tridactylus*), called *kerá* (D) and considered inedible, is said to feed on exactly the same oily seeds as tapir.

8 The name *boráro* is said to be derived from *borá*/housepost, a common phallic symbol, related to the verb *borári*/to shine, to be resplandescent, a metaphor for sexual arousal. The river crab symbolically represents a vagina, a comparison mentioned in many narratives. The crab's name is *gamí*; cf. *kamí*, a word with the alternative meaning of vagina and open wound. See also RD, 1989, p. 357.

9 For more data on *Boráro*, see RD, 1971, pp. 86-88; *idem*, 1989, Index, p. 536; *Boráro*; see also Index, p. 343, Master of Animals. For an 'eyewitness' tale of an encounter with the *Boráro*, see RD, 1991, pp. 140-143.

10 A short hydrographic vocabulary, accompanied by some observations, is of interest. The term *yabú* (D), for a straight stretch of the river, can also mean 'handle' (axe, adze, a phallic metaphor), or can mean 'sleeve', if applied to a Western-style shirt. The corresponding verb is *yabusári*/to put a handle on something, in an erotic context, to copulate. In the three other languages a stretch of the river is called *kusá* (T PT U), cf. the words for 'to bathe' being *kusasé* (T), *kusáye* (PT), *kusáa* (U). The plural of *yabú* is *yabúri*, while *yabuári* refers to a sequence of straight stretches. River braiding is *mera dia maa*, lit. 'ancient-river-path'. A forest corridor that comes to the water's edge, is called *nengero*, lit. 'forest-thing', or *~nëngë nyoro*/forest-peninsula. Other terms are: *diá*/river, *ma*/creek, *ëhtámu*/rapids, falls; *imipáru*/sandbank, *dehkó turáro*, lit. 'water-strong', i.e. rapids; *dehkó turabéro*/water-not strong, lagoon/*dihtáru*. Relict channels and ox-bow lakes are *mera dia maa*, lit. 'ancient-river path' (*vide supra*). An entire meander loop is called *beró*/bow, *dihpá*/headwaters. A small inlet is called *tungú*, a term also used to designate the small compartments inside a maloca.

11 The overhanging vegetation is called *poóru*; cf. *pooresuri*, the smell of dehiscence, of pollen; *poóri*/to inseminate. Fish are 'inseminated' by this riverine vegetation (*dia vehká*).

12 At certain spots along the rivers of the Vaupés territory one can find petroglyphs, pecked or incised on boulders or slabs lying near rapids and falls. Some of the most numerous examples can be seen at Ipanoré, on the Macú-paraná (Uainambí), and near Yavareté. There are many petroglyphs along the Tiquié River. The Rock of Nyí,

situated at the approximate spot where the Pira-paraná crosses the equatorial line, is said to commemorate the episode when *Pamurí-mahsë*'s stick-rattle stood upright and inseminated the primeval womb of the waters. Most petroglyphs are said to be associated with mythological episodes, but it is far from certain that this type of rock art was executed by the Tukanoans; it could have been originated by previous occupants of this part of the Northwest Amazon. No systematic study has been made so far; some sources are: Koch-Grünberg, 1907; Stradelli, 1900, Wallace, 1972, Appendix.

13 The enumeration device is not limited to riverine landmarks. The custom of listing things can be observed in narratives, spells and songs; we find lengthy enumerations of sib ancestors, of sib names of 'our' and 'other' people, lists of fishes, of birds and monkeys. This manner of enumerating things is never gratuitous, but has always had a didactic character. In shamanic spells the enumeration of colour shades, odours, flavours, etc. referring to energies, have to be quoted in a precise sequence. Enumeration and listing is quite definitely part of the ritualisation of ecology.

14 In its image as an umbilical cord, the river connects the nearest maloca with the nearest subaquatic abode of *Vaí mahsë*.

CHAPTER V

1 García Barriga (1975, I, pp. 145-148) quotes bibliographical references on chemical compounds (Lapachol) found in the bark of Colombian species of Tabebuia. See also Schultes and Raffauf, 1990, pp. 107-108. For some additional references see Dominguez, 1985, p. 202, and Mabberley, 1992, p. 260.

2 In Tukano proper the tree is called *dohtogë*, as in Desana, but the Tukano also use the alternative name *buhpu*/thunder-tree, being followed in this by the Uanano who call it *behpe*. Speaking of alternative names, the Desana occasionally say *buíri beróri yukege*, lit. 'arrows-bows-tree', when referring to Tabebuia.

3 On thunder symbolism, see RD, 1989, Index, p. 546, Thunder Person. On the stick-rattle see *ibid*, Index, p. 547, Musical Instruments-Stick-rattle; on rock crystals, *ibid*, Index, p. 549; on ear- pendants, *ibid*, Index, p. 538.

4 The original Desana text reads: '~*igë dohtógë di'í díadige di'í nyidígë iri diíro ~mera diíro moápi muhúkoma.*'

5 Schultes and Raffauf, 1990, p. 247; Wallace, p. 238; Spruce, 1908, pp. 20 & 335.

6 *miúgë* are small understorey trees, the broad leaves of which grow out of the straight and pliable trunk. The leaves are called *miúpu* (D), *miópu* (T PT U), *miápu* (TAT) and are also used for wrapping manioc flour in large storage baskets. Occasionally Heliconia leaves can be used for the same purpose. The entire process of *uacú* seed processing is described in Dufour and Zarucchi (1979), who also give details on nutrient composition. The above-mentioned authors tentatively identify the *miúge* tree as *Clathrotropis macrocarpa* (Leguminosae).

7 Izikowitz (1934, pp. 212-213) gives the distribution of buzz-disks in South America and observes that it coincides with that of the bull-roarer. Small bull-roarers are found among the Desana and their neighbours (RD, 1971; see Index, p. 282).

8 For example the *paxiuba* palm (*Socratea exorrhiza*).

9 *puuri yiádigë* means literally 'leaves-long-tree'; *bohséru*, an unidentified tree.

10 See RD, 1985, pp. 36, 37, Fig. 21.

11 On the variety and dietary significance of Coleoptera larvae, see Dufour, 1987.

12 *gëra*/excrement, bodily secretion; *puririy*/to issue forth, to grow; with a slight change of pronunciation *-puríri-* the meaning changes to 'instill'.

13 Cf. *yeerí*/(D) to copulate; *yërëose*/(T) to copulate; *ohkó yërëáse*/(T) to pass water.

14 RD, 1971, pp. 58-59.

15 See, for example, RD, 1989, pp. 524-526.

16 The original Desana text reads:
 ' *~sií nyama-saa mahsë dohpáta omasërí yúhpë*
 That deer too man like smells he
 ~igë ~gamúri ~nëre. Sií ~sëmé ~sáa
 his copulating day on. That uacú too
 yuhurógeta ~aríka dahá poá sëríro.'
 equally is thus toasted smells.

17 The detailed text, in lingua geral and in Portuguese, is quoted in Barbosa Rodrigues, 1890, pp.106-107. In another mythological text of the same cycle, it is told that some boys came upon a *uacú* tree and toasted the seeds. An old man, affected by the smoke, began to salivate, a common Tukanoan metaphor for ejaculation. Henri Coudreau, a French traveller of the late nineteenth century on the Rio Negro, tells a similar myth: '*...les enfants avant fait du feu sous l'arbre appelé Uacú, il en tomba des fruits que les enfants mangèrent, malgré la défense qu'avait récemment faite Jurupari de manger de ces fruits absolument prohibés pendant le jeûne général qu'on observait alors. Indigné de cet acte de désobéissance, Juruparí tua les enfants et les mangea.*' (Coudreau, 1887, p. 185). Wright, 1981. Wright, 1981.

18 A detailed discussion of the linguistic and semantic aspects of *sëmé*/*semé* relationships would take us too far afield. To mention only a few: *~sëë* (D), *~së'e* (T) is the name of a large snail shell, which is sometimes used as a receptacle for hallucinogenic snuff; metaphorically the shell represents a vulva; *~së'e*, in Barasana, and *~sëë* in Tatuyo, is the name of a mythical progenitor, comparable to *Pamurí mahsë*; *~sëë* (T) is a term used to designate a 'bundle' of palm weevils, ants or small fish, or may refer to the male genitals, especially the scrotum; *së'tisé* (T) means 'to reach puberty'.

19 On *Erisma japura* see, among others, Domínguez, 1985, p. 201; Dufour, 1979; La

Rotta, s.a., pp. 252-253; Schultes and Raffauf, 1990, p. 467; Stafleu, 1954. In Dufour's article Plates 20 and 21 are wrongly identified; Plate 20 shows *Monopteryx angustifolia* seeds, and not *Erisma japura*, which is shown on Plate 21.

20 Quoted in Stafleu, 1954, p. 474. Tukano Indians who have smelled and tasted cheeses of European type find them utterly disgusting, and take a dim view of people who consume them without any preventive measures.

21 For composition analyses (fat, food energy, protein values) see Dufour, 1979, pp. 79-81; *idem,* 1988. The same author (p.78) mentions *batí iía/japurá*-caterpillars. These edible caterpillars are red and black, and measure about 10 cms. in length. They do not feed on the *japurá* tree and are called by that name only because their harvest coincides with that of *japurá*.

22 On *ucuquí*, see, among others: Domínguez, 1985, p. 210; La Rotta, s.a., pp. 224-225; Pires and Schultes, 1950; Schultes, 1989; Schultes and Raffauf, 1990, pp. 412-414; Wallace, 1889, pp. 243-244, 246.

23 Wallace, 1889, p. 243.

24 *puhpiá* is the singular; the plural form is *puhpí* (T PT U). The tree itself is called *puhpíge*.

25 For bilingual (Desana/English) texts of this myth, see RD, 1989, p. 248, 279-309, Marriage to a Fish-Woman. For other mythological contexts of *ucuquí*, see *ibid,* Index, p. 552, on *Ucuqui*.

26 See Galeano, 1991, pp. 88-89 (with illustration); La Rotta, s.a., pp. 224-225; RD, 1989, Index, p. 547; Palms (with illustration, Plate 12). In her botanical description of *ucuquí*, La Rotta, s.a., p. 225, adds somewhat cryptically that: '*This tree is being attributed to the grandparents of the churruco monkey; its guardian animal is tapir.*' The reference is to the Muinane Indians of the Colombian Northwest Amazon (my translation); churruco monkey is *Lagothrix lagotricha*.

27 Wallace's description is quite realistic (Wallace, 1889, p. 245).

28 The sieve is of *seadu* type; see RD, 1985, Plate 42.

29 Tukanoan fork symbolism is complex. Basically, it refers to the human crotch, the genital region. The word *seró* is also the name of the shaman's stool (see RD, 1975, Plate 15) which in one image represents a swallow-tailed kite (*Elanoides forficatus*); on which see RD, 1989, Index, p.536, Swallow-tailed Kites. For additional data, see RD, 1989, Index, p.539, Forked objects, bifurcations. *Bari sero*, lit., 'eat-fork', is the name of the Praying Mantis, a voracious insect whose reproductive habits have been observed by the Indians (see RD, 1971, p. 461). Elbow-handled adzes survive as ritual instruments. During dances related to palm fruit rituals; the men carry them over their left shoulders. The dangerous forest monster *Curupira* (LG), called *boráro* (D T PT U), is said to carry this instrument in order to kill his victims with it, especially women who stray in the forest. Both *boráro* and the adze have phallic connotations).

30 On the botany of *umarí* see Domínguez, 1985, p. 207; Lognay *et al.*, 1988; La Rotta, s.a., pp. 134-135.

31 Wallace, 1889, p. 238.

32 Schultes and Raffauf, 1990, pp. 217-218.

33 RD, 1989, 84ff, 102, 105, 205, 291. On *umarí* in mythological contexts, see RD, 1989, Index, 552: *Umarí*. Several place-names in the Vaupés territory refer to *umarí*, some of them in connection with mythological episodes, for example, the *Umarí* Rapids, upriver from Ipanoré; see RD, 1989, p.154, 211.

34 On botanical aspects, see Schultes and Raffauf, 1990, p.179, 182.

35 The Indians distinguish three classes of *vahsú* trees, according to their habitat: *~nëngë vahsú* (deep forest), *tara boa vahsú* (low open forest with caatinga patches), *diakó peri vahsú* (occasionally flooded riverbanks). Another is *mahá vahsú* (macaw *vahsú*), the small fruits of which are eaten by these birds.

36 From the Desana *ka-sëriri*/raw, referring to uncooked food or to an unmarriageable person. In Tukano proper this would be *kó-siru*, lit. 'she-appetising', with the implied meaning of 'forbidden'. In Desana, *ka-sëriava* means 'cooked', paraphrased by the Indians as *ka sëria va*, lit. 'she-smells-already', alluding to odour compatibility in mate selection.

37 See RD, 1988, p. 188.

38 *~Vahsú* is mentioned in daily conversation and, in one form or another, is always in people's minds. It is a place name (i.e. *~vahsú-nya*/ *~vahsú* creek, RD, 1989, p.76), a sib of the Desana phratry, called *~vahsúpë ~porá*/ 'sons of big *~vahsú*' (RD, 1971, p. 167, 198-199), and is referred to in myths, tales, songs and spells (i.e. RD, 1989, p. 197, 200, 202, 204, 298, 319). A garbled myth referring to a meeting between *~Vahsú* Person and Thunder Person is quoted in RD, 1971, pp. 258-259. The shaft of an elbow-handled adze is made of *~vahsúgë* wood, and in former times the large log-drums were made of the same wood. Another edible fruit, not tripartite, but often mentioned together with *~vahsú*, is *vahsá* (D), called *ëtá nyimí* (T), lit. 'excrement-black', because of its latex which turns black almost immediately after being exposed to air.

39 On *pashiúba* see, among others, Galeano, 1991, p.122, pp. 155-156; Galeano and Bernal, 1987, pp. 148-149, 185-186; La Rotta, s.a., pp. 295-296, 302-303; Schultes and Raffauf, 1990, p. 352, 358; Wallace, 1853, p. 35, 38.

40 The riverine environment of *Iriartea ventricosa* is designated as *dia dehko pee*, lit. 'river-centre part-hole'. This palm is also said to be associated with headwater regions and sandy caatinga forest, but emphatically not with dense forest. The Indians distinguish a smaller variety of *pashiúba* called *uhpú-nyo* (T PT U), with stem diameter of not more than 15 cms. and no swelling. The stems of this palm are used to make blowguns, ritual flutes of *~turirí* type (see Izikowitz, 1934, p. 338),

called *yapurutú* in LG, and fish screens.

41 Wallace, 1853, pp. 35, 37.

42 RD, 1989a. Barbosa Rodrigues, 1903.

43 Botanists occasionally mention odours but, as far as I know, have not established clearly defined odour or colour categories for palm pollen.

44 The original Tukano text reads: '*pahkë too ~anyurí nuhkuapë ~nyehsaré bihperí pahí mi bohsagë vaaya...*'

45 RD, 1979, p. 126a.

46 See for example Hugh-Jones, 1979, on the Barasana Indians.

47 For an introductory bibliography on the *Yurupari* cycle, see RD, 1989a.

48 To quote a specialist: '*...the deer rubs its hindleg over its forehead ... and the fore-head is rubbed against dry twigs... which are sniffed...*' (Müller-Schwarze, 1971, in Wilson, 1975, pp. 233-234). This use of chemical signals corresponds rather to *Odocoileus sp.*, the habitat of which is savannah country and open forest. However not only textual descriptions but also many ancient pictographs found in densely forested regions show unmistakably *Odocoileus*, and not the Brocket deer (*Mazama sp.*) of the forested regions. I have no explanation for this. The rod is called *pahí* (D), a word some informants readily associated with *buhí* (D)/son-in-law, thus suggesting that the girls asked their father for husbands.

49 *~nyohká*; the now detoxified, boiled liquid is called *manicuera* (LG) and constitutes the basic broth for a common dish to which has been added a mash of cooking plantains, or a seasoning made from fermented forest seeds such as *Erisma Japura, Monopteryx angustifolia* or *Hevea pauciflora*. The mixing process is called *~morerí*, and its symbolic significance has been explained in the discussion of the above-mentioned trees. *~Nyohká* is also a good base for beer prepared from manioc, taro, yams, peach palm or sugar-cane, the last two beers being said to be very 'strong'.

50 *Verá*, the white starch obtained from manioc, is commonly compared to human sperm. The phenomenon of precipitation, of starch consolidating at the bottom of the vessel, is called *diaári*, a word expressing fluidity (cf. *dia*/river, *díí*/blood, *díí*/latex). The same word is used to designate a person who, in a narcotic trance, perceives shapes and colours but is unable to order these perceptions into significant images; such a person is said to 'float' and cannot fix the varying impressions into coherent pictures. Starch is used in the preparation of cassava bread, manioc flour, and in *bahurí* fish broth. As another example of the process of a seminal element 'thickening' into a compact mass, *uacú* butter was mentioned; after boiling, the seeds are very bland, but two or three days later they harden into a somewhat elastic mass. The embryogenetic homology of the 'curdling' process was alluded to in several conversations.

51 The verb ~*nyohkaári*/to harden, was said to be composed of *nyuasé* (T)/to copulate, and ~*(v)aari*/to go, in the sense of 'to transform' or 'to become transformed'. In a purely physiological/psychological sense, ~*nyohkaári* can refer to a state that must be called satyriasis, cases of which were mentioned but remainded unexplained. The expression ~*nyokaári* is also used to designate a person who, under the influence of a narcotic drug, has culturally significant visions, who dances, sings, and participates fully in the process of 'transformation'. The relationship with the palm words *nyu, nyo* is suggestive and might indicate a basic sense of fertile creativeness.

CHAPTER VI

1 ~*nëgëre mahsá ohokaríri nye arika*, lit. 'forest in-people-life thing is'.

2 *kunyú* ~*poréro*/heat-incubator. This is rather inadequate translation of a complex concept. The verb ~*kunyúri* means 'to have something in one's mouth', with the implied meaning that this 'something' is being 'warmed' and 'hatched'. The immediate image associated with this expression is that of certain mouth-carrying or mouth-breeding fish, such as *unyú* (Chiclidae), *nimate, vai pora*, and ~*varí*, another Chiclidae, known in the Spanish vernacular as '*Juan Viejo*'. On the level of forest wildlife and plant growth, ~*kunyu poréro*/ 'heat-inseminating' refers to the ground level of the forest where decaying and sprouting vegetation, together with insects and fungi, form a fertile layer. The word *poréro* is the abstract form of *poréri*/to dehisce, related to *poóri*/to inseminate, and alluding to the physical and abstract heat that leads to the abrupt bursting open of a seed vessel. Another model in nature, referred to as ~*kunyúri*, consists in the habit of large game birds (Cracidae) which keep seeds in their gizzards to predigest them. These seeds are mainly unripe berries of *toá* (D) (indet.), *vivapichuna* (LG) or palm seeds (*Jessenia pataua*) (Delacour and Amadon, 1973, Chapter III). '... *guans (Pipile p. cajubi) bear these seeds in their gizzards before swallowing them. Gizzards or mouths transform the hard into soft; heat transforms the crude into the cooked.*' These examples illustrate the Indians' interest in patterns of brood protection in animal population, and in digestive processes, phenomena which lend themselves to the formulation of models and metaphors. Parental care of progeny, as it can be observed in animals, is a frequent topic of conversation. The expression ~*kunyu poréro* is also employed in descriptions of the sex act, when shamans and elders speak of the difference between mere physical satisfaction and conscious impregnation. Another example mentioned shamanic teachings; some people, it was said, followed them closely and were able to 'understand' them, while others did not grasp their meaning and ended up by slandering their elders. We must briefly consider the linguistic/semantic aspects of the *kunyúri* concept. In examining a number of words which seem to show lexical similarities, it appeared that there might also be some semantic links. For example, *unyú* is the name of a short cylindrical fish which is commonly compared with a penis. Its mythical origin is described, in brief, thus: the husband of an adulterous wife emasculated her lover and forced her to eat the boiled penis. The woman went to the port and vomited, thus 'giving birth' to the penis-shaped *unyú* fish (see RD, 1989, pp. 209 and 221-222). *Unyú* fish are described as voraciously persecuting some very small fish called *imiká*; in fact, the presence of *unyú* frightens away these tiny fish. Now *imiká* fish symbolically represent girls of prepubertal age or are asso-

ciated with a generalised concept of 'pure' fertility potential. These small fish swim in dense schools called *ímika*, a word with the meaning of 'smoke', 'cloud', a designation alluding to a glittering mass of tiny fish. The same phenomenon, however, is associated with a glittering quartz crystal used by shamans, a mineral with seminal associations and occasionally designated as 'penis of the sun' (*abé yéru*). The imagery of a voracious penis-like fish, and a seminal element represented by tiny immature fish, is not clear, but it constitutes a well-known model of animal behaviour the Indians discuss in detail. Moreover, the word *unyú*—the fish—is also the name of the avocado (*Persea gratissima*), a tree fruit which combines a very high protein content with an uterine symbolism, and with the widespread belief that a decoction of the seed is an abortifacient or contraceptive. To eat too many ripe avocados is said to unduly stimulate male sexual activities. The three words: *kunyúri, unyú, munyú*, have in common certain connotations which, although not clearly defined, do point to generative concepts. The key to this may be seen in the root *nyu* and this is likely to open an entire semantic field. In Tukano *nyuasé* means 'to copulate', a verb which refers not only to the physical act, but also covers the intricate relationships between people and palms. Palm names usually contain the element *nyu* (D) or *nyo* (T), and palms are closely related to the spheres of sexual initiation, exogamy and shamanic geography. The reader will find a further discussion of palms and palm symbolism in Chapter V.

3   Solar heat/*abé ahsiró*. Temperature categories perceived in the environment are expressed thus: hot (*ahsirí*), torrid (*turáro ahsirí*), warm (*daberó ahsirí*), as applied to dry season temperatures in the forest. Other categories are: firewood heat (*peá ahsirí*), hearthfire heat (*peáme ahsirí*), game animal heat (*vaí mera ahsirí*), fish heat (*vaí ahsiri*). These and many other temperature categories are mentioned in shamanic spells pronounced with the intention to increase and balance the vital energies of the environment. In other words, they form part of Tukanoan ecological theories.

4   The sound described as *dári dári dári nyiiiii* is said to convey the image of energy flow, the cosmic rays striking and 'injecting' their fertilising power into the forest environment. The word *dári* is the plural of *da*/ray, string, vine, duct, flow; *nyiii* is the onomatopoeic rendering of the sound made by attacking wasps (*uhtía*) or perceptible near a wasp nest. '*The dári rays are piercing, inseminating*', it was said.

The insects' song *dári dári dári yoooo* was said to express joy and satisfaction over the abundance of flowers, of pollen, of ripening fruits, especially of *sëmé* (*Monopteryx angustifolia*). It is an insistent call to maintain this state of things by obeying the rules that control overharvesting, and to find contentment in what the forest offers. The longdrawn *yooo* sound was said to refer to this concept of saturation, but the verb *yóri*, it was pointed out, had several other meanings as well. For example, *nomé yóri* means 'woman-to carry', an expression of a man's sexual satisfaction; *vai yorí* means 'to lift up a string of fish' in satisfaction over a good catch, but it can also refer to fish getting caught in a trap. The locution *doré yorí* refers to a relapse suffered by a snake-bite victim who ate some prohibited food, while *behpe yorí* refers to a person being bitten by a poisonous spider. The most frequently mentioned context was that of *mari nomé yóri*/our-women-carry, with the implicit meaning of 'the women of our satisfaction'. The insects' tune was said to contain all these meanings, all of which referred—as far as I could understand—to the rules of exogamy and the dangers of polluting deviations: snake-bite, forbidden food, poisonous spider. The monotonous *yiiiii* sound of nocturnal insects in the forest is said '*to separate day from night*'; *nyíi* is 'black', and many words referring to pain, poison, and darkness seem to contain this root. The wind in the tree tops, the creaking of branches, and the rustling of leaves make up a special sonorous code by which Tree People communicate with humans.

5   The original Desana text reads '*bahá ~nugúri dohpá arika ~nëngëre. ~nëngë yuhú yuhkegë veadígë dohpá. ~nëngë veari táribu dohpá aríro mahsá inyári dihpúru dohpá ariro.*'

6   Table I explains the use of the key verb, in the four Tukanoan languages.

TABLE I

TRIBE	VERBS	MEANINGS
Desana	*su'ari*	to enter, penetrate (forest, woman)
	suári	to pluck fruits
	súari	to thrust into (cleft)
	soári	to cling together
		(lovers, amphibian amplexus, leech)
Tukano	*suáse*	to enter, penetrate (forest, woman)
	suasé	to pluck fruits
	súari	to thrust into (cleft)
Pira-Tapuya	*suáye*	to enter, penetrate (forest, woman)
	súaye	to pluck fruits
	su'áye	to weave basketry
Uanano	*suáa*	to enter, penetrate (forest, woman)
		to pluck fruits (adding name of fruit)
	su'áa	to weave basketry
		to thrust into (cleft)
	*nyuá**	to copulate

* a shift from 'ny' to 's' can be observed with some frequency.

7   In Tukano proper, this reads: *tee ~nëhkëri përe na yáiva mahsá kahtiró ~amásoma.* The same locution was repeated in Desana: *iri ~nëngëri gere irá yéea mahsa ohokariróre.*

8   To hunt is *vai ~mëra gametarári*, lit. 'game animals-to make love to'; from *gamé*/mutually, *tarári*/to pet, to caress, to copulate. For details on Tukanoan hunting practices, see RD, 1968, 218ff. As to the control of body odours, so important in hunting, prudish missionaries have done great damage by obliging the Indians to wear European-style clothing which, if unwashed and not taken proper care of, will scare away most vertebrates.

9   Before an exchange ceremony between two exogamous phratries, or on many other ritual occasions, men and women, or pairs of women, mutually paint their bodies, especially their faces, with various design motifs executed with red or blackish pigments of plant origin. This body paint constitutes a visual code, well-known to all,

indicating male potency and female receptivity. The act of mutual painting is called *~nererí*/to lick, and couples that paint each other are referred to as *~neréri mahsá*/licking people. '*They lick each other as if they were tapir at a saltlick, or like spawning fish.*' Preening and sniffing behaviour, and initial contacts between exogamous units, are very similar. It might be added here that kissing by mouth, as practised by 'civilised' people, is thought by the Indians to be utterly disgusting.

CHAPTER VII

1   RD, 1989, pp.155-160, 168-178.

2   Spruce, 1908.

3   Schultes, 1957; 1988; Schultes and Hoffman, 1979; Schultes and Raffauf, 1992.

4   The corresponding words for cutis in other languages are: *kahséro* (T PT U), *kahéro* (BA, BS).

5   Inside the uterus, the embryo is said to be enveloped by a covering called *suriró* (D), *sutíro* (T PT U), a physical 'clothing'; pronounced *sutiró* (T), this refers to a protective 'shell', a 'hindrance' or 'obstacle' to exterior influences.

6   For a variety of descriptions of *Banisteriopsis* hallucinations, see RD, 1975ff.

7   The original Desana text reads: *gahpi soro ~mahsá dihpuru dohpá ~arí yoró. Gahpí soro gahpí ~mahsó ~porá këri suriró dohpá arí yoró. Gahpí soró ~mahsá ~irá ~pamúra dihtáru dohpá ~arí yoró. Gahpí soró ~ëmëko ëmë ~sii dohpá ~arí yoro. ~mahsá ii ~nyére peé ~nyéa turá ~méra ~irá vahá ~gëra dohpá ~inyakomá iri soró gahpí soró ree.* The shaman added that in daily life people only *talked* about their traditions, but that during their trance states they *saw* them truthfully before them (*gahpí góra ~inyaró*; lit.' 'yajé-truth-vision'). These visions were 'truly the truth' (*~arírota aríri ~gora*).

8   On phosphenes see, among others, the bibliography of RD, 1978.

9   See RD, 1978.

10 The Tukano proper text reads: *kahpí ~siríge ~mari ya viire inyaa mari ya vehesérire ~inyáa ~mari ya nëhkërire ~inyaa ~na vaíre ~inyaa vaí beherãre ~inyaa.*

11 The original Tukano text is: *~kahpí ~mera ~marí ~inyá ~ará vaí vehkerãre náa ya viserire na yehséa náa ~nyamáa na nohpéa nípetiro ~inyá.*

12 The Tukano text reads: *teé kahpí ~sirigeta ~mari kahtíge ba'pátisere ~marí ~inyáa ~marí ~nisére.* The word *kahtisé*/life, was said to be used here in an abstract sense, although imbued with *marári*, *noméri*, and *dobéri* energies. *Nise*, on the other hand, refers to biological existence. The expression *ba'pátisere*, lit. 'accompanying-that', is derived from *ba'pátise*/to accompany, couple with; cf. *ba'pá*/a couple, pair. I have

translated this as concomitance, rather in the theological sense.

13 The root or roots of ~*singá* and their meanings are difficult to trace, but the following suggestions might provide some insights. *Singaári* (D) means 'to crawl', with the implied meaning of the latent presence of an energy (poisonous snake, mythical anaconda, hallucinogenic vine, etc.).

Gahsirú singáari (D), lit. 'canoe-wake', refers to the track left on the surface of the water by a canoe, a sign of some vital energy which remains unexplained. *Simahári* (D)/to crawl and move up (i.e. canoe entering a small creek; a man who rises from his seat and now moves with a certain purpose [i.e. to eat, to rest in his hammock]), cf. *mahári*/to enter a space. ~*Síose* (T)/to stretch out one's hand with a purpose (i.e. to greet, to receive, to threaten); ~*siosé* (T)/to give to drink (i.e. to a visitor, an infant; metaphorically referring to sexual satisfaction); to rid of fibres (i.e. to scrape a green leaf (Bromeliacea) until the yellow or white fibres appear); to uncover something, to bring to light; yellow fibres, which metaphorically represent semen. ~*Sioóse* (T)/to enlighten, to clarify in an authoritative way, to teach, to satisfy intellectually. The expression ~*mëë* ~*sió* (T) means 'my wife's sister'. Let me summarise at this point; we can observe the following underlying concepts: an intentional move toward sensorial satisfaction, an attitude of interpersonal contact, the production of a seminal matter, a state of satisfaction. The objective would appear to be exogamy. The preceding words are mainly taken from Tukano proper, and some Desana comparisons may be of interest in this connection:

Siári (D)/to lie down (alone or with a woman); ~*siarí* (D)/to give birth; *siarí* (D)/to catch up with someone (on the trail, on the river); to fit well (i.e. European-type clothes). The expression *mëë siagó* means 'my-fit she', the particle *go* indicating a female person; it means that she is, culturally, the appropriate wife. This should not be confused with *mëë sëagó*/my desire-she, cf. *sëári*/to desire, to lust after; cf. *sëriri*/fertility. It would seem, then, that the element *si* has a more abstract meaning.

14 The *puíbu* basket and its ethnographic bibliography are discussed in RD, 1985, pp. 8-9, 24; for illustrations, see Plates 3 and 4. For the interested reader, a summary discussion of the *mëhpëri* basket follows. It is made from long splints of *mëhpërigë* wood, a tall forest tree called *turí* in LG. Again, the baskets are not made on the Vaupés or Pira-paraná Rivers, but, in this case, come from the Tiquié River where they are manufactured by the Tuyúka, a Tukanoan tribe closely related to the Desana. They are used like *puíbu* baskets, but since their weaving technique is less dense, they are also used for washing and soaking tubers or palm fruits in the creek. Their symbolic importance can be understood only by analysing their linguistic aspects within certain semantic fields. The name *mëhpëri* is related to the verb *muhpurí*, which refers to the smell of roasting meat. This, in itself, is a 'polluting' smell, being said to be sexually arousing. The act of roasting is associated with the crackling sound of hot fat (*ëye* D, *ë'sé*, T), an element which is associated with sperm, the rock crystal and other seminal elements. When fat begins to crackle, people will say: '*It's going to thunder!*' (*buhpú paári*). Moreover, the related verb ~*mëhteári* means 'to blink', 'to sputter sparks', and is also used to describe a distant flash of lightning. If we add to this the verb *muhturí* (the *e/u* shift is very frequent), meaning 'to make spills', i.e., thin slips of the resinous wood of a *mëhpërigë* tree, used as torches on

nightly fishing or ant-collecting excursions, we begin to recognise the elements of a conceptual field which includes the following aspects: an eroticizing odour, hot fat, a thunderclap (associated with the image of ejaculation), a flash of lightning (lightning produces sperm-like quartz crystals), a slow-burning resinous wood used to 'start a fire' and 'catch fish', i.e. women. *Mëhpëri* baskets are said to exude a strong female smell (*nomé seríri*), very similar to that of *puíbu* baskets. The overall symbolism of the *mëhpëri* basket, as seen from the point of view of the Tukanoans of the Pira-paraná, refers to the seductive fecundity of Tuyuka women. On *mëhpëri* baskets, see RD, 1985, p. 9; illustrations on Plates 5-7. *Teremú* baskets are woven in an openwork lattice technique of three standards forming a pattern of hexagons. Such a grid of hexagons, as seen in honeycombs, rock crystals, or a typical drug-induced phosphene, is called *tere*. This association opens a wide field of analogies. For descriptions and illustrations see RD, 1985, p. 9, Figs, 6-7, Plates 9-10.

15 Of such a knowledgeable person it would be said: '*He is that basket!*' (*~igë ~arimi iri puíbu*).

16 The expression 'to get lost in the forest': *~nëngë vaa dédiri*, does not refer to 'losing one's way' in a spatial sense, but to a psychological state of dissociation.

17 *suriró*/garment. This word has various meanings, depending upon context: a) a garment of daily use, of native or 'European' style; b) a ritual mask made of barkcloth, used by the Cubeo Indians, a Tukanoised Arawakan tribe living on the northern affluents of the middle course of the Vaupés River; c) an investiture, spiritual attribute or ritual state; d) a placenta; e) a psychological dimension of transformation, dissociation, eventually, death. To this we should add the following: a man walking in the forest will, at most, carry a small leather bag containing a few herbs, matches, some cartridges, but certainly not a complete 'garment'. What is suggested here is that the stranger's bag contained a psychotropic drug.

18 Black (melanistic) jaguars (*Panthera onca*), called *yee nyígë* (D), are scarce but are known to exist, and are mentioned in myths and tales. The Indians associate them with rivermouth areas (*dia píro*) and say that they usually migrate to the headwaters (*dihpá*) during the dry season.

19 A thicket in the forest is described with the words *viri-dibu*, lit. 'cutting-thing'; from *viríri*/to cut, a reference to thorny, sharp-edged vines. It is remarkable that in Tukanoan oral literature people almost never hide in caves, but in trees, between buttress-roots, or in thickets, in other words, in vegetation.

20 Jaguar transformation is called *yeeá suri ~mengahári*, lit. 'jaguars-garment'.

APPENDIX NOTES

1   For a short but precise summary, see Descola.

2   The tree frog is probably *Osteocaphalus taurinus* Steindachner; the other species remains unidentified.

3 *piúri*; the following etymology of the word was suggested by the Indians. The verb is related to *viúri*, meaning 'to bring (to light)', 'to uncover something that has gone unnoticed', 'to come to appreciate something'. The image is that no attention is being paid to frogs during the dry season, but when the rains begin they are 'brought to light', and people make contact with them by eating them. It is a meeting of dry season and rainy season, the dry and the wet, men and women.

4 Mortars are of cylindrical shape, short, about 60 cms. high, by 25 cms. in diameter. They are made of *dohtógë* wood *(Tabebuia serratifolia)*. The name of the mortar is *pamúru*, relating to *pamurí*/to mix, to procreate; cf. *Pamurí mahsë*. The process of pounding is called *deári* (D), lit. 'to pulverise'; *dohkesé* (T), *dohkéye* (PT), *dohkea* (U), cf. *dohtó*/bundle, package, container.

5 The leaves are probably from *Phenakospermum guayanense* (see Dufour, 1979; Schultes and Raffauf, 1990, p. 321).

6 On *teremú* baskets see RD, 1985, p. 9, Plates 9-10.

7 Spix and Martius, 1831, pp. 1208, 1218. '*Ueberhaupt habe ich den Yupurá während der Monate December bis Februar an Vögeln jeder Art getroffen* (Footnote) *Die dann zu Tausenden getodteten Vogel werden im Moquem getrocknet, und, aufeinandergepresst, zwischen den Blattscheiden der Pacova Sororoca, einer baumartigen Musacea (Urania amazonica, M.) oder gewiser Palmen im Giebel der Hutte aufbewahrt*'. This refers to the *Uainumá* Indians, whose selfname was *Inabissána*, and who were enemies of the *Umaua* and *Miraña*. The name *Uainuma* sounds Tukano and could be *vaí nomé*, lit. fish-woman, the name of a large eagle that is frequent in the riverine forest from which it suddenly dives down to catch small fish that come to the surface or are near a sandbank. The *Umaua* could be the *omá mahsá* or Frog People, as the Tukanoans call a subgroup of the Karihona. The name *sióroa*, with which the Tukanoans designate the migratory birds that visit the Jirijirimo tunnels, is interesting because *sio* (T PT U) means husband's sister, a term of reference one finds occasionally associated with migratory animals. At present, the Indians living near the Jirijirimo Falls are *Kabiyarí*, an Arawak-speaking group.

8 The following fish are smoked, to be preserved for consumption mainly during the long rainy season: *boréka* (D), *botea* (T PT U), *aracú* (LG) (*Leporinus copelandi*), whole or powdered; *vaipe doróge* (D), *pirahiba* (LG) (*Brachyplatystoma sp.*), whole segments or powdered; *yehéoge* (T), *payára* (LG) (*Chichla ocellaris*); powdered; *uhú* (D T PT U), *pacú* (LG) (*Dorsa dorsalis*), whole or powdered; *unyú* (D), *piranha* (LG) (*Serrasalmus*), whole or powdered; *doé* (D T), *tarira* (LG) (*Erythrinus tarieira*), powdered; *so'o* (T), *peixe espada* (PG), powdered; *~varí* (D), Don Juan (SP) (*Cichlidae*), whole; *bueke* (T), eel (*Synbranchus sp.*), whole, rolled in spirals; *behkavii* (T), unidentified, whole; *~mengá sibá* (D), unident., in creeks, whole; *imiká* (D), unident., in creeks, whole or powdered.

9 Important studies are by Dufour (1987; 1988) who worked among the Tatuyo of the upper Papurí River. Dufour gives quantitative data, tables of nutritional values, and a useful bibliography.

10 The Indians prefer to fell *Mauritia flexuosa, Jessenia pataua* and *Orbignya sp.*, saying that because the larvae thrive on the abundant pith of these palms, they grow fatter and have a better flavour.

11 See, for example, RD, 1989, p. 103.

12 Cf. *mimí*/humming-bird, in which the Indians see a notoriously phallic image.

13 Cf. *pikkoë* (T), *pihkóno* (PT), *pinchón* (U); *pingusée* (D)/Swallow/tailed kite (*Elanoides forficatus*), from *see* (D)/forked, *seéri*/to be pregnant. Kite imagery is very elaborate and includes the bird's spectacular nuptial flight patterns as an image of human exogamy (see RD, 1988, p. 80).

14 On ant exchange between exogamic phratries, see RD., 1989, p. 505.

BIBLIOGRAPHY

Acero D., L.E. 1979 *Principales Plantas útiles de la Amazonía Colombiana*. Proyecto Radargramétrico del Amazonas, Bogotá.

Aguiar Falcão, Martha de, y Eduardo Lleras 1980 'Aspectos fenológicos, ecológicos e de productividade do umari (*Poraqueiba sericea* Tulasne), *Acta Amazónica*, Vol. 10, No. 3, pp. 445-462, Manaus.

Alemán Mosquero, Eduardo, Marion M. Swift de Miller, Leah B. Ellis de Walter. 1986 *Si puede leer en castellano puede leer en desano!* Summer Institute of Linguistics, Lomalinda, Colombia.

Amorim, Antonio Brandão de 1928 'Lendas em Nhenengatú e em Portuguez', *Revista do Instituto Histórico e Geographico Brasileiro,* tomo 100, Vol. 154, pp. 3-475, Rio de Janeiro.

Ardila, Olga 1992 'Las lenguas Tucano-Orientales: Elementos para un estudio comparativo', *Lenguas Aborígenes de Colombia: Memorias: II Congreso del Centro Colombiano de Estudios de Lenguas Aborígenes*, Universidad de los Andes, Bogotá.

Århem, Kaj 1981 *Makuna Social Organisation: A Study in Descent, Alliance and the Formation of Corporate Groups in the North Western Amazon,* Uppsala Studies in Cultural Anthropology, 4, Almquist and Wiksell International, Stockholm.

Århem, Kaj 1987 'Wives for Sisters: The Management of Marriage Exchange in Northwest Amazonia', in: Skar, Harald O, and Frank Salomon (editors), *Natives and Neighbors in South America: Anthropological Essays*, pp. 130-177, Etnologiska Studier 38, Goteborgs Etnografiska Museum, Goteborg.

Århem, Kaj 1990 'Ecosofía Makuna', in: Corréa, François (editor) *La Selva Humanizada*, pp. 105-122, Instituto Colombiano de Antropología, Bogotá.

Bailey, Robert C., Genevieve Head, Mark Jenike, Bruce Owen, Robert Rechtman, and Elzbieta Zechenter 1989 'Hunting and Gathering in Tropical Rain Forest: Is it possible?' *American Anthropologist*, Vol. 91, No. 1, pp. 59-81.

Barbosa Rodrigues, João 1890 *Poranduba amazonense ou Kochiyma-Uara due 1872-1887*. Buenos Aires.

Barbosa Rodrigues, João 1903 *Les noces des palmiers. Remarques préliminaires sur la fécondation*, Imprimerie Ad. Mertens, Brussels.

Barnes, Janet D., Alva L. Wheeler, and Margaret A. Powel Wheeler 1992 *Estudios comparativos: Proto Tucano*. Editorial Alberto Lleras Camargo, Bogotá.

Bates, Henry Walter 1975 *The Naturalist on the River Amazons*, fourth edition, Dover Publications, New York.

Beckerman, Stephen 1979 'The Abundance of Protein in Amazonas: A Reply to Gross', *American Anthropologist*, Vol.81, pp. 533-560.

Beckerman, Stephen 1983 'Does the Swidden Ape the Jungle?' *Human Ecology*, Vol. 11, No. 1, pp. 1-12.

Bernal, Rodrigo G. 1992 'Colombian Palm Products', in Plotkin, Mark, and Lisa Famolare (editors) *Sustainable Harvest and Marketing of Rain Forest Products*, pp. 158-172, Island Press, Covelo, California.

Betancur, Alberto 1985 *Región del Papurí y Paca: su tierra y su gente*. Coordinación de Educación Nacional, Oficina de Supervisión Escolar (mimeographed), Mitú, Vaupés.

Bidout, Patrice 1985 'Le chemin du soleil: Mythologie de la création des Indiens Tatuyo du Pira-Paraná, Amazonie Colombienne', *L'Homme*, Vol. 93, pp. 83-103, Paris.

Bidout, Patrice 1989 'Du mythe a la légende: La naissance de la parole dans le village des Bianacas', *Journal de la Société des Américanistes*, Vol. LXXV, pp.63-90, Paris.

Bodley, John H., and Foley C. Benson 1979 'Cultural Ecology of Amazonian Palms', *Report of Investigations*, No. 56, Laboratory of Anthropology, Washington State University, Pullman.

Bolens, Jacqueline 1967 'Mythe de Jurupari-Introduction à une analyse', *L'Homme*, Vol. VII, No. 1, pp.50-66, Paris.

Brüzzi Alves da Silva, Alcionilio 1962 *A civilisação indigena do Uaupés*. São Paulo.

Brüzzi Alves da Silva, Alcionilio 1966 *Observações gramaticais da lingua daxseyé ou Tukano*. Centro e Pesquisas de Iauretê (Amazonas).

Buchillet, Dominique 1988 'Interpretação da doença e simbolismo ecológico entre os índios Desana', *Boletim do Museu Paraense Emilio Goeldi, nova serie, Ser. Antropol.* 4 (1), pp. 27-42, Belém.

Buchillet, Dominique 1991 'Pari Cachoeira: o laboratório Tukano do projto Calha Norte', in Ricardo, Carlos A. (editor): *Povos Indígenas no Brazil*, Centro Ecoménico de Documentação e Informação, Rio de Janeiro, pp. 107-115.

Carneiro, Robert L. 1961 'Slash-and-burn Cultivation among the Kuikuru and its Implications for Cultural Development in the Amazon Basin', in: Wilbert, Johannes (editor), *The Evolution of Horticultural Systems in Native South America: Causes and Consequences—A Symposium*, pp. 47-67, Sociedad de Ciencias Naturales La Salle, Caracas.

Carneiro, Robert L. 1970 'The Transition from Hunting to Horticulture in the Amazon Basin', *Proceedings, VIIIth International Congress of Anthropological and Ethnological Sciences, 1968, Tokyo and Kyoto,* Vol. III, Ethnology and Archaeology, pp.344-348, Science Council of Japan, Tokyo.

Cerqueira Leite Zarur, George 1979 'Ecological Need and Cultural Choice in Central Brazil', *Current Anthropology*, Vol. 20, No. 3, pp. 249-253.

Chagnon, Napoleon, and R. Hames 1980 'La "Hipótesis Protéica" y la adaptación indígena en la cuenca Amazonas: Una revisión crítica de los datos y de la teoría', *Interciencia*, Vol. 5, pp. 346-358, Caracas.

Chernela, Janet N. 1989 'Managing Rivers of Hunger: The Tukano of Brazil', in Posey, D.A., and W., Balée (editors): *Resource Management in Amazonia: Indigenous and Folk Strategies*, pp. 238-247, The New York Botanical Garden, New York.

Chernela, Janet M. 1992 *The Wanano Indians of the Brazilian Amazon: A Sense of Space*, University of Texas Press, Austin.

Cochran, Doris M. 1972 *Living Amphibians of the World*, Doubleday & Company, Inc., Garden City, New York.

Corréa, François (editor) 1990 *La Selva Humanizada: Ecología alternativa en el trópico húmedo colombiano*, Instituto Colombiano de Antropología, Bogotá.

Contreras Vásquez, Julián 1991 *Diccionario de regionalismos y terminología del Vaupés: El Vaupés en su mitología*. Instituto Colombiano de Cultura, Editorial FUDESCO, Armenia.

Delacour, Jean, and Dean Amadon 1973 *Curassows and Related Birds*. American Museum of Natural History, New York.

Descola, Philippe 1986 *La nature domestique: symbolisme et praxis dans l'écologie des Achuar*, Editions de la Maison des Sciences de l'Homme, Paris.

Descola, Philippe 'Le déterminisme famélique', in Dominguez, Camilo, A. 1985 *Amazonia Colombiana: Visión General*, Biblioteca Banco Popular, Textos Universitarios, Bogotá.

Domínguez, Camilo, and Augusto Gómez 1990 *La economía extractiva en la Amazonía colombiana 1850-1930*, Corporación Colombiana para la Amazonia Araracuara, TROPENBOS, Bogotá.

Dufour, Darna L. 1983 'Nutrition in the Northwest Amazon Household Dietary Intake and Time-Energy Expenditure', in Hames, Raymond B., and William T. Vickers (editors), *Adaptive Responses of Native Amazonians*, pp. 329-355, Academic Press, New York.

Dufour, Darna L. 1987 'Insects as Food: A Case Study from the Northwest Amazon', *American Anthropologist*, Vol. 89, No. 2, pp. 383-397.

Dufour, Darna F. 1988 'The Composition of Some Foods Used in Northwest Amazonia', *Interciencia*, Vol. 13, pp. 83-86, Caracas.

Dufour, Darna L. 1990 'Uso de la selva tropical por los indígenas Tukano del Vaupés', in Corréa, François (editor) *La Selva Humanizada: Ecología alternativa en el trópico húmedo colombiano*, Instituto Colombiano de Antropología, Bogotá.

Dufour, Darna L., and James L. Zarucchi 1979 '*Monopteryx Angustifolia* and *Erisma Japura*: Their Use by Indigenous Peoples in Northwestern Amazon', *Botanical Museum Leaflets*, Vol. 27, No. 3-4, pp. 69-91, Harvard University, Cambridge, Mass.

Eichmeier, Joseph, and Oscar Hofer 1974 *Endogene Bildmuster*, Urban & Schwarzenberg, Munich/Berlin/Vienna.

Emmons, L. 1990 *A Field Guide of Neotropical Rain Forest Mammals*, University of Chicago Press, Chicago.

Eu, Geoffrey (editor) 1992 *Amazon Wildlife*, APA Publications, Singapore.

Ferguson, R. Brian 1989 'Game Wars? Ecology and Conflict in Amazonia', *Journal of Anthropological Research*, Vol. 45, No. 2, pp. 179-206, University of New Mexico, Albuquerque.

Flowers, Nancy M., Daniel R. Gross, Madeline Ritter, Dennis W. Werner 1982 'Variation in Swidden Practices in Four Central Brazilian Indian Societies', *Human Ecology*, Vol. 10 No. 2,, pp. 203-217.

Fulop, Marcos 1954 'Aspectos de la cultura Tukana: Mitología, Parte I', *Revista Colombiana de Antropología*, Vol. III, pp. 335-373, Bogotá.

Fulop, Marcos 1956 'Aspectos de la cultura Tukana: Cosmogonía', *Revista Colombiana de Antropología*, Vol. V, pp. 121-164, Bogotá.

Galeano, Gloria 1991 *Las palmas de la región de Araracuara*, Estudios de la Amazonía Colombiana, Vol. I, TROPENBOS, Bogotá.

Galeano, Gloria, and Rodrigo Bernal 1987 *Palmas del Departamento de Antioquia: Región Oriental*. Universidad Nacional de Colombia, Bogotá.

Galvão, Eduardo. 1959 'Aculturação indigena no Rio Negro', *Boletim do Museu Paraense Emilio Goeldi*, No. 7, nova serie, Belém.

Gallo M., Carlos I. 1972 *Diccionario Tucano-Castellano*, Prefectura Apostólica de Mitú, Multigráficas, Medellín.

García Barriga, Hernando 1975 *Flora medicinal de Colombia: Botánica médica*, 2 vol., Universidad Nacional de Colombia, Instituto de Ciencias, Bogotá.

Gawthorne, Linda Anne (editor) 1976 *Estudios Tucanos IV*, Summer Institute of Linguistics, Lomalinda, Colombia.

Giacone, Antonio 1949 *Os Tucanos e outras tribus do Rio Uaupés afluente do Negro-Amazonas. Notas etnográficas e folcloricas de un missionario salesiano*, São Paulo.

Giacone, Antonio 1967 *Pequeña gramática e diccionário da lingua Kótira ou Uanano*, Imprenta Universitaria, Belém.

Giacone, Antonio 1976 *Trentacinque anni fra le tribu del Rio Uaupés (Amazzonia-Brasile)*, Centro Studi di Storia delle Missioni Salesiane, Roma.

Goehner, Marie, Birdie West, and William R. Merrifield 1990 'Tucano (Tucanoan) Kinship Terminology', *Journal of Contemporary Ethnography*, Vol. 19, No. 1, pp. 55-69, Sage Publications.

Goldman, Irving 1963 *The Cubeo: Indians of the Northwest Amazon*, Illinois Studies in Anthropology 2, Urbana.

Golley, Frank B., and Ernesto Medina (editors) 1975 *Tropical Ecological Systems: Trends in Terrestrial and Acquatic Research*, Springer Verlag, Berlin-Heidelberg-New York.

Gomez, Elsa 1982 *De la forme et du sens de la classification nominale en Tatuyo (Langue Tukano Orientale d'Amazonie colombienne)*, doctoral dissertation, Université de Paris IV.

Gómez-Imbert, Elsa 'Problemas en torno a la comparación de las lenguas Tukano-Orientales', in: *Estado actual de la clasificación de las lenguas indígenas colombianas: Familia Lingüística Tukano*, s.1.

Gómez-Imbert, Elsa 1991 'Force des langues vernaculaires en situation d'exogamie linguistique: le cas du Vaupés colombien, Nord-Ouest amazonien', *Cahiers des Sciences Humaines*, Vol. 27, No. 3-4, pp. 535-559.

Gómez-Imbert, Elsa, and Dominique Buchillet 1986 'Propuesta para una grafía Tukano normalizada', *Amerindia*, No. 11, supplement 3, pp. 1-30, University of British Columbia, Vancouver.

Gross, Daniel 1975 'Protein Capture and Cultural Development in the Amazon Basin', American Anthropologist, Vol. 77, pp. 526-549.

Guerrero M., Mario de J. 1990 *Quejti cuori turi 2: Libro de cuentos en tucano*, Summer Institute of Linguistics, Acaricuara, Vaupés.

Guille-Escuret, Georges 1989 *Les sociétés et leurs natures*, Armand Colin, Paris.

Hames, Raymond B., and William T. Vickers 1982 'Optimal diet breath theory as a model to explain variation in Amazonian hunting', *American Ethnologist*, Vol. 9, No. 2, pp. 358-378.

Hames, Raymond B., and William T. Vickers (editors) 1983 *Adaptive Responses of Native Amazonians*, Academic Press, New York.

Hamlett, William C. (editor) 1992 *Reproductive Biology of South American Vertebrates*, Springer Verlag, New York.

Henderson, Andrew 1985 'Pollination of *Socratea exorrhiza* and *Iriartea ventricosa,*' *Principes*, Vol. 29, No. 2, pp. 64-71.

Hildebrand, Patricio von 1975 'Observaciones preliminares sobre utilización de tierras y fauna por los indígenas del río Mirití-paraná', *Revista Colombiana de Antropología*, Vol. XVIII, pp. 183-291, Bogotá.

Howes, David (editor) 1991 *The Varieties of Sensory Experience: A Sourcebook in the Anthropology of the Senses*, University of Toronto Press, Toronto-Buffalo-London.

Hugh-Jones, Christine 1978 'Food for Thought: Patterns of Production and

Consumption in Pira-paraná Society', in La Fontaine, editor, (J.S.) *Sex and Age as Principles of Social Differenciation* pp. 41-66, Academic Press, New York.

Hugh-Jones, Christine 1979 *From the Milk River: Spatial and Temporal Processes in Northwest Amazonia*, Cambridge University Press, Cambridge.

Hugh-Jones, Stephen 1979 *The Palm and The Pleiades: Initiation and Cosmology in Northwest Amazonia*, Cambridge University Press, Cambridge.

Ihering, Rodolpho von 1968 *Diccionário dos animais do Brasil*, Editora Universidade de Brasilia, São Paulo.

Izikowitz, Karl Gustav 1935 *Musical and Other Sound Instruments of the South American Indians*, Goteborgs Kungl. Vetenskaps-och Vitterhets Samhalles Handlingar, Femte Foljden, Ser. A, Band 5, No.1, Goteborg.

Jackson, Hean J. 1983 *The Fish People: Linguistic Exogamy and Tukanoan Identity in Northwest Amazonia*, Cambridge Studies in Social Anthropology 39, Cambridge University Press, Cambridge.

Jackson, Jean E. 1984 'Vaupés marriage practices', in Kensinger, Kenneth M. (editor) *Marriage Practices in Lowland South America*, pp. 156-179, Illinois Studies in Anthropology No. 14, University of Illinois Press, Urbana and Chicago.

Jackson, Jean E. 1988 'Gender relations in the Central Northwest Amazon', *Antropologica*, Vol. 70, pp. 17-38, Caracas.

Janzen, Daniel H. 1975 *Ecology of Plants in the Tropics*, The Institute of Biology's Studies in Biology No. 58, Edward Arnold.

Johnson, Allen 1982 'Reductionism in Cultural Ecology: The Amazon Case', *Current Anthropology*, Vol. 23, No. 4, pp.413-427.

Junk, Wolfgang J., and Karin Furch 1985 'The Physical and Chemical Properties of Amazonian Waters and their Relationship with Biota', in Prance, Ghillean T., and Thomas E. Lovejoy (editors), *Amazonia*, pp.3-17, Pergamon Press, Oxford.

Kahn, Francis (editor) 1992 *Palms in Tropical Forests*, Simposio Internacional, Iquitos, 18-24 de Septiembre de 1991, *Bulletin de l'Institut Français d'Etudes Andines*, tome 21, No. 2, Lima.

Kaye, Jonathan 1970 *The Desana Verb: Problems in Semantics, Syntax and Phonology*, Doctoral dissertation, Columbia University, University Microfilms, Ann Arbor.

Kaye, Jonathan 1971 'Nasal Harmony in Desana', *Linguistic Inquiry*, Vol. 2, No. 1, pp. 37-56.

Kensinger, Kenneth M. (editor) 1984 *Marriage Practices in Lowland South America*, Illinois Studies in Anthropology, No. 14, University of Illinois Press, Urbana.

Kensinger, Kenneth M. 1984 *Sex Ideologies in Lowland South America*, Working Papers on South American Indians, No. 5, Bennington College, Benington, Vermont.

Koch-Grünberg, Theodor 1907 *Sudamerikanische Felszeichnungen*, Verlag Ernst Wasmuth, Berlin.

Koch-Grünberg, Theodor 1909 *Zwei Jahre unter den Indianern: Reisen in Nordwest-Brasilien 1903/1905*, Verlag Ernst Wasmuth, Berlin.

Koch-Grünberg, Theodor 1913/16 'Betoya-Sprachen Nordwestbrasiliens und der angrenzenden Gebiete', *Anthropos*, Vol. VIII (1913), pp. 944-976; Vol. IX (1914), pp. 151-195, 569-589, 812-832; Vol. X-XI (1915-1916), pp. 114-158, 421-449, St. Gabriel-Modling.

Koch-Grünberg, Theodor 1922 'Die Volkergrupierung zwischen Rio Branco, Orinoco, Rio Negro and Yapurá', in (Walter Lehmann, editor): *Festschrift Eduard Seler*, pp.205-266, Verlag Strecker & Schroder, Stuttgart.

Köster, Friedemann, and Wolfgang Bohme 1975 'Die mythologische Bedeutung des Baum-Leguans *Plica plica* bei den Tucano-Indianern aus ethno-zoologischer Sicht', *Salamandra*, Vol. II. No. 2, pp. 99-104, Frankfurt am Main.

Kricher, John C. 1989 *A Neotropical Companion: An Introduction to the Animals, Plants, and Ecosystems of the New World Tropics*, Princeton University Press, Princeton.

La Rotta, Constanza, *et. al* s.a. *Especies utilizadas por la comunidad Miraña: Estudio Etnobotánico*, World Wildlife Fund, FEN, Editorial Presencia, Bogotá

Lévi-Strauss, Claude 1964 *Le crue et le cuit*, Plon, Paris.

Linares, Olga F. 1976 ' "Garden Hunting" in the American Tropics', *Human Ecology*, Vol. 4, No. 4, pp. 331-349.

Lizot, Jacques 1979 'On Food Taboos and Amazon Cultural Ecology', *Current Anthropology*, Vol. 20, No. 1, pp. 150-155.

Lognay, G., E. Trevejo, M. Marlier, S. Flores-Paitan, M. Mary-Laura et M. Severin 1988 'Etude de nouvelles ressources en matières grasses de l' Amazonie péruvienne. Investigation sur l'huile de umari (*Poraqueiba sericea* TUL.)', *Bull. Rech. Agron.* Vol. 23, No. 3, pp. 271-282, Gembloux, Belgium.

Mabberley, D.J. 1992 *Tropical Rain Forest Ecolology*, 2nd edition, Blackie, Glasgow and London.

Magaña, Edmundo, and Peter Mason (editors) 1986 *Myth and the Imaginary in the New World*, Latin American Studies, 34, Centre for Latin American Research and Documentation, Dordrecht.

Martius, Carl Friedrich Phil. von 1867 *Beitrage zur Ethnographie und Sprachenkunde Amerikas*, Vol. I, Leipzig.

McDonald, David R. 1977 'Food Taboos: A Primitive Environmental Protection Agency (South America)', *Anthropos*, Vol. 72, pp. 734-747.

Meggers, Betty J. 1971 *Amazonia: Man and Culture in a Counterfeit Paradise*, Aldine-Atherton, Chicago.

Meggers, Betty J. 1975 'Application of the Biological Model of Diversification to Cultural Distributions in Tropical Lowland South America', *Biotropica*, Vol. 7, No. 3, pp. 141-161.

Meggers, Betty J. 1984 'Resource Optimization and Environmental Limitation in Lowland South America', *Reviews in Anthropology*, Vol. 11, pp. 288-293.

Meira, Márcio 1991 'Baniwa, Baré, Warekena, Maku, Tukano...: Os povos indígenas do "baixo rio Negro" querem ser reconocidos', in: Ricardo, Carlos A. (editor), *Povos Indígenas no Brasil*, pp. 135-140, Centro Ecuménico de Documentação e Informação, Rio de Janeiro.

Meyer de Schauensee, Rodolphe 1964 *The Birds of Colombia and adjacent areas of South and Central America*, Livingston Publishing Company, Narberth, Pennsylvania.

Milton, K. 1984 'Protein and Carbohydrate Resources of the Maku Indians of Northwestern Amazonia', *American Anthropologist*, Vol. 86, pp. 7-27.

Müller-Schwarze, D. 1971 'Pheromones in black-tailed deer (*Odocoileus hemionus Columbianus*), *Animal Behaviour*, Vol. 19, No. 1, pp. 141-152.

Moran, Emilio F. 1990 'Levels of analysis and analytical level shifting: Examples from Amazonian Ecosystem research', in Moran, Emilio F., (editor), *The Ecosystem Approach in Anthropology: From Concept to Practice*, pp. 279-308, University of Michigan Press, Ann Arbor.

Moran, Emilio F. (editor) 1990 *The Ecosystem Approach in Anthropology From Concept to Practice*, University of Michigan Press, Ann Arbor.

Murphey, Robert M. 1976 'Mammalia Americae Australe: A Table of Taxonomic and Vernacular Names', *Ciencia Interamericana*, Vol. 17, Nos. 1, pp. 16-32; 2, pp.18-30; 3, pp. 26-35, Secretaría General, Organización de los Estados Americanos, Washington.

Neira R., Daniel 1975 *Mari Weese: Lo que hacemos en tucano*, Summer Institute of Linguistics, Lomalinda, Colombia.

Neira, R., Faustino *et. al.* 1975 *Wa'i; Descripciones en tucano de los hábitos de algunos peces*, Summer Institute of Linguistics, Lomalinda, Colombia.

Norton, John 1984 'The Domestication of the Savage Pig: The Role of Peccaries in Tropical South and Central America and Their Relevance for the Understanding of Pig Domestication in Melanesia', *Canberra Anthropology*, Vol. 7, Numbers 1 and 2, pp. 20-70, Special Volume: Pigs, Australian National University, Canberra.

Olivares, Antonio, and Jorge Hernández 1962 'Aves de la Comisaría del Vaupés (Colombia), *Revista de Biología Tropical*, Vol. 10, No. 1, pp. 61-90, Universidad de Costa Rica, San José.

Posey, D.A., and W. Balée (editors) 1989 'Resource Management in Amazonia: Indigenous and Folk Strategies', in *Advances in Economic Botany*, Vol. 7, The New York Botanical Garden, New York.

Prance, Ghillean T., and Thomas E. Lovejoy (editors) 1985 *Amazonia*, Pergamon Press, Oxford.

Rappaport, Roy A. 1968 *Pigs for the Ancestors: Ritual in the Ecology of a New Guinea People*, Yale University Press, New Haven and London.

Rappaport, Roy A. 1971 'The Flow of Energy in an Agricultural Society', in: *Energy and Power*: A Scientific American Book, pp. 69-80, W. H. Freeman and Company, San Francisco.

Rappaport, Roy A. 1979 *Ecology, Meaning, and Religion*, North Atlantic Books, Berkeley.

Regal, Philip, J. 1977 'Ecology and Evolution of Flowering Plant Dominance', *Science*, Vol. 196, No. 4290, pp. 622-629.

Reichel, Elizabeth 1987 'Asentamientos prehispánicos en la amazonia colombiana' and 'Etnografiá de los grupos indígenas contemporáneos en amazonia', in Colombia Amazónica, Universidad Nacional y Fondo FEN, Bogatá.

Reichel, Elizabeth 1989 'La Danta y el delfín: Manejo ambiental e intercambio entre dueños de malocas y shamanes', Revista de Antropología, vol. V no. 1-2, Universidad de los Andes, Bogotá.

Reichel, Elizabeth 1992 'La Eco-política en conceptos indígenas de territorio en la amazonia colombiana', in Antropología jurídica, E. Sanchez (editor), PARCO-MUN, Bogotá.

Reichel-Dolmatoff, Gerardo 1967 'A Brief Report on Urgent Ethnological Research in the Vaupés Area, Colombia, South America', *Bulletin of the International Committee on Urgent Anthropological and Ethnological Research*, No. 9, pp. 53-61, Vienna.

Reichel-Dolmatoff, Gerardo 1971 *Amazonian Cosmos: The Sexual and Religious Symbolism of the Tukano Indians*, University of Chicago Press, Chicago.

Reichel-Dolmatoff, Gerardo 1975 *The Shaman and the Jaguar: A Study of Narcotic Drugs Among the Indians of Colombia*, Temple University Press, Philadelphia.

Reichel-Dolmatoff Gerardo 1976 'Desana Curing Spells: An Analysis of Some

Shamanistic Metaphors', *Journal of Latin American Lore*, Vol. 2, No. 2, pp. 157-219, University of California, Los Angeles.

Reichel-Dolmatoff, Gerardo 1978 'Desana Animal Categories, Food Restrictions and the Concept of Color Energies', *Journal of Latin American Lore*, Volo. 4, No. 2, pp.243-291, University of California, Los Angeles.

Reichel-Dolmatoff, Gerardo 1978 'Drug-induced optical sensations and their relationship to applied art among some Colombian Indians', in Greenhalgh, Michael, and Vincent Megaw, (editors) *Art in Society: Studies in Style, Culture and Aesthetics*, Duckworth, London.

Reichel-Dolmatoff, Gerardo 1978 *Beyond the Milky Way: Hallucinatory Imagery of the Tukano Indians*, UCLA Latin American Studies, Volume 42, Los Angeles.

Reichel-Dolmatoff, Gerardo 1979 'Conceptos indígenas de enfermedad y de equilibrio ecológico: Los Tukano y los Kogi de Colombia', in *Simposio Internazionale sulla Medicina Indigena e Popolare dell' America Latina, Roma 1977*, pp. 151-162, Instituto Italo/Americano, Roma.

Reichel-Dolmatoff, Gerardo 1979 'Desana Shaman's Rock Crystals and the Hexagonal Universe', *Journal of Latin American Lore*, Vol. 5, No. 1, pp. 117-128, University of California, Los Angeles.

Reichel-Dolmatoff, Gerardo 1979 'Some Source Materials on Desana Shamanistic Initiation', *Antropológica*, Vol. 51, pp. 27-61, Fundación La Salle, Instituto Caribe de Antropología y Sociología, Caracas.

Reichel-Dolmatoff, Gerardo 1985 *Basketry as Metaphor: Arts and Crafts of the Desana Indians of the Northwest Amazon*, Occasional Papers of the Museum of Cultural History, No. 5, University of California, Los Angeles.

Reichel-Dolmatoff, Gerardo 198 'Tapir Avoidance in the Colombian Northwest Amazon', in Urton, Gary (editor): *Animal Myths and Metaphors in South America*, pp. 107-143, University of Utah Press, Utah.

Reichel-Dolmatoff, Gerardo 1986 'Algunos conceptos de geografía chamanística de los indios Desana de Colombia', in Magaña, Edmundo, and Peter Mason, (editors): *Myth and the Imaginary in the New World*, Centre for Latin American Research and Documentation, Amsterdam.

Reichel-Dolmatoff, Gerardo 1986 'A Hunter's Tale from the Colombian Northwest Amazon', *Journal of Latin American Lore*, Vol. 12, No. 1, pp. 65-74, University of California, Los Angeles.

Reichel-Dolmatoff, Gerardo 1987 *Shamanism and Art of the Eastern Tukano Indians: Colombian Northwest Amazon*, Iconography of Religions IX:1, State University Groningen, Institute of Religious Iconography, E.J. Brill, Leiden.

Reichel-Dolmatoff, Gerardo 1988 *Goldwork and Shamanism: An Iconographic Study of the Gold Museum*, Editorial Colina, Medellín, Colombia.

Reichel-Dolmatoff, Gerardo 1989 'Biological and Social Aspects of the Yuruparí Complex of the Colombian Vaupés Territory', *Journal of Latin American Lore*, Vol. 15, No. 1, pp. 95-135, University of California, Los Angeles.

Reichel-Dolmatoff, Gerardo 1989 *Desana Texts and Contexts*, Acta Ethnologica et Linguistica No. 62, Series Americana 12, Vienna.

Reichel-Dolmatoff, Gerardo 1990 'Algunos conceptos de los indios Desana del Vaupés, sobre manejo ecológico', in Corréa, François, (editor) *La Selva Humanizada: Ecología alternativa en el trópico húmedo colombiano*, pp. 35-41, Instituto Colombiano de Antropología, Bogotá.

Reichel-Dolmatoff, Gerardo 1991 *Indians of Colombia: Experience and Cognition*,

Villegas Editores, Bogotá.

Reichel-Dolmatoff, Gerardo 1996 'Yuruparí: Studies of an Amazonian Foundation Myth, in *Religions of the World*, Harvard University Centre for the Study of World Religions.

Renard-Casevitz, France-Marie 1991 *Le banquet masqué: une mythologie de l'étranger*, Lierre & Coudrier Editeurs, Paris.

Ribeiro, Berta G. 1989 'Rainy Seasons and Constellations: The Desana Economic Calendar', in Posey, D.A., and W. Ballée, editors *Resource Managements in Amazonia*, pp. 97-113.

Ricardo, Carlos A. (editor) 1991 *Povos Indigenas no Brasil*, Centro Ecuménico de Documentação e Informação, Rio de Janeiro.

Rivière, Peter 1987 'Of Women, Men and Manioc', in Skar, Harald O., and Frank Salomon (editors) *Natives and Neighbors in South America: Anthropological Essays*, pp. 178-201, Etnologiska Studier 38, Goteborgs Etnografiska Museum, Gothenburg.

Robinson, John G., and Kent H. Redford (editors) 1991 *Neotropical Wildlife Use and Conservation*, University of Chicago Press, Chicago.

Rodrigues, W.A. 1975 'Contribução para o estudo do genero Monopterix Spr. ex Benth. (Leguminosae) da Amazonia', *Acta Amazonica*, Vol. 5, No. 2, pp. 153-155, Manaus.

Rojas U., and Carlos Castaño U. (editors) 1990 *Areas protegidas de la cuenca del Amazonas*, Red Latinoamericana de Cooperación Técnica en Parques Nacionales, Otras Areas protegidas, Flora y Fauna silvestres, Bogotá.

Ross, Eric Barry 1978 'Food Taboos, Diet, and Hunting Srategy: The Adaptation to Animals in Amazon Cultural Ecology', *Current Anthropology*, Vol. 19, No. 1, pp. 1-36.

Schultes, Richard Evans 1957 'The Identity of the Malpighiaceous Narcotics of South America', *Botanical Museum Leaflets*, Vol. 18, No. 1, pp. 1-56, Botanical Museum, Harvard University.

Schultes, Richard Evans 1974 'Palms and Religion in the Northwest Amazon', *Principes*, Vol. 18, No. 1, pp. 3-21.

Schultes, Richard Evans 1988 *Where the Gods Reign: Plants and Peoples of the Colombian Amazon*, Synergetic Press, Oracle, Arizona.

Schultes, Richard Evans 1989 '*Pouteria ucuqui* (Sapotaceae), a little-known Amazonian fruit tree worthy of domestication', *Economic Botany*, Vol. 43, No. 1, pp. 125-127.

Schultes, Richard Evans, and Albert Hofmann 1973 *The Botany and Chemistry of Hallucinogens*, Charles C. Thomas, Publishers, Springfield, Illinois.

Schultes, Richard Evans, and Albert Hofmann 1979 *Plants of the Gods: Origins of Hallucinogenic Use*, McGraw-Hill Book Company, New York.

Schultes, Richard Evans, and Robert F. Raffauf 1990 *The Healing Forest: Medicinal and Toxic Plants of the Northwest Amazon*, Dioscorides Press, Portland, Oregon.

Schultes, Richard Evans, and Robert F. Raffauf 1992 *Vine of the Soul: Medicine Men, their Plants and Rituals in the Colombian Amazon*, Synergetic Press, Oracle, Arizona.

Siegel, Ronald K., and Louis Jolyon West (editors) 1975 *Hallucinations: Behavior, Experience, and Theory*, John Wiley & Sons, New York-London-Sidney-Toronto.

Sioli, Harald 1975 'Tropical Rivers as Expression of Their Terrestrial Environments', in Golley, Frank B., and Ernesto Medina (editors) *Tropical Ecological Systems*, pp.

275-285.

Silverwood-Cope, Peter 1972 *A Contribution to the Ethnography of the Colombian Maku*, Doctoral Dissertation, Cambridge University.

Skar, Harald O., and Frank Salomon (editors) 1987 *Natives and Neighbors in South America: anthropological Essays*, Etnologiska Studier 38, Goteborgs Etnografiska Museum, Gothenburg.

Skutch, Alexander F. 1977 *A Bird Watcher's Adventures in Tropical America*, University of Texas Press, Austin.

Sorensen, Arthur P. 1984 'Linguistic exogamy and personal choice in the Northwest Amazon', in Kensinger, Kenneth, editor: *Marriage Practices in Lowland South America*, pp. 180-192, Illinois Studies in Anthropology No. 14, University of Illinois Press, Urbana and Chicago.

Spix, Johann Baptist von, and Martius, Karl Friedrich Phil. von 1823-31 *Reise in Brasilien auf Befehl Sr. Majestat Maximilian, Joseph I. Konigs von Baiern, in den Jahren 1817 bis 1820 gemacht und beschrieben* (etc.), 3 vol., Atlas, M. Lindauer, Munich.

Sponsel, Leslie E. 1986 'Amazon Ecology and Adaptation', *Annual Revue of Anthropology*, Vol. 15, pp. 67-97.

Spruce, Richard 1908 *Notes of a Botanist on the Amazon and Andes*, 2 vol., Macmillan, London.

Stafleu, F.A. 1954 'A Monograph of the Vochysiaceae IV. Erisma', *Acta Bot. Neerl.* vol. 3, No. 4, pp. 459-480.

Stolte, Joel A. 1980 'La nasalización en las lenguas tucanas orientales', *Artículos en Lingüística y Campos Afines*, No. 7, pp. 1-27, Summer Institute of Linguistics, Bogotá.

Stradelli, Ermanno 1890 'Leggenda del Jurupary', *Bollettino della Societa Geografica Italiana*, anno XXIV,Vol. XXVII (Serie III, Vol. III), pp. 659-689, 798-835, Roma.

Summer Institute of Linguistics 1973 *Sistemas fonológicos de idiomas colombianos*, Vol. II, Lomalinda, Colombia.

Summer Institute of Linguistics 1972 *Sistemas fonológicos de idiomas colombianos*, Vol. I, Lomalinda, Colombia.

Summer Institute of Linguistics 1976 *Sistemas fonológicos de idiomas colombianos*, Vol. III, Lomalinda, Colombia.

Summer Institute of Linguistics 1974 *Folclor indígena de Colombia*, Vol. 1, Editorial Towhsend, Colombia.

Trupp, Fritz 1977 *Mythen der Makuna*, Acta Ethnographica et Linguistica No. 40, Series Americana 8, Vienna.

Van der Hammen, María Clara 1991 *El Manejo del mundo: Naturaleza y sociedad entre los Yukuna de la Amazonia colombiana*, Doctoral Dissertation, University of Utrecht, 1991.

Van der Hammen, Thomas 1992 *Historia, ecología y vegetación*, Corporación Colombiana para la Amazonia, Fondo FEN Colombia, Bogotá.

Wallace, Alfred Russel 1853 *Palm Trees of the Amazon and their Uses*, John van Voorst, London.

Wallace, Alfred Russel 1972 *A Narrative of Travels on the Amazon and Rio Negro*, second edition of 1889, Dover Publications, New York.

Waltz, Nathan 1991 *Ahri yehpa, apeye yehpari guhu ijire La tierra y los planetas en piratapuyo*, Editorial Alberto Lleras Camargo, Bogotá.

Waltz, Nathan, and Carolyn 1991 *wahi cjãna yere buheihna: Cartilla Piratapuya*,

Editorial Alberto Lleras Camargo, Lomalinda, Colombia.

Waltz, Nathan E., and Alva Wheeler 1972 *Proto-Tukanoan*, in *Comparative Studies in Amerindian Languages*, Janua Linguarum, 127, pp. 119-149, Mouton, The Hague.

Welch, Betty, and Birdie West 1974 *Te'a wesepu wa'ara: Vamos a la chagra en tucano*, Summer Institute of Linguistics, Lomalinda, Colombia.

Welch, Betty, and Birdie West 1983 *Te'a abu'era mari mari 1: Cartilla pre-lectura y pre-escritura en tucano*, Summer Institute of Linguistics, Lomalinda, Colombia.

West, Birdie 1980 *Gramática Popular del Tucano*, Summer Institute of Linguistics, Lomalinda, Colombia.

Whitmore, T.C. 1992 *An Introduction to Tropical Rain Forests*, Clarendon Press, Oxford.

Wilson, Edward O. 1971 *The Insect Societies*, Harvard University Press, Cambridge, Mass.

Wilson, Edward O. 1975 *Sociobiology: The New Synthesis*, Harvard University Press, Cambridge, Mass.

Wright, Robin Michael 1981 *History and Religion of the Baniwa Peoples of the Upper Rio Negro Valley*, 2 vol., Doctoral Dissertation, Stanford University, 1981, University Microfilms International, Ann Arbor.

Zerries, Otto 1954 *Wild-und Buschgeister in Sudamerika. Eine Untersuhung jägerzeitlicher Phänomene im Urbild sudamerikanischerIndianer*, Studien zur Kulturkunde, 2, Wiesbaden.

Zerries, Otto 1990 'Die Rolle des Tapirs bei ausserandinen Indianern', in *Circumpacifica, Festschrift fur Thomas S. Barthel*, pp. 589-626, Peter Lang Verlag, Frankfurt-Bern-New York-Paris.

INDEX

Related titles from Themis Books:

COOL TOBACCO, SWEET COCA
*Teachings of an Indian Sage
from the Colombian Amazon*

Hipólito Candre (Kɨneraɨ)

"What comes across in this book, perhaps better than in any other, are the crucial moral and ethical dimensions of what to most would seem to be merely ordinary practical activities. Through such 'Words of Life', a genre found throughout the north-western Amazonia, peoples such as the Uitoto convert the practice of living into a true art of life in which ethics and aesthetics are conjoined... This book steers a fine course between the exotic and the everyday, bringing them together in a powerful synthesis."
Dr. Stephen Hugh-Jones, University of Cambridge

ISBN 0 9527302 1 9 £11.95 pb

THE WAY
An Ecological World-View

Edward Goldsmith

'A unique, extraordinary and profoundly challenging book... Goldsmith's urgent and prophetic book is destined to disturb the dogmatic slumbers of all the conventional philosophies."
John Gray, Times Literary Supplement

"Goldsmith has written a masterpiece... Every writer of environmental philosophy from now on will have to take Goldsmith's work into account."
J. Donald Hughes, author of 'Ecology in Ancient Civilizations'

"It is a delight to see so many dogmas of the scientific faith thrown to the winds by a mind of such precise critical intelligence and large understanding."
Kathleen Raine, poet and Blake scholar

ISBN 0 9527302 3 5 £14.95 pb
ISBN 0 9527302 2 7 £25.00 hb